Derek Conrad Murray is Assistant Professor of History of Art and Visual Culture at the University of California, Santa Cruz and is one of the foremost experts on the subject of contemporary African-American art. He completed a Ph.D. in the Department of History of Art, Cornell University in 2005.

'With lucidity, eloquence and sophistication, Murray shifts the question of identity away from the dictates of racial solidarity and toward a sensitive commitment to form, style, and the material and affective properties of blackness. He shows how, by being committed to attending to difference within difference, post-black artists' formal experimentation, satire, playfulness, and assertive vision articulate a sophisticated critical engagement with canonical art and scholarship. A beautifully argued book, sensitive to both the semiotic vulnerability and the futurity of the post-black imagination, *Queering Post-Black Art* effectively queers and blackens art discourse while casting both blackness and queerness as expansive artistic vanguards. Critical race theory at its best.'

Alessandra Raengo, Assistant Professor of Communication, Georgia State University

Queering Post-Black Art

Artists Transforming African-American Identity after Civil Rights

Derek Conrad Murray

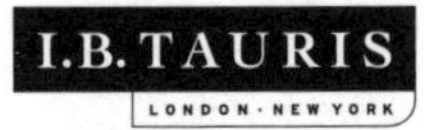

Published in 2016 by
I.B.Tauris & Co. Ltd
London • New York
www.ibtauris.com

International Library of Modern and Contemporary Art 30

ISBN: 978 1 78453 287 1
eISBN: 978 0 85772 989 7

A full CIP record for this book is available from the British Library
A full CIP record is available from the Library of Congress

Library of Congress Catalog Card Number: available

Typeset by Aptara
Printed and bound in Great Britain by T.J. International, Padstow, Cornwall

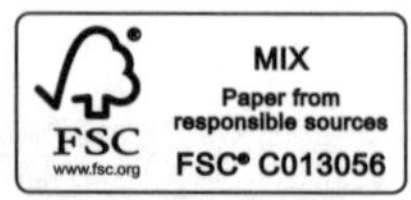

Contents

List of Illustrations

Figures

Plates

Acknowledgements

Over the course of writing this book, I have had the benefit of much support from teachers, colleagues, students, and family. There are too many individuals to thank here, but I would like to begin by acknowledging the support of Professors Abbas Daneshvari, Mika Cho and Julie Trager from California State University, Los Angeles, whose encouragement early in my educational career, gave me the courage to pursue doctoral study in the history of art. I must also thank my mentor and graduate advisor at Cornell University, Salah Hassan, as well as my dissertation advisors Laura Meixner and Amy Villarejo, who provided invaluable support and professional guidance from which I continue to benefit. During my time at Cornell, I was given the opportunity to publish actively within the journal *Nka: Journal of Contemporary African Art*. Along with Professor Hassan, I must also thank Okwui Enwezor who was always supportive of my developing research. I owe a special thanks to Patricia Phillips who, during her time as Editor of the College Art Association's *Art Journal*, published two feature-length articles of mine. These early publishing opportunities led to the research contained within this manuscript. Earlier versions of my writings on the artist Kehinde Wiley were published in the pages of *Nka* and were later anthologized by my colleague Julia Kim Wertz. I owe a debt of gratitude to Chantal Pontbriand, Editor of the Montréal-based Contemporary Art magazine *Parachute*. It was in the pages of *Parachute* where many of my ideas were fostered and where my political approach to contemporary art was encouraged and nurtured.

Since 2011, I have been writing almost exclusively on the subject of contemporary African-American art – specifically on the controversial and polarizing term post-black. I must thank Thelma Golden and Glenn Ligon, the individuals who launched this terminology, propelling it into the public consciousness, but also the journalist and author Touré, who interviewed and enlisted me as an informant in his important book *Who's Afraid of Post-Blackness: What It Means to Be Black Now* (2001). It was my contribution to Touré's book that led to the current direction of my research on African-American art. It's essential that I express a heartfelt thanks to scholars Cherise Smith and Jessica Horton. Their support was invaluable and led to my inclusion in their special issue of the journal *American Art* on the subject of post-identity. I also must express my additional appreciation to Cherise Smith for inviting me to give a lecture in her panel 'The Particulars of Postidentity' held at the College Art Association conference in New York in 2013. The current direction of my research was greatly informed and inspired by this event and it gave me a forum to explore new and challenging ideas.

This book would not have been possible without the guidance of my editor Anna Coatman, as well as the mentorship, support, and scholarship of art historian Amelia Jones. I additionally benefitted from the support of scholars Derek C. Maus and James J. Donahue who published an earlier version of my research on post-black art and African-American satire in their edited volume *Post-Soul Satire: Black Identity after Civil Rights* (2014). I would be remiss if I did not also thank the brilliant scholar Alessandra Raengo who invited me to be the keynote at her conference *Liquid Blackness*, an event that was at the vanguard of critical ideas about black identity. The *Liquid Blackness* conference (and collective of scholars and artists of the same name), have been essential to my intellectual evolution and have inspired the direction of this research. The College Art Association (CAA) has been contributory to the development of this book, allowing me to present papers and on two occasions, to chair my own session, most notably 'Contemporary Black Art and the Problem of Racial Fetishism' (2014). The session enabled me to work through many of the key themes addressed in *Queering Post-Black Art* and so I must thank my co-chair Andrianna Campbell, as well as the panelists Soraya Murray, Jillian Hernandez, Daniel L. Haxall, Charlotte Ickes, and Grace Yasumura. I also thank the Townsend Working Group in

Contemporary Art at the University of California, Berkeley, for supporting my research in post-black with an invitational lecture that helped me to further push the ideas contained within this manuscript.

I am grateful to the various artists discussed in this volume, Glenn Ligon, Kehinde Wiley, Mickalene Thomas, and Kalup Linzy. Without their creative visions and undeniable courage, a project like this one could not have been realized. In the years leading to this book's completion, I was both assisted and inspired by several of my students, including Kathleen Reinhardt, Denise Reso, Mia D'Avanza, Eleanore Hopper, Ace Lehner, and Vivian Fu. I would also like to acknowledge the support of my colleagues who over the years have offered invaluable insights and mentorship: Lewis Watts, John Brown Childs, and David Marriott. Thank you to Jesi Khadivi for her careful editing of this manuscript.

Last, but certainly not least, none of this research would have been possible without the love and support of my partner, collaborator, and colleague Soraya Murray.

This book is dedicated to my father, Spencer Jack Murray.

Introduction

> Demanding respect for people as blacks and as gays requires that there are some scripts that go with being an African-American or having same-sex desires. There will be proper ways of being black and gay, there will be expectations to be met, demands will be made. It is at this point someone who takes autonomy seriously will ask whether we have not replaced one kind of tyranny with another. If I had to choose between the world of the closet and the world of gay liberation, or between the world of *Uncle Tom's Cabin* and Black Power, I would of course, choose the latter. But I would like not to have to choose. I would like other options.[1]
>
> – K. Anthony Appiah, *Multiculturalism*

What is Post Blackness?

So often misunderstood, post-black is a term that has found an unlikely critical space in the lexicon of ideas about African-American art and culture. When I travel around the USA attending conferences about African-American art, and the subject emerges, I encounter a contradictory mix of responses. Generally, there is great interest in the topic, and it inspires heated and lively discussion. In other contexts, I've experienced a range of more negative, or cynical responses, from dismissiveness to outright expressions of vitriol and condemnation – yet the term has paradoxically become the most talked about and debated issue in contemporary African-American art. I am deeply interested in what I often see as a desire to maintain a kind of embarrassed distance from post-black in social space, while embracing and advancing the values it exemplifies within the milieu of intellectual debate and creative endeavour. To publicly embrace post-blackness is to potentially be subject to a particular kind of suspicion in the African-American community, because for many, the term signifies at best the rejection of blackness, and at worst, a naiveté regarding an ennobled history of struggle and resistance. In certain segments of black intellectual culture, to be thought of as embracing post-blackness is tantamount to being a racial turncoat who rejects their community. In the black community, solidarity is sacrosanct, and therefore there are limits on the degree to which self-criticality can be expressed. This anxiety is compounded by a great fear of falling out with the group. Despite this fear, post-black continues to thrive in intellectual and creative discourse and is the major driving force behind the most avant-garde forms of contemporary African-American art. The desire to seek a comfortable distance from post-black most clearly affirms its reason for being, and the necessity for many artists and intellectuals to resist the stifling dictates of racial obligation, and its attendant socio-political dogmas. One of the more significant aspects of post-black is that it makes visible a set of ideological and political differences between generations: those who were born and raised prior to the passing of the Civil Rights Act of 1964 (that ended legal segregation) and those who were born and raised in its wake. The significance of this demarcation lies in the lived experiences of individuals, whose encounters with racism vary in severity, and are informed not just by age, but also by other factors like class and geographic location.

Post-black discourse contends that the pre-Civil Rights generation's hold over the political agendas and cultural values of African-American life is so all-encompassing that, until the last ten years or so, there has been hesitation to advance any new ideas – or present challenges to historical dogma. A fear festers within the younger generation of being branded as silly and petulantly misguided in their allegedly post-racial dreams of assimilation – even if that characterization is entirely false. To be clear, post-black is not about post-racialism. It is on the contrary a term that signifies a desire to question constructions of African-American identity that negate forms of difference, particularly the subjectivities of women and those who are queerly identified. For many in the African-American community, the visual and ideological emblems of normative blackness have not spoken to the complexities of their experience. In fact, official forms of resistance and radicalism have historically regarded the concerns of gender and queerness as a threat to its aims. If post-black represents a threat, it is to the hegemony of hetero-patriarchal expressions of blackness that, in their essentialist logics and racial nostalgia, relegate African-American identity to a series of limiting scripts. In response, I argue that post-black is simply a notion. It is an idea that allows for intellectual discussion to occur. There is nothing to be feared or reviled, because at its most incendiary, it challenges an existing intolerance that has led to forms of erasure and neglect. It is only a threat to those who adhere to an essentialist cultural politics of the past – those whose romantic nostalgia for a black liberation of yesteryear would transform blackness into a type of theology to be worshipped and feared, but never questioned.

For the purpose of this investigation, I use the terms 'blackness' and 'African-American' interchangeably, because I want to make a corollary, as well as a distinction between African-American identity and what could be described as a *cultural politics of blackness*. To be African-American does not mean that one inherently embraces a cultural politics of blackness – even while considering themselves to be black. For this reason, blackness is a slippery term, and an identification that is often embraced or rejected depending on the circumstance. Blackness holds a special place in African-American history as a form of resistance and socio-political uplift, yet (in a contemporary context) its aims are often thought of as passé and mired in the past. There is pride in blackness, because it has become *culture* – it is an expressive mode of being and a form of cultural distinctiveness that allows for collective identification and a sense of membership and community. It is therefore possible to embrace blackness *as culture*, while rejecting many of its more politically problematic associations and values. Along these lines, I believe it important to acknowledge that terms like 'African-American' and 'blackness' are either accepted or refused for a range of reasons – but perhaps more significantly, they are both contested and utilized with trepidation. Labels are always problematic, and while they may provide context for understanding particular historical shifts and ways of being, they can also be incredibly confining and restrictive.

The emergence of post-black in North American art discourse is now widely known and debated, yet it warrants further unpacking because within this divisive terminology lies a set of concerns that are of central importance to understanding the ever-evolving complexities of African-American life. Art historian Robert Farris Thompson was first credited with using the term in a 1991 *Artforum* article in which he stated: 'A retelling of modernism to show how it predicts the triumphs of the current sequences would reveal that "the Other" is your neighbour – that black and Modernist cultures were inseparable long ago. Why use the word, "post-Modern" when it may also mean "post-black"'.[2] In its more current and notorious usage, post-black emerged in the wake of the 2001 exhibition *Freestyle* at the Studio Museum in Harlem. Organized by celebrated curator Thelma Golden, the exhibition launched a group of emerging African-American artists into the public consciousness. But perhaps overshadowing the impact of the works themselves, was Golden's mention of the term post-black in her catalogue essay: 'It [post-black] was a clarifying term that had ideological and chronological dimensions and repercussions. It was characterized by artists who were adamant about not being labelled as "black" artists, though their work was steeped, in fact deeply interested in redefining complex notions of blackness.'[3] These often recited words have been the catalyst for an entire discourse that extends far beyond the limits of African-American art, though when Golden went on to say, 'post-black was the new black', she ignited a divisive debate about the parameters of blackness as a visually expressive form. The critical response to the curator's statement attempted to characterize the text as a flippant and ill-conceived sentiment – yet while the curator's words were relatively brief, what was articulated was actually more substantive than is often recollected.[4] In fact, what Golden stated prior to the above citation is arguably of greater intellectual heft, yet it has gone largely unacknowledged. In her recollections of conversations with her friend and celebrated artist Glenn Ligon, Golden discusses their shared love of absurd uses of language and their use of the term post-black, which was shorthand for post-black art:[5] 'As a child born in the mid-1960s, I imagine I hold a certain degree of nostalgia for the passion and energy that created the nationalist/aesthetic dogma of the 1970s Black Arts Movement . . . which allowed me to thrive in the words and actions of late 1980s multiculturalism.'[6] In Golden's formulation, post-black didn't simply signify a generational and aesthetic shift, but rather a divergent set of values that were cognizant of the Black Arts Movement's political limitations. The *black* in post-black is more than an umbrella term signifying the African-American experience, but is actually a more pointed reference to a particular *regime of representation*: specifically, the history of images depicting black men in the throes of collective resistance. The visual culture of normative blackness has been defined through the representation of black men as the defiant leaders of their beleaguered communities. We see this exemplified in images of the Black Panthers, clad in leather jackets and berets, as they stand in militant opposition to racial oppression – or in iconic photographs of 1960s era race-men like Martin Luther King, Jr., and Bayard Rustin, as they bravely protest bigotry in the American South.

The African-American liberation struggle was visually defined by depictions of black hyper-masculinity, which for Golden, signified a change in the American consciousness among both white and black communities. These codified images served as inspiration for Golden's 1994 exhibition *Black Male: Representations of Masculinity in Contemporary American Art*. In *Black Male*, Golden questioned the hegemony of hetero-normative representations of black masculinity that always defined popular understandings of African-American men. These Black Power era images became a touchstone for Golden's critical investigation into the historical construction of black masculinity: 'The black leather jackets, dark sunglasses, big afros, and bigger guns made visual the myths of uncontrollable aggression and rampant sexuality.'[7] Golden's criticality around the representation of black men was informed by the work of British scholar Kobena Mercer, whose writings on the intersection of masculinity, race, and representation powerfully explored the 'regimes of truth' that produce damaging social definitions about black men.[8] For Mercer, these social definitions have either kept these men from achieving the social and economic markers of normative masculinity, or they have encouraged them to embody its more pernicious and damaging expressions.[9] In its recuperative elements, black liberation movements in the USA aggressively took on and naturalized an expression of male power that was patriarchal at its core – and solidified a set of gender roles that were largely about black male virility and reclaimed dominance. As Mercer articulates, 'black male gender identities have been culturally constructed through complex dialectics of power'.[10] Mercer makes a significant point that a byproduct of Black Power's masculinist dictates was the formation of a regressively hetero-patriarchal value system that was subsumed within a visual regime of images meant to signify radical resistance and uplift.

In his collaborative writings with the queer black British artist Isaac Julien, Mercer references the iconic photograph from the 1968 Olympics in Mexico City that depicts African-American athletes

Tommy Smith (Gold medallist) and John Carlos (Bronze medallist) as they raise a defiant fist (known as the Black Power salute). With heads down, fists adorned with black gloves, and human rights badges on their jackets, the gesture is often regarded as the most overtly political statement in the history of the modern Olympic Games. Still, despite the ascribed political efficacy of this occurrence, Mercer suggests that sports is one of the few arenas in which black men have historically been able to excel, and that in 'classical racism's dominant regimes of truth' African people were defined as having bodies but not minds – which aided the 'super-exploitation' of the black body as a 'muscle machine'.[11] The point here is that while Smith and Carlos' protest brings consciousness to the exploitation and dehumanization of oppressed peoples, it does so (in its rapacious masculinity) at the expense of other constituencies (primarily women and homosexuals) who struggle under the duress of those very same conditions. Making reference to the Black liberation movement's mantras of collective resistance, Mercer and Julien are critical of their hidden biases:

> Slogans such as 'Black is Beautiful,' and new idioms of cultural and political expression like the Afro hairstyle, signified the rejection of second-class citizenship and 'negative self-image.' The movement sought to clear the ground for the cultural reconstruction of the black subject – but because of the *masculinist form* this took, it was done at the expense of black women, gays, and lesbians. Figures such as Eldridge Cleaver promoted a heterosexist version of black militancy which not only authorized sexism – Stokely Carmichael said the only position of black women in the movement was 'prone' – but a hidden agenda of homophobia, something which came out in Cleaver's remorseless attack on James Baldwin. Revolutionary nationalism implied a very macho-oriented notion of black struggle . . . and this has been taken, rather romantically, by some black male activists and intellectuals to embody the 'heroic' essence of black people's resistance.[12]

In the aforementioned quotation, Mercer and Julien express critical concern around constructions of black masculinity that are damaging in their patriarchal logics, but also directly negate women and queerly identified subjects. We see a similar line of thought advanced in the writings of black feminist thinkers who rallied against a legacy of black political resistance that relegated them to the margins. American political activist and scholar Angela Davis, whose radicalism in the

1960s positioned her in close proximity to the Black Panther Party, has written about (through the lens of personal experience) the often fraught role of women during the period of black liberation struggle:

> The sisters who were my closest comrades, in SNCC, in the Black Panther Party, in the Communist Party, fought tenaciously – and we sometimes fought tenaciously among ourselves – for our right to fight. And we were sometimes assisted in this by sympathetic men in these organizations. We may not have been able to talk about gendered racism, 'sexuality' may have still meant sexiness, homophobia, as a word, may not yet have existed, but our practice, I can say in retrospect, was located on a continuum that groped and zigzagged its way toward this moment of deliberation on the pitfalls of nationalism and essentialism.[13]

Davis' recollections align with black feminist re-assessments of Civil Rights and Black Power era political movements that, in their revisionism, interrogate the repressive patriarchal masculinity of the period.[14] The notion that black power was synonymous with misogyny and homophobia has produced a rather vibrant intellectual discourse, as well as a representational counter-politics that examines the role of images in the ideological construction of black personhood.

Golden's curatorial efforts have been greatly influenced by feminist and queer revisionist approaches to the black liberation struggle, including critical reassessments of its corollary, the Black Arts Movement, or BAM (1965–1975). Considered the artistic branch of the Black Power Movement, BAM was fundamentally an essentialist crusade that sought to elevate black culture above its historical debasement. Its platform hinged upon revolutionary politics and a black cultural nationalism that established links between African-American life and a mythical African past from which they were forcibly exiled. The movement demanded that all creative expressions work to evoke the dictates of black cultural nationalism – and African-American art forms that were resistant to this agenda were largely dismissed.[15] According to bell hooks, the consequence of these values was that artistic creativity (as a powerful form of individual expression) became secondary to the aims of nationalist politics.[16] The dogma of black cultural nationalism was artistically stifling, but also repressive in its marginalization of any expression of African-American identity that was antithetical to a hetero-patriarchal value system. We see this also in the emergence of various disciplinary formations within academia in the 1960s and 1970s, specifically 'Black Studies' (also known as Afro-American Studies, Africana Studies, and African-American Studies).[17] According to E. Patrick Johnson, the rise of Black Studies was the result of the volatile and ever-shifting political climate that saw black students and faculty applying pressure against the administrations of predominantly white institutions to create a more diverse and equitable academic culture.[18] The Civil Rights and Black Power movements were the fuel that drove the origins of these burgeoning academic disciplines, yet the concerns of women (within these departmental formations) were dismissed, and they were subject to blatant forms of sexism and misogyny.[19] As a result, the histories and lived experiences of black women were understudied and devalued – however, as Johnson attests, homosexuality (within the dictates of black cultural nationalism) was regarded as corrosive and part of a larger infestation (a 'white' disease) that was diminishing African-American dignity.[20] Within Black Studies, the effort to subvert a lengthy history of stereotypes around black male sexual deviance encouraged a heterosexual politics that had no room for queer subjectivities, which were already viewed as part of a plot to emasculate African-American men.[21]

Many scholars have written about the origins of the black liberation movement in the USA and its eventual formation of what is called the black aesthetic: a constructed visual and representational expression of racial authenticity and political solidarity that was (as we have seen) hetero-patriarchal at its core. But even if we go back further to the writings of W.E.B. Du Bois, we see a desire to subvert the 'image problem' of the American Negro, by creating empowering representations to counteract the negative effects of racial stereotypes. Historian Shawn Michelle Smith reminds us that, even as far back as the 1920s, intellectuals (most notably Du Bois) called upon artists of all types to use their creativity to subvert the preponderance of negative representations of black people: 'Du Bois argues that African-American art must testify to African-American identities, providing a record to challenge a long legacy of racist representation.'[22] In fact, Du Bois used the tradition of ethnographic photography to re-inscribe African-American identity by presenting the 'human face of blackness' so forcefully hidden behind 'representations of blackness as absence, as nothingness, as deformity and depravity'.[23] One of the assertions of post-black is the idea that mainstream African-American life, as well as normative conceptions of blackness, have always been resistant to difference. It is for this very reason that post-blackness is ideologically incompatible with mainstream African-American art history, which is primarily celebratory of black resilience and creative prowess – while being less committed to aggressive anti-racist thought, or challenging (in a self-reflexive manner) its own gender and sexual biases.

One might ask how a movement dedicated to a politics of black liberation could be hostile to forms of difference – yet we see that in its hetero-patriarchal logics, and in the fact that women and homosexuals, in particular (as well as a range of other illegible black subjectivities), were excised from the movement's political agendas. One of the major concerns that post-black puts forth is that the political, intellectual, cultural, and aesthetic dictates of African-American life are so tightly controlled by the sensibilities of the pre-Civil Rights generation, that there is little room for younger generations to engage in self-definition. However, more pertinent perhaps, is the notion that the aims of the Black Arts Movement were never fully realized because of the intolerances that lingered within it. Therefore at the most basic level, post-black is an effort to redefine the parameters of blackness in the twenty-first century, and to push it beyond the stifling dictates of nostalgia for past political movements.

Old Black/New Black

In the wake of Thelma Golden's controversial introduction of the term post-black into the lexicon of contemporary art discourse, intellectuals and cultural commentators (outside of the arts) began to respond to the debate. One of the most significant interventions was made by Touré in his book, *Who's Afraid of Post-Blackness?: What It Means to Be Black Now* (2011).[24] The American writer and journalist Touré wrote the most substantial text on the subject and he endeavoured to push the discussion of post-blackness beyond the subject of African-American art and aesthetics. *Who's Afraid of Post-Blackness?* consists of a series of personal anecdotes by the author, as well as excerpts of interviews he conducted with 105 luminaries in the African-American community including Cornel West, Henry Louis Gates, Jr., Malcolm Gladwell, Kara Walker, Glenn Ligon, and Melissa Harris-Perry, among many others. In the book's introductory pages the author dedicates the manuscript to 'everyone who was ever made to feel "not black enough." Whatever that means.'[25] For Touré post-blackness means the possibility to aggressively resist those individuals who attempt to create confining definitions of what it means to be black in America: 'There is no dogmatically narrow, authentic Blackness because the possibilities for Black identity are infinite. To say something or someone is not black – or is in-authentically Black – is to sell Blackness short. To limit the potential of Blackness . . . if there are forty million black Americans then there are forty million ways to be Black.'[26] The focal of Touré's ire are those whom he calls the 'self-appointed identity cops' (within the African-American community) who write 'Authenticity Violations as if they were working for Internal Affairs making sure everyone does Blackness in the right way'.[27] Touré's 'identity cops' echoes a similar characterization made by writer John Blake in his 1992 essay 'Running Afoul of the Soul Patrol', an impassioned treatise assailing black folks who oppressively impose their racial definitions onto others: 'I call them the Soul Patrol. They are the legions of black people who impose their definition of blackness on other black people. They scorn and reject those who don't act "black enough."'[28] Both Blake and Touré express disdain for the essentialist dictates of African-Americans who wield blackness as a restrictive, yet esoteric set of guidelines and cultural codes that are nearly impossible to fully comprehend or adhere to. However, Touré's definition is clearly generational and demarcates a shift in thought away from a cultural politics of trauma and a compulsory racial solidarity that is rooted in nostalgia.[29]

In the introduction to *Who's Afraid of Post-Blackness?*, noted scholar Michael Eric Dyson echoed Touré's sentiment by harshly critiquing those who attempt to create a limiting lens through which to define what blackness is and can be:

> The sheer plasticity of blackness, the way it conforms to such a bewildering array of identities and struggles, and defeats the attempt to bind its meanings to any one camp or creature, makes a lot of Black folk nervous and defensive. Sometimes the transfer of power to define Blackness is a bloodless affair where one meaning peacefully succeeds the next, as in the shift from coloured to Negro to Black as a self-identifier among African-Americans . . . but the very malleability of Blackness permits Black Folk to shape it into weapons to fight on all sides of the debate about what Blackness is or isn't.[30]

He further elucidated:

> That's why post-Black is so suggestive a term: It clearly doesn't signify the end of Blackness; it points, instead, to the end of the reign of a narrow, single notion of Blackness. It doesn't mean we're over Blackness; it means we're over our narrow understanding of what Blackness means. Post-Blackness has little patience for racial patriotism, racial fundamentalism and racial policing. Racial patriotism builds on the parallel between loyalty to the race and loyalty to the nation. Loyalty isn't the problem, but rather the sort of racial fidelity that often flies under the banner of Blackness.[31]

Dyson's powerful assessment of post-black bolstered Touré's argument that African-American identity is so multifarious and so varied, as to defy any attempts to lock it down to any one definition. In a sense, post-blackness has an air of cynicism to it – a defiant willfulness that is fed up with the intra-cultural mandate to be *down* so to speak, to adhere uncritically to the dogmas of community and racial allegiances. To be down is to *keep it real*: to be a part of the collective and to be authentically black – which is a comforting notion indeed, even if it restricts and limits.[32] As the debate over Touré's book evolved, it became more of an argument over the perils and merits of racial belonging: a rather heated conversation that staked out generation-defining positions about the proper expression of blackness.

Harvard Law Professor Randall Kennedy (b. 1954) posed the most significant challenge to Touré's post-blackness theory. The often-contentious Kennedy is the author of the controversial book *Sellout: The Politics of Racial Betrayal* (2009), which took on many of the problems that Touré explored, namely the charge of being read (by members of the African-American community) as a racial turncoat (a *sellout*) who, for various reasons, is viewed as injurious to the collective.[33] A product of the pre-Civil Rights generation, the Harvard professor has been on both sides of the debate: a proponent of racial freedom from the dictates of intra-community essentialism, yet also a defender of the black community's right to establish and produce boundaries. Kennedy is used to being at the centre of the racial melodrama and has written passionately about his personal experiences with racism, both within and beyond the black community.[34] However, in response to Touré, Kennedy sharply criticized the journalist's assailment of the black community's racial chauvinism, even while acknowledging its often-problematic presence:

> African-Americans fight a multi-front struggle in pursuing their ambitions. Along with the difficulties that others face – bad luck, personal deficiencies, talented competitors – blacks face additional obstacles. On one front they encounter prejudiced Caucasians. On another they encounter Negroes who, attached to stunted conceptions of racial solidarity, habitually castigate as disloyal blacks perceived as 'acting white,' being 'Oreos,' 'selling out.'
>
> Blacks characteristically confront white racism with uninhibited fury. With black critics, however, they often display ambivalence. Even when chafing miserably from constraints imposed by racial solidarity, many blacks nonetheless bite their tongues. They refrain from speaking openly and frankly because the rhetoric and performance of racial solidarity occupies an honoured position in black American circles. It has claims on blacks' psyches even as they wrestle with the restraints that solidarity entails.[35]

Kennedy makes a compelling argument about the merits of community loyalty as a barrier against racial attack – which he sees as a necessary evil that is opposed to Touré's more liberal notion of blackness as porous and without restriction: 'No restriction? But what about an African American who expresses racial hatred for blacks? Or what about an African American who joins a legitimate black-uplift organization for the purpose of crippling it? Blacks (or anyone else) who do or say such things ought to be shunned as forcefully as possible in order to punish them, render them ineffective and dissuade others from following a similar course.'[36] Kennedy's impassioned response castigates Touré's *new* and less restricted blackness, characterizing it as a hypocritical position that seeks to 'escape the fundamental aspects of any community: boundaries and discipline'. Kennedy elaborates: 'Every community – be it a family, firm or nation-state – necessarily has boundaries that distinguish members from non-members. That boundary is a constituent element of the community's existence . . . Racial solidarity will always depend to some extent on self-appointed monitors of racial virtue.'[37] From the character of Kennedy's comments, it is clear that the discussion of post-black tends to devolve into an age-old debate about racial fidelity and the boundaries of cultural authenticity – which are often a fragile a set of visual and behavioural markers that define one's rootedness in blackness. Cornel West has termed this set of qualities 'black cultural distinctiveness'.[38] West makes a distinction between black cultural distinctiveness and black nationalism, which he sees as an essentialist viewpoint that advocates for a mythical notion of black authenticity: 'I don't like the term "black authenticity" because it implies that there has been and is one black essence, one black core, one black centre – and that one group has a monopoly on that centre ... Black nationalism can fall into traps of nostalgia and romanticism as they attempt to generate their own myths, their own fictions.'[39] As a counter to the nationalist impulse, West describes his notion of cultural distinctiveness as a history of black styles and mannerisms: ways of communicating that, in his estimation, have created a certain sense of community and sustained sanity.[40]

As exemplars of this quality, West cites acclaimed jazz musicians Louis Armstrong and Wynton Marsalis, as individuals who – in their ways of walking, talking, and composing – behave in a manner that has deep roots in the tradition of black cultural distinctiveness though, despite that quality, they could not be accurately characterized as nationalists. West makes this distinction out of a firm belief that the embodiment of this distinctiveness in no way designates an essentialist, or fundamentalist attitude towards blackness – but rather a rootedness in a specific cultural history where black styles and mannerisms are deeply engrained.[41] While I agree that there is a profound difference between 'black nationalism' and 'black cultural distinctiveness', within these seemingly benign qualities of ethnically specific folksiness (that the scholar valorizes), are often a series of judgements that allow for the designation of those who are wielding blackness in the proper or improper way. Black cultural distinctiveness is not without its own biases and hegemonies, even if it does not indulge in the more structured essentialisms of a nationalist value system. Many of the strongest abuses take place, not in the arena of political or intellectual debate, but rather in social and interpersonal encounters where the simple (yet ideologically violent) act of looking is the most powerful means of inflicting judgement upon those who do not appear to embody the black styles and mannerisms (the cultural distinctiveness) necessary to achieve racial legitimacy. In simpler terms, black cultural distinctiveness does not have to be nationalist in order to be abusive and to provide the foundation and justification for alienation, judgement, and condemnation. I say this because, within these characteristics, is a notion of interpellation in which an authentically black subject becomes socially constituted.[42] To be hailed in the ocular location of racial veracity or illegibility is a violent and often self-effacing process that produces lasting psychic wounds. That said, I am more concerned with the incongruity between black cultural distinctiveness and black queerness, because lingering within these folksy embodiments, is a hetero-patriarchal expressiveness that has never had room for homosexuality. Even if we think about West's evocation of Louis Armstrong and Wynton Marsalis as individuals with a black style, they are also heterosexual men who are comfortably expressive of normative blackness. West is a progressive thinker who has spoken passionately in favour of universal human rights – including those of women and homosexuals, so his notion of black cultural distinctiveness should not be taken as a form of callousness against any particular constituency. On the contrary, this critique aims to ponder the more subtle ways in which social norms are policed and maintained – and black cultural distinctiveness is perhaps one of the ways in which this process unfolds.

I am troubled by the devolution of these authenticity debates as exemplified by Touré's book and the responses to it – particularly because they never seem to address what is most pressing about post-blackness, which is the gender and sexual politics at its core. We can spend considerable time arguing the parameters of blackness and debating who lays claim to it, but I am more interested in thinking critically about the way queerness seems to always fall outside the auspices of normative blackness. Even in Touré and Kennedy's contentious debate, there is no mention of the fact that the origins of post-blackness lie in the aesthetic and conceptual dimensions of mostly queer artists. Impatient with the signifiers of hetero-masculinity that always inform the construction of normative blackness, Afro-British artist Isaac Julien discusses the importance of de-essentializing black identities and the necessity for new definitions to be 'liberated enough to include "queerness" in its "blackness"'.[43] Julien elaborates: 'In the debris of this postmodern moment, the rise of essentialist black thinking is in part a reaction to a decade of Reagan-Bush-Thatcherite policies. And in the response to the AIDS crisis, the rise of Queer Nationhood lends itself to a similar form of identity politics in aligning itself with an anti-heterosexual essentialism.'[44] Julien rightly criticizes the essentialist impulse in so-called progressive black thought – even within the more politically radical sectors of the gay community. However, I'm more concerned that that heterosexuality is taken for granted within discussions of blackness – that it is taken as a kind of precondition that goes un-problematized. Put more directly, I am disturbed that, as E. Patrick Johnson puts it, 'black authenticity has increasingly become linked to masculinity in its most patriarchal significations.'[45] In Johnson's estimation, this particular brand of masculinity 'epitomizes the imperialism of heterosexism, sexism, and homophobia'.[46] Post-blackness, as it has been constructed in the writings and curatorial efforts of Thelma Golden, are perhaps more productive and politically urgent than the recuperative efforts of Touré, precisely because they are more unapologetically queer in their effort to radically re-envision blackness beyond compulsory heterosexuality. *Who's Afraid of Post-Blackness?* is more concerned with healing the racial wounds of privileged African-Americans who have found themselves thrust outside the comforts of authenticity and membership: those individuals who, for one reason or another, are devoid of the black cultural distinctiveness necessary to *be down*. Touré's message is an important one and speaks to an enduring intra-cultural challenge that is certainly destructive, if not also self-annihilating. However, despite its more meaningful interventions, it does not acknowledge what Johnson calls the 'imperialism of hetero-normativity' that continues to plague conceptualizations of black authenticity.[47]

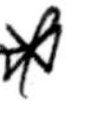

When we think critically about the relationship between black masculinity and hetero-normativity, it is imperative to remember that the origins of black liberation in the USA worked to solidify traditional gender roles, even despite their unwavering commitment to upending legal forms of oppression. In that regard, while the black liberation movement posed a challenge to structural racism, it tended to share with its antagonist an interest in maintaining a deep belief and investment in the discourses and practices of hetero-patriarchy.[48] We see this manifested throughout the black liberation struggle, yet it expressed itself notoriously in the 1970s era of black power. According to Roderick A. Ferguson, the Black Panther Party, as a national liberation movement, embraced an oppressive and hegemonic logic as it normalized a hetero-patriarchal brand of revolutionary agency.[49] E. Patrick Johnson's close reading of performances and iconic written works by heterosexual black men like political activist Eldridge Cleaver and contemporary comedians Damon Wayans and David Alan Grier echoes this point. Johnson draws a corollary between how the black liberation struggle of the 1960s–70s adopted and advocated an abusive hetero-patriarchal value system and the eventual culturalization of queer debasement. Filmmaker Marlon Riggs named this impulse 'negro faggotry':[50] a visual and performative regime that functioned to demean and disparage black gays from authentic blackness – but also to render what is perceived as a *feminized* queerness, ideologically synonymous with the emasculation of black men.[51] Johnson's referencing of comedic performance is interesting when considering a history of deeply homophobic rhetoric within the black liberation struggle. The increasing popularity of 'negro faggotry' in African-American comedy – particularly the tradition of male performers either lampooning black queer swishiness, or appropriating drag – is certainly a post-Civil Rights/post-Black Power phenomenon. As exemplars, Johnson recalls the satirical skit *Men on . . .* (otherwise known as *Men on Films*): a series of comedy sketches that aired on the Fox Network's variety show *In Living Color* (1990–1994). In *Men on . . .* flamboyantly gay film critics Blaine Edwards (Damon Wayans) and Antoine Merriweather (David Alan Grier) critique popular cinema 'from a male point of view'. The point of these skits is not just the ridicule of queerness, but a very specific attack on the effete, or swishy black gay man, whose effeminate manner is considered a signifier of disempowerment.[52] The point here is that, at the root of its construction, authentic blackness has theorized queerness in such a manner as to exclude it from its borders. To further bolster this point, Johnson recalls the writings of activist Eldridge Cleaver in his famous 1968 book *Soul on Ice*. Earlier in this chapter, I cited a quotation from Kobena Mercer and Isaac Julien that makes a similar reference to Cleaver's expressed homophobia, which notoriously took the form of an attack on the celebrated openly gay African-American writer and social critic James Baldwin. Written during his time in Folsom Prison, *Soul on Ice* is a memoir that chronicles the author's transformation from a convicted drug dealer and rapist to a Marxist revolutionary. It is a treatise that is regarded as one of the seminal and most widely read works in the African-American literary tradition. One of the original leaders of the Black Panther Party, Cleaver fully embodied the hyper-masculine black revolutionary ethos that was rabidly patriarchal, misogynistic, and homophobic – but, in a more contradictory sense, it was also emblematic of an organic intellectualism and an authentic

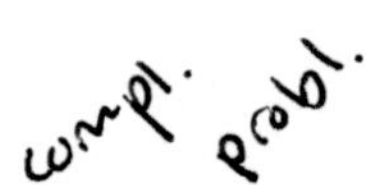

outsiderness. Cleaver's transformation from convicted criminal with no formal education to highly articulate black revolutionary was the stuff of legend – and linked him to comparable narratives like that of slain African-American human rights leader Malcolm X (1925–1965). The similarity between Cleaver and Malcolm X is significant, because the legends surrounding both men personify (and ultimately solidify) the heterosexual, hyper-masculine, black revolutionary ideal that provided the blueprint for a particular kind of normative, patriarchal father/leader/rebel archetype that aggressively defied the dictates of white racism.

Establishing a compelling link between authentic blackness (as an ideal normative heterosexual masculinity) and its aberrant opposite, black homosexuality, Johnson recounts a notorious passage from Cleaver's *Soul on Ice*, in which the activist equates Baldwin's feminized homosexuality with black queer self-hatred:

> The black homosexual, when his twist has a racial nexus, is an extreme embodiment of this contradiction. The white man has deprived him of his masculinity, castrated him in the centre of his burning skull, and when he submits to this change, and takes the white man for his lover as well as Big Daddy, he focuses on 'whiteness' all the love in his pent up soul, and turns the razor edge of hatred against 'blackness' – upon himself, what he is, and all those who look like him, remind him of himself. He may even hate the darkness of night.
>
> The racial death wish is manifested as the driving force in James Baldwin. His hatred of blacks, even as he pleads what he conceives as their cause, makes him the apotheosis of the dilemma in the ethos of the black bourgeoisie who have completely rejected their African heritage, consider the loss irrevocable, and refuse to look again in that direction.[53]

Johnson is correct that in Cleaver's formulation, the black homosexual is 'not only a race traitor, but also a feminized version of a white man'.[54] However, what is most problematic is that the activist's logic insists that middle-class status and homosexuality are inherently and unequivocally anti-black.[55]

The relation that Johnson advances here is useful when thinking about polemical discussions around contemporary post-blackness, specifically in relation to its gender and sexual politics. The race-man archetype of black leadership, personified in the legacies of slain leaders

Martin Luther King, Jr., and Malcolm X, endures to this day and still provides the model (a very hetero-patriarchal one) for African-American uplift. Even in more mainstream definitions, as exemplified in Touré's book, post-blackness is configured as inherently heterosexual – and its most vaunted embodiment is America's first African-American President, Barack Obama. In *Who's Afraid of Post-Blackness?*, Touré dedicates an entire chapter to Obama that hails his presence as a post-black politician distinguished by his remarkable and transformative ability to embody black cultural distinctiveness, while never posing a threat to whites. Entitled 'How to Build More Baracks', the chapter cautiously suggests that 'the more a black person can learn to put the whites around them at ease, and also to feel comfortable doing so, the more powerful they can become'.[56] However, what Touré implies is that Obama's ability to let whites off the hook, so to speak, has rendered him ineffective as a racial saviour for black people. Touré states that, unlike past presidents, Obama cannot be perceived as favouring the underclass, especially the African-American poor, for fear of alienating liberal whites, whose votes he desperately needs. For this reason, he has always been under suspicion by the black community – not least because his aggressively normative and bourgeois, black family man image, is perceived as pandering to white sensibilities in its quest for their approval. Viewed within the logic of Cleaver's 1960s–70s-era political radicalism, Obama's middle-class conservatism represents, at least in symbolic terms, a feminized blackness that ultimately panders to the values of white America. However, I want to also suggest that, under Touré's model of post-blackness, Obama represents a new and emergent blackness that – even in its capitulation and apparent racial inaction – is clever enough to forgo the self-defeating limitations of African-American essentialism and reactionary anger. What is odd about both Cleaver and Touré's ideologically opposing, yet hetero-patriarchal characterizations, is that they both tend to view the kind of black masculinity that Obama represents as somehow compromised: a type of feminization for Cleaver and for Touré, one that is defined by racial conciliation (even if the journalist ultimately hails the politician as brilliant).

Golden's post-blackness suggests that we need to rethink the models of authentic blackness that represent us, and acknowledge the simple fact that – for many in the African-American community – the symbolic markers of normative heterosexual blackness fail to resonate with, or even speak to, the histories and lived experiences of female and queer subjectivities. Interestingly, the rise of Barack Obama occurred at roughly the same time as the emergence of post-black, and for many, these developments signalled a new blackness that was free of racial obligation and the burden of historical trauma. In *Who's Afraid of Post-Blackness?*, Touré interviews former Mayor of Washington D.C., Sharon Pratt, who intimated that Obama's having been raised in a racially diverse home (and in the era of post-Civil Rights optimism) was visible in his political approach:

> One reason he was so good is he could soar above the pain. You watch his manners, his energy – he doesn't have those scars. He didn't have to worry about the police. He didn't have to worry about whether he could use the water fountain. He didn't have to stay on a road and try to figure out where you go to a restroom. He had none of that and he was reared by a very loving white family from Kansas, so he doesn't bring that to the party . . . There was clearly no bias, no cruelty, no 'got you,' no nothing. He just said, 'Folks, these are the facts. This is where we are, this is who we've been,' and it was so masterful because he is so centred and he can sail and navigate above the sky.[57]

In the above quotation, Pratt makes reference to Barack Obama's presidential campaign, when the candidate uttered the now famous words: 'There is not a Black America and a White America and Latino America and Asian America – there's the United States of America.'[58] As scholar Tavia Nyong'o reminds us, Obama's optimistic rhetoric promised to thrust the racial dialogue in a new direction by making 'blackness secondary to Americanness',[59] but most importantly, he was a candidate with the ability to transcend race. Obama's seemingly evolved attitudes about race were met with widespread approval by a public eager to move beyond a troubling history of oppression – but for more conservative commentators in the African-American community, his words were cause for scepticism and ill-tempered speculations about the politician's authenticity. Stanley Crouch, in his 2006 *New York Daily News* article entitled 'What Obama Isn't: Black Like Me On Race', suggested that Obama's mixed race heritage invalidates him as an authentically black American: 'His father is a black Kenyan. Other than colour, Obama did not – does not – share a heritage with the majority of black Americans, who are descendants of plantation slaves.'[60] Crouch, an African-American poet and cultural critic, was born in 1945 and came of age in a legally segregated America – a stark and contrasting experience to Obama's more inclusive and less turbulent, post-Civil Rights era of racial hopefulness. Having been born in 1961, as many commentators have acknowledged, Obama was not raised under the duress of structural racism, and his views reflected that reality. Nyong'o makes an important point that the president's softer approach resonates more with a sentiment held by many whites that 'a robust sense of minority or racial identity was not fully compatible with being a proud American'.[61] Crouch, on the other hand, held firm to his belief that Obama's blackness was a fraudulent construction, wielded opportunistically when necessary, and discarded when politically inconvenient:

> So when black Americans refer to Obama as 'one of us,' I do not know what they are talking about. In his new book, *The Audacity of Hope*, Obama makes it clear that, while he has experienced some light versions of typical racial stereotypes, he cannot claim those problems as his own – nor has he lived the life of a black American.[62]

Crouch's words clearly speak to generational divisiveness in the African-American community on the issues of racial legitimacy and authenticity. Obama's mixed race heritage has been the cause of speculation about his authenticity – even if it is precisely that quality that has made him a symbolic beacon for America's history as an ethnic melting pot. Assessments of Barack Obama's authenticity are extremely significant to understanding the nuances of post-blackness, because there is a urgent necessity to redefine and broaden cultural understandings of African-American identity to be much more inclusive. This is especially germane to an intra-cultural climate in which 'one's allegiance to "race" is critical to one's in-group status'.[63] Much of the speculation about Obama's racial allegiances surfaced during his 2008 campaign when, during many of his rousing speeches, he seemed to evoke the spirit and oratory genius of civil rights leader Martin Luther King, Jr. The brilliantly calibrated contrast between his inclusive racial rhetoric and the Southern-inflected folksiness of the black preacher tradition was an irresistibly potent combination that seduced an entire nation. For some it was hucksterism, but for others it was a masterful calculation – yet Obama was keenly aware of the rhetorical and spiritual force of the MLK image. The morally upright, family-oriented-community-based-African-American leader archetype is a beloved personage that is deeply engrained in the American historical consciousness. However, while the hetero-patriarchal race-man endures, it is perhaps an outmoded figure, and one that (as many of his critics and devotees have noted) the politician has only embodied symbolically. Obama's resuscitation of MLK's image has an eerie resonance with the critical intent of this book, which is to reconsider post-blackness as a particularly queer phenomenon: one where the masculinist dogma surrounding black authenticity has outlived its usefulness – but more significantly, has never really acknowledged the true diversity of the black American experience.

In the twenty-first century era of increased focus on gay rights, a new hero has emerged that personifies both the genius of the 1960s race-man and the oppressive intolerances that lingered within the black liberation struggle. Civil rights leader Bayard Rustin (1912–1987) – the architect of the 1963 March on Washington for Jobs and Freedom, and staunch advocate for non-violent resistance – was a gay man whose sexuality was considered a political liability among the leaders of the Civil Rights Movement. Scholar Henry Louis Gates, Jr. said it well when he stated that 'Bayard Rustin lived and worked in the deepest shadows, not because he was a closeted gay man, but because he wasn't trying to hide who he was.'[64] A pacifist and follower of the writings of Henry David Thoreau and Mahatma Gandhi's principles of nonviolent civil disobedience, Rustin travelled to Alabama in 1956 (at the request of activist and labour leader A. Philip Randolph) to support Dr King's efforts during the Montgomery bus boycott. It was during this pivotal time that Rustin introduced Gandhi's teachings to King and his followers – forever altering the movement's aims and strategies. Despite his prominence as an activist and civil rights leader, Rustin was always at the centre of controversy. In 1944 he was convicted for violating the Selective Service Act and spent two years in federal prison, after which he travelled to India, Africa, and Europe, convening with other activists and political radicals – as well as lending support to various independence and peace movements.[65] Nevertheless, it was his sexuality that led to his marginalization and public shaming, due in large part to the legal prohibitions of the time, which criminalized homosexuality in almost every state. Rustin was always open about his life with those close to him, but in 1953 he was arrested in Pasadena, California while having sex with a man in a parked car and was charged with public indecency. The criminal charge proved too much for movement leaders to publicly stand by Rustin and he was ultimately pushed to the background and viewed as a political liability. Despite the impact of his arrest, he continued to be a vital member of the movement, becoming Dr King's strategist and ghostwriter. In support of Rustin, A. Philip Randolph sought to have the controversial activist appointed as head of the March on Washington, an event that was initially not supported by then President John F. Kennedy. In fact, several weeks before the march, as Peter Dreier recounts, Senator Strom Thurmond, a segregationist from South Carolina, 'publicly attacked Rustin on the floor of the Senate by reading reports of his Pasadena arrest for homosexual behaviour a decade earlier – documents he probably got from FBI director J. Edgar Hoover'.[66] The result of Thurmond's very public attack was that 'Rustin had become perhaps the most visible homosexual in America.'[67]

It is only in the last decade that Rustin's legacy has been recovered and chronicled in several biographies,[68] though what is most striking about his resurgence, is that he has become a beacon for both racial equality, as well as for the continuing struggle for LGBT rights around the world. Growing public interest in Rustin's contributions to human rights led President Barack Obama to posthumously award the late activist the Presidential Medal of Freedom on 8 August. Throughout his career, Rustin was thrust into the shadows because of his sexuality, and it wasn't until late in his life that the Civil Rights activist spoke openly about the importance of acknowledging the full humanity and legal rights of the gay community. In an 1987 interview, Rustin prophetically stated the following words, which in so many ways, sums up what is so incredibly urgent about this thing called post-blackness:

> Twenty-five, thirty years ago, the barometer of human rights in the United States were black people. That is no longer true. The barometer for judging the character of people in regard to human rights is now those who consider themselves gay, homosexual, lesbian.
>
> We are all one. And if we don't know it, we will learn it the hard way.[69]

Queering Post-Blackness

Keeping in mind the highly nuanced, yet ever-evolving discourse on the African-American experience (particularly the contentious debate about racial authenticity) – post-blackness speaks not only to sexual marginality, but also ways of being and modes of expressiveness that lack cultural distinctiveness, yet are still very much rooted in the complexities of black life. Throughout this book, I characterize the aesthetic strategies of post-black artists as creating a *semiotic vulnerability*, or, in other words, a liquidity or porousness in the semiotic function of blackness that transcends its historical and ideological opacity. When considering the nuances of the post-black aesthetic, it bears understanding that for many of its practitioners, *blackness* – as Thelma Golden suggests – is something to be embraced, but is not necessarily autobiographical, or specific to their individual experience.[70] In an interview with Touré, one of the major artists associated with post-blackness, Rashid Johnson, said the following about the way his contemporaries wield blackness:

> There's a generation of black artists before me who made work specifically about the black experience, but I think for my generation, having grown up in the age of hip-hop and Black Entertainment Television, there's less of a need to define the black experience so aggressively to a white audience. I think it gives us a different type of opportunity to have a more complex conversation around race and identity. It's not a weapon for me, it's more of an interest.[71]

Post-blackness resonates because it articulates the frustrations of young African-American artists (the post-Civil Rights generation) around notions of identity and belongingness that they perceived to be stifling, reductive, and exclusionary. For artist Glenn Ligon post-black means a more individualized notion of blackness:

> I just think we're getting beyond the collective notion of what blackness was. Blackness was about group definitions so there could be black leaders who spoke for black people in total. And I think we've moved beyond that and we're entering the space where more individualized conceptions of blackness will be the rule and not the exception. I think that's where we're headed.[72]

For many African-American artists, blackness (as it was historically constructed and mobilized) is a nationalist cultural politics that produced a set of values and visual expressions overly concerned with recovering black male dignity – by advocating for traditionally heterosexual archetypes of patriarchal strength, domination, and virility (i.e., Civil Rights and Black Power Movement representations). While post-black can be understood as a rejection of this history – particularly the politically-urgent dictates of the black aesthetic movement – it is an approach to artistic production that continues to thrive all around the USA. Ennobling, colourful, and largely figurative artworks with an Afrocentric sensibility are perhaps the most ubiquitous and prolifically produced forms of African-American art in circulation today. Thelma Golden has termed this style of art 'black romantic': an honorific and celebratory form of cultural production that is sold in neighbourhood galleries, black art fairs, and in shopping malls with primarily African-American clientele. In 2002, The Studio Museum in Harlem, under the direction of Golden, staged an exhibition entitled *Black Romantic.* According to the curator, the exhibition was designed to explore a type of African-American art that – while celebrated and collected across the nation – falls outside of the elitist high-art circuits that The Studio Museum operates within. There is such disregard among the post-black generation for the black romantic aesthetic that its absence speaks to a form of marginalization that occurs within the African-American arts community. The contradiction is of course that, in Golden's words, The Studio Museum itself was designed to function as 'a corrective to the exclusion of African-American artists from the canon of American art'.[73] Therefore it was problematic that the museum, in its focus on what Golden characterized as artists who are at the vanguard of post-modern discourse, would exclude an African-American cultural form that spoke to the values of everyday black folks – not just to the esoteric proclivities of the cultural elite.[74]

The black romantic genre is a direct descendant of the black aesthetic movement. It is a genre that is about the visualization of racial fidelity, which deeply believes that art holds the potential for racial uplift and should produce positive, affirming representations of African-American identity. In her catalogue essay for the exhibition entitled *To Be Real*, Golden spoke frankly about her distaste for the art she reluctantly put on display:

> I was often physically unsettled by what I perceived to be the overwrought sentiment, strident essentialism, and problematic authenticity that is the lingua franca of this world. I shuddered at the crass commercialism, the rampant reproduction, and the bombastic self-promotion I often encountered. I seemed caught in a clash of values and I could not read past any of that. Mostly, I was suspicious of the notion of the 'real' or the authentic that many of the artists strive to present. The 'real' seemed based on a mixture of revisionist history and wilful fantasy, weirdly combined with reportage. The absence of irony is profound. Directly translating or visualizing the language of black empowerment, the art operates as an antidote to perceptions of a conspiracy to promote 'negative' images in the mainstream press, black popular culture, and even in the work of other African-American artists.[75]

It's interesting that, in Golden's stated impatience with and distaste for the essentialist dictates of black romanticism, she would choose to title her essay 'To Be Real', which appears to be a cheeky reference to the 1978 disco song 'Got To Be Real' by Cheryl Lynn. A queer anthem, Lynn's popular hit was featured in the groundbreaking 1990 documentary *Paris Is Burning* (Dir. Jennie Livingston) about the heyday of New York City drag balls, in which mostly working class gay black and Latino men performed various states of 'realness' (slang for mimicking hetero-normativity). It would seem that Golden's title contains a double meaning that, on the one hand, indicts the black romantic genre's fixation with mythically constructing a regressively hetero-normative brand of black authenticity – and on the other, it is a thinly veiled and rather sarcastic reference to its erasure of queerness.

As a generationally-specific ethos, post-blackness can be understood as issuing from a general attitude of ambivalence towards everything that black romantic art stands for: compulsory solidarity, insularity, and the intra-community demands to maintain a sense of racial pride. It could also be said that there is a broad rejection of the generational passing down of racial trauma and the expectation that the post-Civil Rights contingent will carry the torch of survivorship and anti-racist politics. The elusiveness of post-blackness makes it difficult to pin down, and certainly not all African-American artists grouped under this banner can easily be encapsulated by it. It is more of an ethos than a dictum; nevertheless it continues to define a generation of artists, many of whom seek to escape the limitations imposed by race.

What is perhaps most urgent about post-black artistic production is the sexual politics that inform the work. Many of the most notable artists within this genre are descendants of oppositional and politically engaged critical practices of the previous generation that explored themes related to gender and sexual discrimination that were ultimately marginalized and relegated to a peripheral position within the art world of the 1980s and early 1990s. During this period, few African-American artists took on such themes aside from notable contributions from photographer Lyle Ashton Harris, documentarians Marlon Riggs and Thomas Allen Harris, and multi-media artists like Glenn Ligon, Iké Udé, and poet Essex Hemphill. Much of this work was informed by debates in UK-based cultural studies (such as the writings of scholars Stuart Hall, Paul Gilroy, Homi Bhabha, and Kobena Mercer) and the representational strategies of British artists Isaac Julien and Rotimi Fani-Kayode. The expanded notion of identity that post-blackness gestures towards (the decentralizing of the African-American experience), has roots in British cultural studies, specifically Gilroy's anti-essentialist notion 'the Black Atlantic', which is a diasporic and trans-national approach to studying African identities.[76] Gilroy's radical new position was forcefully against all expressions of ethnic absolutism and provided inspiration to artists and intellectuals interested in breaking free from the dogmas imposed by essentialist conceptualizations of identity. Intellectually, Gilroy's Black Atlantic was a space for transnational exchange that sought to disrupt forms of cultural nationalism. Artist Glenn Ligon (while in conversation with art historian Huey Copeland and curator Thelma Golden) discussed the importance of Gilroy's Black Atlantic to his eventual formulation of post-black:

> I first encountered the term in relationship to an exhibition created by David A. Bailey at the Institute of Contemporary Arts in London called *Mirage: Enigmas of Race, Difference and Desire*.[77] What was interesting about the exhibition was that it brought together a number of artists who were prominent in Britain alongside artists from the United States, myself included. In addition to the show there was a conference organized around the issues raised by the Black Atlantic, which introduced me to scholars like Paul Gilroy, Kobena Mercer, Stuart Hall, and Homi Bhabha. I realized that London was an intellectual hotbed, and being in that environment made me think about my relationship to black British cultural studies and to the work of artists like Isaac Julien and Steve McQueen.[78]

Golden echoed Ligon's sentiment when she stated 'the Black Atlantic allows us to rewrite and reflect on our own history in a more expanded way'.[79] The notion of a globalized and expanded blackness, as formulated by Gilroy, is central to understanding the eventual evolution of post-blackness as a means to open-up African-American identity to be more inclusive – and this process of expanding coincides with a historical moment, marked by the intensifying social and political struggle for LGBT rights. In that regard, post-black is at the vanguard of a civil rights struggle that endeavours to transform the social, political, and cultural life of the nation. For the sake of context, Gilroy's *Black Atlantic* was published in 1995, a moment in which debates around the de-essentializing of identity and nationhood were intensifying in the UK and were beginning to have a major impact on artists and intellectuals in the USA. At the same, leading intellectuals in North America were beginning to seriously reconsider the presence of heterosexism and homophobia in the African-American community in the face of shifting public sentiment around gay and lesbian rights. In 1995 Dr Cornel West gave a groundbreaking and polarizing lecture at the Harvard Graduate School of Education in which he made connections between white supremacy, patriarchy, and heterosexism. But he also spoke very personally about the troubling relation between organized religion and homophobia and the manner in which 'various institutions have promoted unjustified suffering and unmerited pain'.[80] In interrogating the presence of homophobia in religious communities, West spoke about encountering resistance, and at times condemnation, for doing so:

> Any time you offer a serious critique of the systems of power and privilege, be it compulsory heterosexuality, be it white supremacy or what have you, you're going to catch some hell. There's no doubt, both within the black community and the black church, as well as outside, that I tend to catch hell on this issue.[81]

West recounts that his evolution on the issue homosexuality necessitated that he recognize his own homophobic tendencies, because he 'grew up in the black community, in the black church, on the black block and there's a lot of homophobia in all three sites'.[82] So, as he states, 'I'm quite candid about the internal struggle that I undergo because of my own homophobic socialization.'[83] In terms of the black community, West debunks the notion that homophobia is more rampant than in other communities – though he admits that for many years he felt that, within African-American life, homophobia was dealt with quietly, and in a manner that would not disunite the black community.[84]

One of the more significant aspects to West's admission is the notion that homophobia was cast as *subordinate* to the survival of the black community – and this led to the scapegoating of constituencies who are most vulnerable: black women, gays, and lesbians. The scholar believes this situation constitutes a deep crisis that the black community must seriously contend with.[85] The fear of disunity that West discusses is significant and has consistently been a barrier to more progressive action. In the striving for equality is an effort to both illustrate and perform social norms – and to present a stable and hetero-normative image of black life. The consequence is that homosexuality is pushed into the closet and subordinated, in a larger quest to present an image of appropriateness. The anger this causes was well articulated by filmmaker and gay activist Marlon Riggs in a lecture and essay entitled 'Unleash the Queen'. Struggling with declining health due to AIDS, Riggs spoke forcefully about the closeted position that homosexuality occupies in American society, but even more specifically, within the arena of black avant-garde intellectual culture where in his words, the black queer subject is merely 'a pawn in someone else's cultural war game, and thus expendable'.[86] While speaking at a conference on the subject of black popular culture, Riggs articulated the following:

> At these conferences, I am typically called upon to speak on matters of race and sexuality in queer media; race and sexuality in black culture; race and sexuality in Western cinema. But increasingly, of late, this Snap Queen harbours the sneaking suspicion that the measure of her acceptance into various critical in-crowds has less to do with any vital concern with black gay subjectivity and its intrinsic value in black social/cultural expression than with how well she has mastered, and now mimics, the critical language of her newfound tribe . . .
>
> Here we sit assembled, the newest of the New Negroes (the Niggerati of the Nineties), preening and posturing in our fanciful display of cultural literacy, the command of language, the strategic deployment of so many elegant words. Again I witness how casually, how unself-consciously, the faggots and dykes have been left in the woodshed – or is it the closet?[87]

In this quotation, Riggs angrily speaks to what he forcefully calls the 'the insult' of being relegated to a 'cultural ghetto' or more specifically to the condition of 'total erasure'.[88] In a sense, post-blackness carries with it the bitterness of past erasures even if (in an a contradictory sense) it rejects the onus of political obligation. The queerness of post-black is taken as a matter of fact, in that it is never overtly spoken about, and despite the fact that the work is openly expressive of its unique aesthetics and satirical attentiveness. One of the thorny dimensions of post-black – and in the histories and critical discourses of African-American art in general – is that queerness is rarely discussed openly. As quiet as it's kept, post-black is a corrective to the very ghettoization and erasure that Riggs bemoaned and, in its silences and appropriateness, is a framework that allows for queer artists to achieve a visibility and centrality that is unprecedented. On the other hand, I don't wish to assert that the artist's identity politics (as a queer subject) drives post-blackness, per se . . . or in other words, claim that post-blackness is synonymous with queer art. I want to emphasize the notion that post-black *queers* (as an operation) the black romanticism in African-American art (the hetero-patriarchal logics that subtend its values systems and aesthetics). As a critical project, *Queering Post-Black Art* unpacks the impact that sexual politics and queer identities have on our understanding of blackness as a set of visual, cultural, and intellectual concerns. The artists chosen for this investigation (Glenn Ligon, Kehinde Wiley, Mickalene Thomas, and Kalup Linzy) exemplify a dramatic conceptual and thematic shift in contemporary African-American Art. In its intersectional engagement with sexuality, gender, and African-American identity in the arts, *Queering Post-Black Art* stands apart.

I have focused my inquiry upon artistic and critical interventions that consider the construction of identity and difference and how these interventions influence contemporary artistic production. There have been no critical projects to date that have explored the shifting (and at times radical) sexual projects implicit within post-black artistic production and therefore, this book is of vital importance to discussions about the current state of black art in the USA. The success of African-American gay and lesbian artists has played a significant role in re-conceptualizing blackness as a set of visual and critical rhetorics. The book proposes to unpack what these changes mean and to explore their potential ramifications for the study of African-American art and its historicization. *Queering Post-Black Art* asserts that the innovative conceptual strategies of these artists not only indict and break down the barriers of sexual and gender-based exclusions, but simultaneously create a new notion of blackness: one that is less readily knowable and evades the easy process of ideological over-determination key to the formation of stereotypes. This treatise is unique in its effort to bring such criticalities to the forefront of African-American art historical debates.

The art of Glenn Ligon is crucial to this discussion because, as an originator of the term 'post-black', the artist's production truly exemplifies the basic qualities of the genre – particularly the satirical engagement with race and sexual difference. Chapter 1 focuses on an interpretation of key works by Ligon including, *Notes on the Margin of the Black Book* (1991–93) and *Untitled* (*Malcolm X*) (2008). *Notes on the Margin of the Black Book* is a groundbreaking work that critically reassesses the late photographer Robert Mapplethorpe's 1988 photographic series *The Black Book*, a series of mostly nude and eroticized depictions of black men. Widely considered fetishistic, objectifying, and indulging in racial stereotypes, Mapplethorpe's series catalyzed an entire generation of black queer intellectual and artistic production. In *Untitled* (*Malcolm X*), Ligon repurposes an iconic image of the late Civil Rights leader, Malcolm X, characterizing it as a fraught and potent symbol for a type of ethnic authenticity that negates sexual difference. In a sense, the artist reduces Malcolm X's image as a visual signifier of a certain kind of blackness and then defaces it, a gesture that signifies both its malleability and its inability to fully encapsulate the complexity of the African-American experience. This chapter directs significant attention towards the semiotic complexity of Ligon's highly conceptual body of work, but the intention is to explore the formation of the artist's uniquely queer critique of normative blackness: a gesture that is not simply embodied in his more literal text-based paintings, but is also realized as an affective material presence. The brilliance of these works is connected to the artist's willingness to mine the roots of his ambivalence towards blackness – an attitude that ultimately led to the formation of post-blackness, which has become a generation-defining ethos.

Chapter 2 is dedicated to the iconic painter Kehinde Wiley, an artist who is perhaps the best-known and most successful post-black artist to date. His paintings are some of the most unapologetically satirical in subject matter and tone, while at the same time elevating the formal over the political. The chapter looks at the evolution of his work, beginning with his early portraits of urban-attired black men, set against decorative backgrounds. Wiley's signature style of melding the masculine pose of classical Western art, with the African-American male body, paved the way for a more nuanced vision of black male subjectivity. The contrasting of black male bodies, with the signifiers of European male dominance becomes a pairing of two ideologically determined fictions – one considered low culture, the other considered high. Their juxtaposition creates a clever visual pun that speaks to the desirability of the black body as a commodity fetish in the era of hyper-capitalism. Wiley's work is often characterized as post-political in its formalist engagement with the history of Western painting; however, the satirical *queering* of hip-hop culture's masculinist pose sheds a critical light on the performance and maintenance of gender norms and pernicious racial stereotypes. His paintings wield the black male body not in the service of making a meta-commentary on the plight of the urban underclass, but rather as a glorious fantasy or as a phantasmagoric and brand-able good to be exchanged in the global marketplace. The politics embedded in Wiley's satire (like that of many of his post-black contemporaries) is perhaps more focused on the aggressiveness of a rapacious capitalism that commoditizes the black male body as an imago to be fetishized and exchanged. His paintings also effectively dislodge the African-American male from the now-mythical backdrop of urban blight, violence, and social discrimination – though his images are not meant to function as an idealistic corrective to a history of racially demeaning stereotypes. Like many of his post-black contemporaries, Wiley manages to break free from an aesthetics of racial obligation and the hetero-patriarchal logics of normative blackness to create a representational counter-narrative in which queer desire can be visualized.

Chapter 3 considers the work of artist Mickalene Thomas, paying particular attention to the feminist and queer-feminist conceptual strategies in her production. Thomas is widely known for her large-scale and highly decorative images of black women. Her work references a history of black female representation, from the modernist odalisque to the iconic heroines of the Blaxploitation era. In many respects, Thomas recovers the black female body from a history of neglect and debasement, in what amounts to a powerful re-inscription of black female subjectivity. However, her aesthetic and conceptual sensibility interrogates multiple erasures: among them the exclusion of queer women of colour from mainstream feminism, from a history of black liberation struggle, and from normative conceptions of black authenticity. While Thomas' ennobling images are often read as a celebration of female strength, they also forcefully advance a queer feminist gaze that makes visible the desires of black women. This significant dimension of the artist's work highlights the hetero-normative dictates of black feminist representational strategies that, despite their interrogation of gender and racial inequity, fail to acknowledge the lives and critical concerns of queer women of colour. Through an assessment of the artist's key works, the chapter explores how Thomas creates an oppositional worldview that challenges historical dogmas around sexuality and race, while also reimagining blackness as a visually expressive form.

Kalup Linzy's video and performance-based work explores the complicated terrain of race, sexuality, class, and popular media. Chapter 4 unpacks the specificities of the artist's conceptual approach, from his unconventional use of sound and voice-over, to drag, and his meditations on class and soap opera aesthetics. Linzy's production also represents a turn towards the performative in current African-American art and the mobilization of stereotypical notions (and visual markers) of blackness onto white bodies. Linzy is known for provocatively taking racially specific codes (gesture, speech, dress, music, and mannerisms) and mobilizing them across gender, race, and nationality. In the process, he makes an effective commentary on the nature of social division. Significant attention will be given to mining Linzy's fascination with soap operas – specifically the manner in which popular soaps engage in the mythologizing and hyper-visualization of affluent whiteness. The artist is widely recognized for taking the kitschy formal and narrative tropes of soap operas and inserting black bodies into them. In the process Linzy advances a powerful critique on the erasure and marginalization of difference in popular media – as well as on the aspirational longing (through media consumption) of black communities in the American South. By critically examining Linzy's use of drag, the chapter delves into the artist's imaging of black queer subjectivity – most notably against the backdrops of Southern rural life and the high culture circuits of the New York art world. The chapter also addresses the formal and political relationships between Linzy's moving images and those produced by Andy Warhol in the 1960s–1970s, in terms of their fixation with celebrity, kitsch, and the vulgarity of popular culture.

Each of the above artists, in their own inimitable way, represents the ever-evolving sexual and gender politics that have come to define the notion of post-black art. My aim here is to produce new, innovative interpretive possibilities that will elucidate the specific conceptual, aesthetic, and political concerns of post-Civil Rights generation visual artists. Specifically, *Queering Post-Black Art* is concerned with the manner in which gay and lesbian artists seek to redefine the visual and intellectual rhetorics of blackness – and by extension, open it up to new interpretive possibilities. Nevertheless, if one was to characterize post-blackness as a type of collective consciousness – the satirical and often contradictory engagement with the signifiers of blackness renders it more porous and open to the process of signification: a queering of blackness, so to speak.

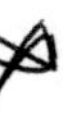

The rise of female, gay, and lesbian artists as legitimate African-American creative voices is essential to the development of black art. Their work resonates with present-day cultural imperatives to finally bring an end to gender inequity and legalized homophobia, in addition to interrogating their spectral presence within the black community. However, we should not believe that these imperatives simultaneously signal that the battle against racism has been won (a critique that is often levelled against the notion of post-black). Post-racial and post-black are not the same thing, and I would venture to say that few African-American artists believe that racism in American society is a thing of the past. The four selected artists employ a type of queer satire that never fails to fascinate and infuriate – while simultaneously transgressing the boundaries of taste and decorum. Both celebrated and reviled, post-black art embodies all of these characteristics, while simultaneously managing to give us pleasure and make us rethink the ideological boundaries we prescribe to our identities. In doing so, this investigation acknowledges how the rise of black gay and lesbian artists impacts the intellectual consideration, historicization, and display of African-American art. In so doing, this research moves away from discussions of African-American identity rooted in notions of cultural authenticity and hetero-normativity, as well as essentialist and rigidly ethnocentric expressions of community and belongingness. Along those lines, this research also departs from multiculturalism-era attitudes around difference that seem to advocate for the celebration and preservation of those differences, while functioning as a means to maintain the status quo of social, cultural, and historical division. With an eye towards a future rich with those 'other options' invoked by Appiah and many others, *Queering Post-Black Art* presents a perspective on contemporary visual production that resonates beyond identity politics of the past, and models useful interpretive strategies across cultural boundaries.

1

Looking for Ligon: Towards an Aesthetic Theory of Blackness

> I am an invisible man. No, I am not a spook like those who haunted Edgar Allan Poe; nor am I one of your Hollywood-movie ectoplasms. I am a man of substance, of flesh and bone, fiber and liquids – and I might even be said to possess a mind. I am invisible, understand, simply because people refuse to see me . . .[1]
>
> – Ralph Ellison, *Invisible Man*

Blackness, Formless, Invisible

In the work of Glenn Ligon, language hovers like a spectre, looming over us hauntingly – beckoning the viewer to confront the darkest and most troubling regions of the African-American experience. While the artist excels at mining the history of black folk, it is perhaps the formal dimension of his work that speaks most effectively to the complexities and contradictions of race in America. If there is a core tension that resides at the centre of Ligon's production, it is the manner in which form and materiality undercut the political. As a result, there is a need to address 'the historical flattening' of Ligon's production that so often plagues its critical interpretation.[2]

It is certainly true that Ligon's practice has been comprehensively detailed – particularly the artist's social and political concerns, while the material processes become somewhat secondary to its unpacking. Curator Okwui Enwezor has sought to recover the work's formal dimension in his reflections on the artist's impressive career, highlighting the fact that Ligon's work is in fact a 'relentless reflection on the legacies of postwar art... and that the legacies of minimalism and late-abstraction pervade his often celebrated text-based paintings'.[3] Enwezor rightly reminds us that the work of post-Abstract Expressionist artists like Ad Reinhardt, Jasper Johns, Robert Rauschenberg, Robert Ryman and Frank Stella, were key influences on young Ligon's formal development – while the text-based production of artists John Baldessari, Mel Bochner, Joseph Kosuth, and Ed Ruscha greatly impacted Ligon's conceptual approach.[4] Ligon's use of language aligns with the politically charged moment of the late 1980s, when identity politics gained an increasing legitimacy in the New York art world. Socially engaged conceptualists like Barbara Kruger and Félix González-Torres, and contemporary African-American artists Adrian Piper, Lorna Simpson, and Carrie Mae Weems, all employed text and image as a means to confront the construction and representation of identity.[5] Much of the artwork produced during the identity debates of the late 1980s through the 1990s explored a relation between text and image that was deeply informed by post-structuralist theories of language. This was a period heavily influenced by a critical engagement with the formation of pernicious ideologies around race, gender, and sexual orientation – although these explorations were not always met with enthusiasm.

Ligon's work emerged quite brilliantly from the wreckage caused by the 1993 instalment of the Whitney Biennial. Curated by Elisabeth Sussman, Thelma Golden, John G. Hanhardt, and Lisa Phillips, the biennial represented the museum's attempt to address the political concerns of minority artists – to grant them a legitimacy that had, up to that point, been elusive. From the perspective of more conservative critics and scholars, the 1993 biennial was an epic failure, borne out of liberal guilt and political correctness run amok. Art historian Robert Hughes famously proclaimed that the exhibition was a 'fiesta of whining' by what he characterized as a gaggle of malcontents and angry outsiders.[6] It was a sentiment shared by many, but such views proved to be neither effective countermeasures, nor capable of stemming the tide of artwork dedicated to commenting upon the mechanisms of social inequity.

Ligon's contribution to the biennial, a conceptual work entitled *Notes on the Margin of the Black Book* (1991–93), was a critical meditation

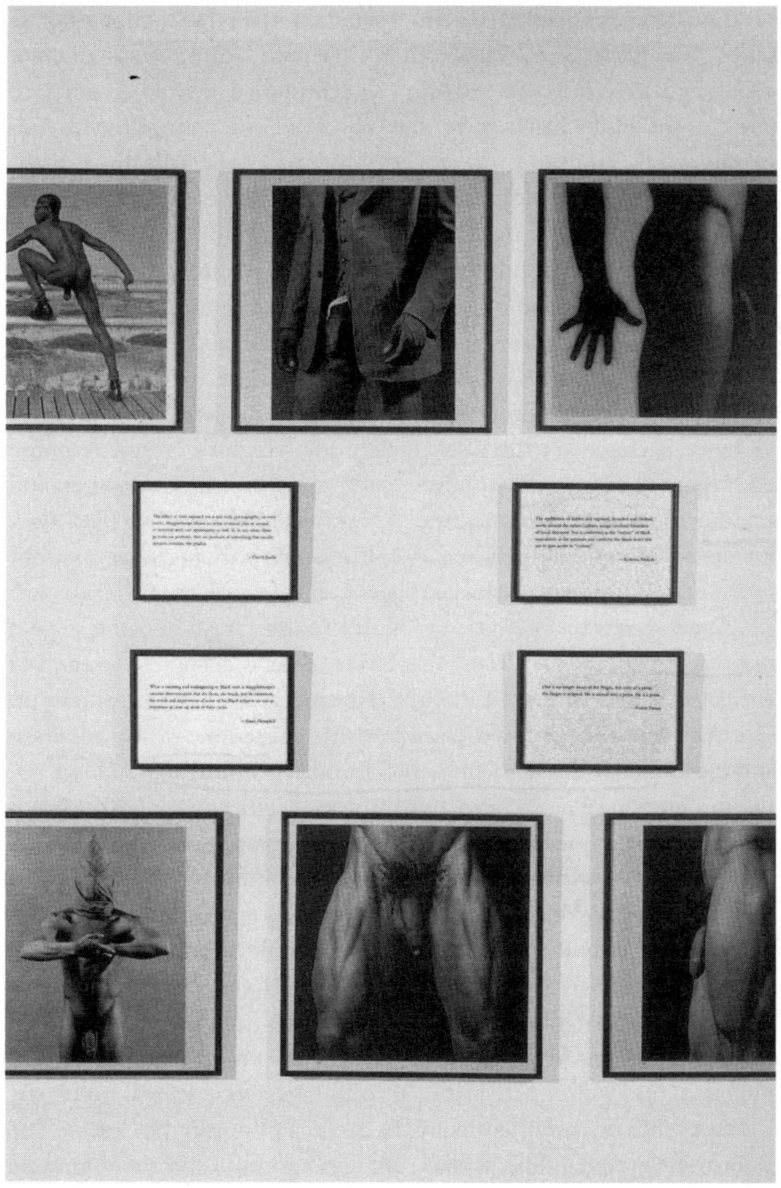

Figure 1 Glenn Ligon, *Notes on the Margin of the Black Book* (1991–1993). Ninety-one offset prints $11\frac{1}{2} \times 11\frac{1}{2}$ in. each (framed); seventy-eight text pages $5\frac{1}{4} \times 7\frac{1}{4}$ in. each (framed). Solomon R. Guggenheim Museum, New York. © Glenn Ligon/Regen Projects, Los Angeles

on the late photographer Robert Mapplethorpe's 1988 photographic series *The Black Book*. Mapplethorpe, a noted queer photographer and gifted formalist and provocateur, composed a striking series of portraits of nude black men – most of whom were close friends of the artist. The series drew sharp criticism, especially from black queer communities, most notably for their fetishistic and objectifying representation of black male bodies. The emphasis on genitalia and the cropped-away heads of his subjects seemed to self-consciously deny his models personhood and interiority – ultimately reinforcing stereotypes about black male aggressiveness and hyper-sexuality. Scholars from Kobena Mercer to David Marriott have written extensively about Mapplethorpe's homoerotic gaze and the particular brand of ideological violence it enacts on the black male body.[7] Ligon's critical response endeavoured to identify with Mapplethorpe's 'portrayal of gayness and critique the portrayal of blackness'.[8] *Notes on the Margin of the Black Book* juxtaposes Mapplethorpe's images of black men with personal reactions to the series' problematic racial suggestiveness.

Margin seems to foreshadow Ligon's future forays into the subject of black gay identity – a topic that has received a negligible amount of critical attention in the art world's response to his prodigious output. Greater emphasis has been placed on his epistemological playfulness and the linguistic dexterity of his sociopolitical commentary. However, Ligon's interest in racial formations and their self-definition have taken a diverse array of visual and conceptual forms, from prints and drawings to neon signs. Arguably, it is his text-based paintings that have garnered the most fervent critical attention and acclaim. It was in the late 1980s when Ligon debuted as a maker of large-scale text-based paintings, most of which were initially black and white. Incorporating fragments of racially charged jokes and literary quotations from notorious cultural commentators like James Baldwin and Richard Pryor, Ligon repeatedly stenciled the appropriated text directly onto the canvas until the words eventually lost their legibility in a sea of murky blackness. The paintings were incredibly formal, but also conceptual in their semiotic and linguistic emphasis – a strategy that enabled the artist to engage with structures of identity, while thinking seriously about colour, materiality, and the sensuousness of form.

It is in this content-versus-form binary that Ligon's work provokes us and frustrates attempts to easily affix meaning. Since late modernism, form and identity have no doubt been theorized as polar opposites,

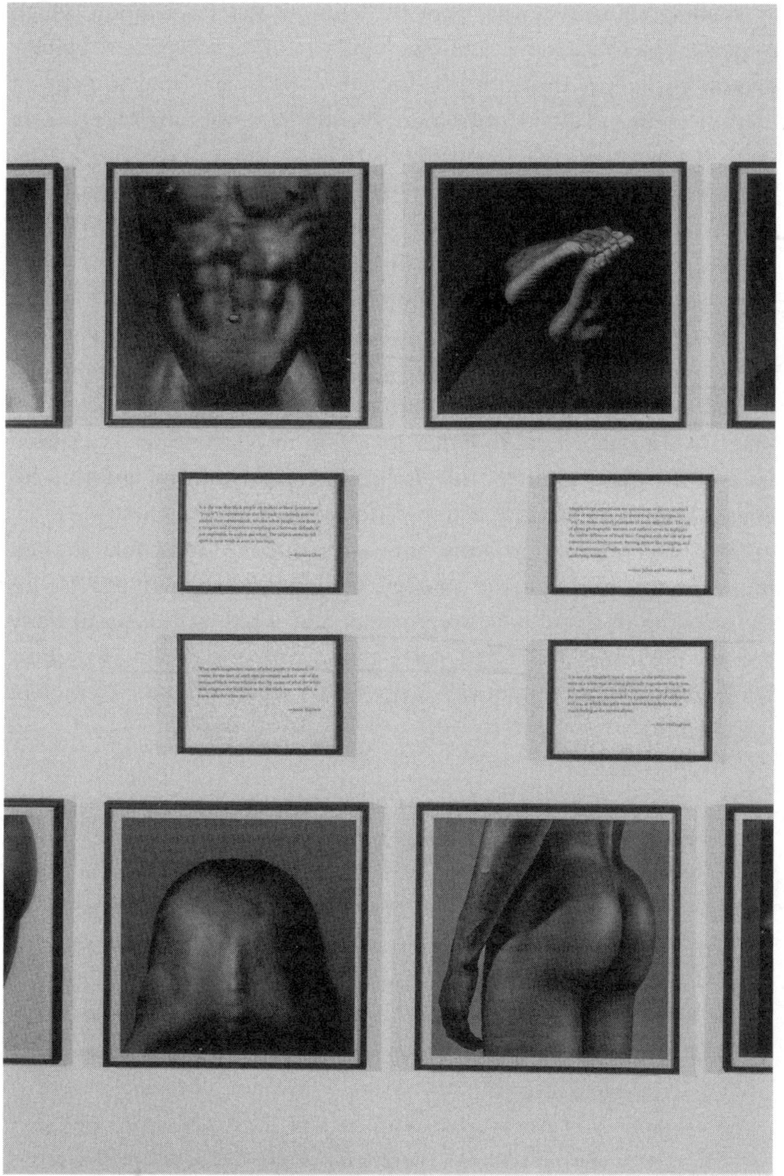

Figure 2 Glenn Ligon, *Notes on the Margin of the Black Book* [Detail] (1991–1993). Ninety-one offset prints $11^1/_2 \times 11^1/_2$ in. each (framed); seventy-eight text pages $5^1/_4 \times 7^1/_4$ in. each (framed). Solomon R. Guggenheim Museum, New York. © Glenn Ligon/Regen Projects, Los Angeles

as duelling value systems meant to delineate the terms upon which important art can achieve legitimacy and canonical acceptance. Ligon's oeuvre challenges these efforts through a well-calculated strategy of identification and dis-identification. Neither race nor form takes centre stage. Rather, there is an oscillation between a self-reflexive meditation on race and sexuality, and an intervention into the falsity of formalism's mythic universality. It is in this quality that Ligon breaks from his contemporaries, namely conceptualists David Hammons and Gary Simmons, as well as the late painter Jean-Michel Basquiat. I would argue that Ligon denies both oppositional archetypes of the conceptually inclined, identity-conscious ethnographer and the enlightened formalist in favour of a much more nebulous creative identification – one that disrupts efforts to either lock him into a confining racialized state of marginality, or to universalize his production by ignoring his engagement with identity and the condition of his blackness.[9]

In many respects, as Enwezor states, Ligon's resistance to easy pigeonholing (through the strategy of linguistic slipperiness) has its roots in the distinction between black and white artists, particularly the ideologically prescribed roles that grant universality to some, while relegating the minority artist to a perpetual state of inherent marginality:

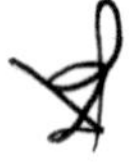

> The distinction between white and black artists, however, is not meant to separate Ligon's work from the seemingly universal tendencies often ascribed to the work of white American artists, nor is it meant to isolate Ligon exclusively in the category of non-universality often reserved for the work of black and minority artists in the discourses of American art and letters. Rather the distinction demonstrates how his work is entangled not only in the formal, conceptual, and epistemological systems within which the work of African-American artists has been received, but equally how it constantly negotiates the diverse conceptual, philosophical, and formal grounds of American art since at least the 1960s, at the height of the civil rights movement. The impact of the civil rights movement so completely transformed the American sociopolitical landscape that it would be a matter of extreme intellectual blindness not to notice the shifting historical differences in the linguistic emphases placed on African-American identity as the ground of self-definition moved from one racial category to the next: from *coloured* to *negro*, *black*, *Afro American*, and *African American*.[10]

In Enwezor's critical framework, the significance of Ligon's intervention resides in his rather uncanny capacity to challenge easy racial categorization: his 'racial self' in the ideological box of so-called *authentic* African-American identity.[11] The embodied and over-determined archetype of the *black artist* is one of his foils, but his satirical approach to slaying this demon doesn't just come from his more literal brand of linguistic and conceptual gymnastics. It also finds its resonance in form itself: in the legibility/illegibility of his text-based paintings. Blackness holds its metaphorical meanings in our understanding of race. But the stark muddiness of Ligon's constructing of blackness, as abject formlessness, potentially conveys something much more profound.

I argue that Ligon images blackness *as an affective material presence* – something that isn't simply visual, but also something we can feel and smell: a presence that embodies the horror of detachment that Julia Kristeva so effectively allegorizes in her theory of abjection.[12] Art historians Rosalind E. Krauss and Yve-Alain Bois have written about this quality in their book *Formless: A User's Guide.*[13] These contrasting understandings of abjection – one concerned with gender, the other with material form – are both rooted in the writings of Georges Bataille. This dualism provides a nice little irony that conveniently captures the impasse at the heart of Ligon's production: the demand for racial fidelity versus the mythic emancipatory potential of form. Kristeva theorizes the abject as that which is cast off, a difference (or Otherness) that cannot be assimilated into the self. In her allegory, she speaks of a traumatic encounter with the corpse, or with bodily excess (spittle, blood, urine, faeces, or tears) as symbolism for a difference that becomes abjected or expelled. But it also speaks to the psychological condition of embodying the position of the social Other (the shame of alterity or lack).[14] This model is useful when discussing the formation and maintenance of difference, especially in oppressive cultural climates where physically identifiable forms of difference (i.e. racial, ethnic, gender, sexual) determine levels of enfranchisement or disenfranchisement. However, it is also meaningful when thinking about the psychological relationship between the self and Other – and the way that interaction takes shape in material form.[15]

It is nonetheless important to think about the relationship between abject form (as a material presence) and the social condition of being abject (embodying physical difference) when discussing the work of Glenn Ligon – not least because the tension between content and form often becomes apparent in an opposition between the condition of marginality (experienced by minorities) and the universality granted to so-called normative subjectivities. The impasse between content and form (the political and formal) that takes precedence in Ligon's art exacerbates ongoing tensions around the presence and canonical viability of minority artists. As Krauss and Bois have pointed out, Georges Bataille used the term *informe* (formless) to allegorize 'that which is other' in the form of base materialism – a scatological presence that is abject. Abjection is not so much a thing in itself, 'it is an *operation* (which is to say, neither a theme, nor a *substance*, nor a concept)'.[16] Krauss and Bois have taken this notion of abjection (as an *operation*) to think about materiality in a manner that vulgarizes the impasse between content and form that has plagued art discourse since early modernism. Their notion of formlessness (*informe*) is the unverifiable, the un-hierarchized, that insults the binary logic central to the modernist opposition between form and content.[17] If they endeavour to render this enduring antagonism obsolete, Krauss and Bois have also taken aim at several other art historical pretentions, namely 'artistic autonomy' and 'significant form' – terminologies that have served the function of elevating the formal dimension of a work of art (the quest for the essential, or the pure), at the expense of more overtly political or identity-based concerns.[18] *Informe*, as defined by Bataille, is subversive in its articulation of the belittled, the denigrated, and the repressed – it is excremental form, but not in a literal sense, because it resembles nothing. It has autonomy from fixed meanings. There is perhaps a utopian impulse at the heart of Krauss and Bois' attempt to sublimate Bataille's *informe* into art discourse, which seeks to elevate materiality (in the evaluative stances and critical agendas of art), while still rejecting the binary logic of content versus form.

It is my contention that Ligon's artistic approach wields the base materialism of abjection as an *operation* – as a means to frustrate the binary-based value systems of art. He uncannily renders blackness as a material presence that is tactile, yet also intervenes in the ideological meanings that blackness so powerfully evokes. In his abjection, there is no elevation of content over form, but rather a base materialism of blackness *as an operation*: it is the unverifiable and the uncategorized that Krauss and Bois theorized in their articulation of Bataille's *informe*. However, Ligon is all too aware of abjection's metaphorical usage in a Kristevian engagement with embodied forms of difference. It is certainly true that his imaging of blackness contains its material pleasures – although he still acknowledges its historical and ideological allusions that posit it as a belittled, denigrated, and repressed presence that is embodied in *certain* subjectivities. It is here where Ligon intervenes into the archetype of the *black American artist*. To be a black artist is to produce art concerned with the state of being black (a cultural politics of race) that has, in much of its history, been thought of as an inferior social condition: a condition defined by marginality and various forms of social obligation. Further, to be a black artist is to foreground one's racialized identity at the expense of more universal aesthetic concerns – it is to place the political over the formal.

Ligon's paintings, as Okwui Enwezor reminds us, use the vitality of colour (in this instance, *blackness*) as a social trope in the looking, seeing, reading, and comprehending of a black formal language.[19] He further states, 'In the majoritarian culture of whiteness, in which race becomes a barometer of value, for obvious reasons blackness becomes a value against which the primacy of whiteness as a literal and metaphorical universal sign of aesthetic value is defined and measured.'[20] This engagement with blackness as a sign of aesthetic value is precisely how the notion of post-blackness derives its epistemological and polemical significance. Ligon, like many of his contemporaries (i.e. Kerry James Marshall, Kara Walker, and Michael Ray Charles) uses blackness as a trope of racialized communication. Unlike the others, he perverts its meaning by complexifying the ideological legibility that restricts its expressive potential.[21] As previously articulated, one of the operations of post-black is to question the problem of intra-cultural obligation and the demand for racial fidelity. It wouldn't be a stretch to suggest that Ligon's production wrestles with that same demand by muddying our understanding of the aesthetic possibilities of blackness – *queering* it by endowing it with a semiotic vulnerability. The queering of blackness in Ligon's production is a topic I will return to in the proceeding pages, but this chapter largely endeavours to create an aesthetic theory of blackness – and to explore how this quality finds its rhetorical force in the artist's impressive body of work.

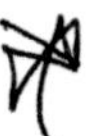

On Black Cultural Distinctiveness

There is a lengthy history of black visual artists who have contemplated blackness as a visual sign: William H. Johnson, Jacob Lawrence,

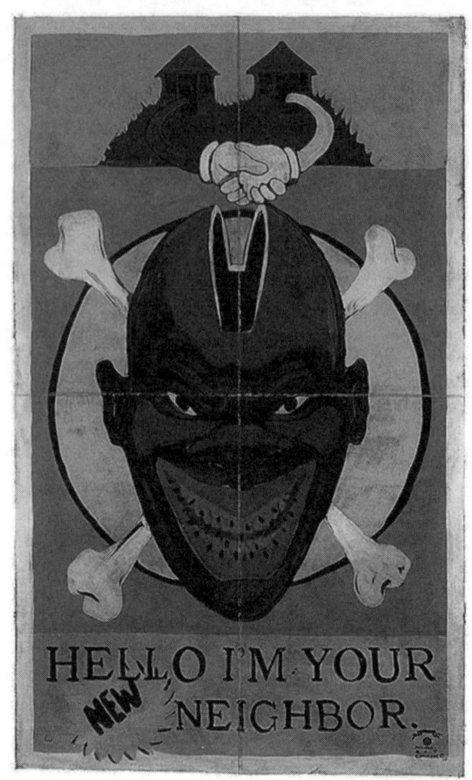

Figure 3 Michael Ray Charles, *(Forever Free) Hello I'm Your New Neighbor*, (1997). Acrylic latex, stain, and copper penny on paper, 60¼ × 36 in. © Michael Ray Charles/Tony Shafrazi Gallery

Romare Bearden, Charles White, Daniel LaRue Johnson, Betye Saar, Jean-Michel Basquiat, and David Huffman come to mind – but there are scores of others whose iconography, conceptual approaches, and colour choices have been dominated by a struggle with blackness. There is no more powerful signifier than blackness, a fact that speaks to its enduring presence in visual, literary, and linguistic forms of cultural production. The list of visual artists, filmmakers, poets and novelists, historians, philosophers, and cultural theorists that have explored this powerful social construction is too vast to mention. However, my interest here is in contemplating the base materialism of blackness as an affective tactile form. Conventional readings of

Ligon's pictures locate their political dimensions in the more overt and primarily linguistic references to black culture. Ligon has relentlessly grappled with blackness as a powerful racialized construct, exploring its visual presence as well as how blackness functions as a linguistic form. My reading of Ligon's work challenges the uncritical and rather unimaginative reduction of his political intervention to the realm of linguistic play. The appropriated text by Richard Pryor, for example, endows Ligon's paintings with a black style – what Cornel West has termed 'black cultural distinctiveness'.[22]

There is no doubt that this quality enables the artist to contemplate the social status of the black subject. We have seen this done quite successfully in works such as *Mudbone (Liar)* (1993), a square format painting composed of acrylic and oil stick on linen. *Mudbone (Liar)* adopts Pryor's off-colour humour for its satirical send up of black stereotypes – in this instance mythologies about black male endowment and sexual prowess. Pryor, as Thelma Golden notes, perpetuates stereotypes as he debunks and critiques them, a strategy that has its roots in the rich tradition of African-American satire.[23] Scholar Darryl Dickson-Carr characterized the controversial nature of black satire as an incendiary mode of intra-cultural critique, suggesting that its critical gaze looks outward – skewering the dominant culture's racist antics, while also satirizing the foibles and intolerances within the black community.[24] For this reason, satire has not always been widely accepted among African-Americans. In its use of text, Ligon's *Mudbone (Liar)* is a picture that is about reading as much as it is about looking. This crucial distinction lies at the core of Ligon's aesthetic and conceptual approach. Set against hot red-orange text, the painting's muddy red background possesses a scatological quality: an abject smudgy materiality that compliments the obscenity of the text itself. The opening phrase of Pryor's satirical joke, '*Niggers had the biggest dicks in the world . . .*', is where Ligon mobilizes the signifiers of identity as a racially specific trope.[25] Most critical reflection locates the artist's political commitments in precisely this visual and linguistic element of his work. Contrary to this notion, it is perhaps necessary to look deeper into Ligon's materially affective processes – because I argue that blackness more accurately resides in the base materialism of his objects: the *informe* that Krauss and Bois have endeavoured to theorize. The satirical text is only one dimension of his self-conscious brand of racial

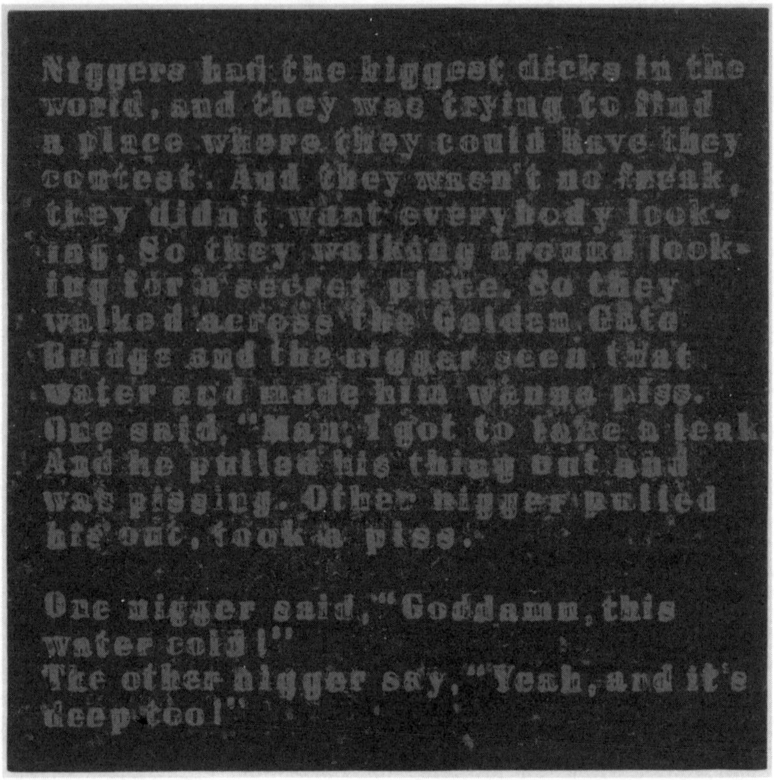

Figure 4 Glenn Ligon, *Mudbone Liar* (1993). Oil stick, synthetic polymer and graphite, 81.3 × 81.3 cm. © Glenn Ligon/Regen Projects, Los Angeles

signifying – though it is arguably in the object itself where the blackness truly resides.

The apparent tension between form and content in Ligon's oeuvre must take us back to the notion of the black male artist, an archetype that is so over-determined that it has become the focus of considerable debate. Art historian Darby English, like Okwui Enwezor, challenges the popular notion of 'black art' and rather pointedly asks: 'What makes "black art" black?'[26] English acknowledges the deceptive simplicity of his query, yet he doesn't ignore the fact that works of art produced by black people are routinely, and rather matter-of-factly, socially understood this way.[27] His impatience around the ghettoization of black art reflects the fact that, all too often, art produced by white heterosexual men has enjoyed a cultural universality that is never afforded minorities. The stain of racial particularity has always been a barrier to the cultural neutrality that so-called normative whiteness contains. This has never been more evident than in the history of high modernist abstraction. Formalism (and formal analysis in general) has long been the domain of Euro-ethnic subjectivities and has tended to negate the possibility that works by black artists could produce more complex and esoteric meanings.

Dominant rhetoric in the visual arts has continually positioned formalism as the antidote to identity politics, but this is in fact untrue. Whether we look at formalism's early iterations in the nineteenth-century or the 1950s era of high modernist abstraction, identity and ethnicity were at the forefront of its formulations. Jewish critics like Harold Rosenberg and especially Clement Greenberg were instrumental to the evolution of formalism as a value system that advocated for universality and anti-essentialist attitudes (while still remaining rooted in a self-conscious oppositional engagement with anti-Semitism and the postwar Jewish experience).[28] The art historian Louis Kaplan has written meaningfully about Greenberg's modernist formalism in light of Jewish identity: ultimately characterizing the notorious critic's formalism as a kind of Jewish unconscious. I mention this because blackness – with its ideological legibility – tends to enslave us. Formalism has always represented a point of departure from the limitations imposed by the body. It's a utopian strategy, but it nonetheless functions as a gesture towards a more open-ended engagement with the complexities of culture.

Formalism also resides within the ideological engagement with blackness employed by Ligon and his contemporaries. Most often, this engagement rests in the self-conscious imaging of the black body. The representation of blackness is usually about *skin* as a marker of difference: the *epidermal schema* that Homi Bhabha discusses in his writings on the black subject under the duress of colonialism. Bhabha's notion of *fixity*, the process upon which markers of difference and degeneracy are affixed onto black bodies, is a means to establish systems of domination and subordination.[29] Within an oppressive colonial context, black skin is a visible and verifiable form of difference that contains damaging stereotypes. Within such a climate, blackness is always *lack* and as Bhabha instructs: '[t]he difference of the object of discrimination is at once visible and natural – colour as the cultural/political *sign* of inferiority or degeneracy, skin as it natural "*identity*"'.[30] Cultural theorist Stuart Hall has written about the relationship between power and fantasy within racialized regimes of representation. Hall identifies fantasy as one of the *operations* of racist systems of power – it mobilizes stereotypes to create and maintain misperceptions about the Other.[31] Blackness as a *trope of racialized communication* is as much about a politics of difference as it is about formalism. We must be wary of value systems in the arts that seek to create binaries and hierarchies that falsely grant formalism a type of universalizing neutrality. The representation of blackness (as an ideologically loaded marker of difference) by black artists does express political concerns – there is no disputing that fact. However, their intellectual and conceptual interests in the historical problem of racism neither negate, nor undermine the material force of their objects. In fact, the political potency of black art may actually reside in form and not the more overtly politicized elements (racialized bodies or didactic text).

Regardless, the archetypal black artist trope that Ligon complicates isn't simply a condition that impacts the social and economic possibilities of cultural producers, of which he himself is included – it is also the mythologized form of difference that fantasy and stereotype is projected onto. The black artist has a cultural capital that expects certain clichés and certain forms of visual expressions to be articulated. Black art comes with a particular set of conceptual expectations and representational demands, among them the visualization of racial stereotypes, predictable political positions, and cheap liberal sentiment about the condition of marginality. These sentiments may take the form of social symbolisms that are visually resplendent – but at their root, they tend to trap the black artist in a position where creative freedom is stifled and the spectacle of racial stereotype is their product. We might benefit by refusing to separate the ideologically over-determined archetype of the black artist from the formal rhetorics of the objects they produce. The politicizing of the black artist is inextricably bound to the materiality of their work and vice versa. Ligon appears to understand this, and so he has created a body of work that always acknowledges the fetishization and fantasy that subtends the critical reception of his production. An anxiety about racial stereotypes lingers uncomfortably in all of Ligon's pictures. Perhaps more specifically, these works express an uneasy awareness of society's phobic condemnation of black men. Ligon tends to skewer and reject the tragic heteronormative construction of black maleness, opting instead to satirically queer it. Nevertheless, he always ponders how the black man has been represented in Western culture 'as the central enigma of a humanity wrapped in the darkest and deepest subliminal fantasies of Europe and America's collective id'.[32] Ligon, as curator Thelma Golden reminds us, recognizes the role racial stereotypes play in our collective psyches – while bearing in mind the specific violence inflicted by images that depict black people as debased and devoid of reason. As Kristeva has aptly illustrated, humanistic engagements with identity inherently connect to relations between bodies. The socially committed artist always aims to examine how we see others and ourselves – but in Ligon's case, anti-racism also comprises a formal project that explores the affective irrationality of blackness as a sensory experience.

Art historian Michael D. Harris, in his writing on the satirical work of artists Kara Walker and Michael Ray Charles, takes aim at post-Civil Rights artists' re-appropriation of racial stereotypes and caricatures. Aunt Jemimas, Sambos, and Coons have always populated the imaginations of these artists, often to controversial and polarizing results. When Kara Walker won the coveted MacArthur Foundation 'Genius' Grant in 1997 at the age 27, she found herself the object of a vicious attack by fellow black female artists Betye Saar and Howardena Pindell. The elder artists characterized her bacchanalian scenes of racialized depravity and violence as injurious to the black community, and the artist as a willing enabler in its destruction. The drubbing took the form of a letter-writing campaign calling for Walker to be blackballed from the art world, but also served as a warning to the younger artist, and those of her generation, to step lightly when dealing with America's history of anti-black racism.[33] The result was a generational rift between pre- and post-Civil Rights generations and a sense that young black artists should labour under a stifling climate of racial obligation. Michael D. Harris' critique of Walker claims that her images are harshest on black folks, in what he characterizes as her petulant lampooning of racial folly. For Harris, Walker is 'not rooted in an African sensibility and her fascination with history is not based in African-American feeling and pathos ... her work offends many who have those roots and understandings'.[34] It is clear that Harris sees Walker's historical interest residing in a fascination with blackness as a debased presence –

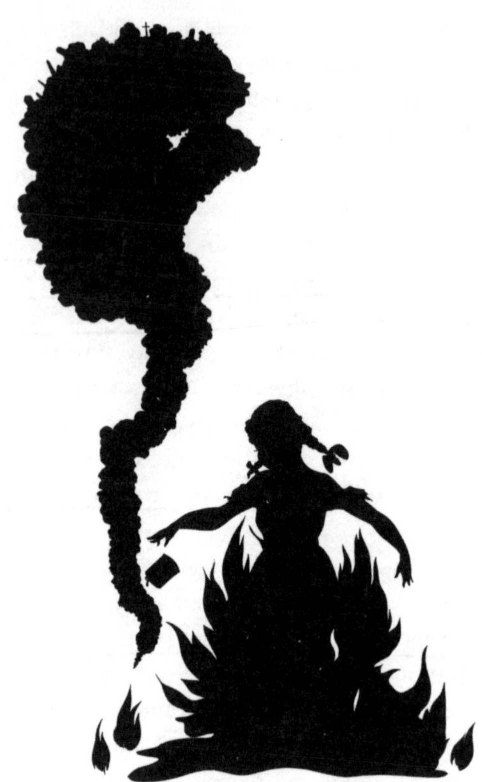

Figure 5 Kara Walker, *Burn* (1998). Cut paper and adhesive on wall, 92⅛ × 48 in. Collection of Jerry and Katherine Speyer. © Kara Walker/Sikkema Jenkins & Co

as something that is 'always dependent on the existence of whiteness for meaning, so it offers no means of transcendence'.[35] There is some merit to the art historian's characterization of Walker's engagement with blackness, which she represents as a kind of ideological *heart of darkness*.[36] Her stark black cutouts set against pristine white walls and the dusty charcoal drawings that depict the nastiest side of human behaviour all image blackness as a fraught spectre that haunts the deepest regions of our collective imagination.

It is often suggested that the blackness on display in the work of Walker and Ligon is not reverent enough to satisfy the dictates of racial obligation. Indeed, these artists do not attempt to soothe the sensibilities of those who demand that images of black people function as uplifting tributes to resilience and survivorship in the face of intolerance. Their post-blackness contains a collective shrugging off of racial obligation, as a means to create the intellectual space to say something meaningful about the insanity of racism. It is perhaps in the materiality of blackness, where they forgo a romanticized relationship to the past. Scholar bell hooks, in her contemplation of African-American creativity and the formation of a black aesthetic, suggests that the historical assault on black intelligence and imaginative potential has placed undue pressure on black artists to produce racially affirming and politicized art:

> Whatever African-Americans created in music, dance, poetry, painting, etc., it was regarded as testimony, bearing witness, challenging racist thinking which suggested that black folks were not fully human, were uncivilized, and that the measure of this was our collective failure to create 'great' art. White supremacist ideology insisted that black people, being more animal than human, lacked the capacity to feel and therefore could not engage the finer sensibilities that were the breeding ground for art ...[37]
>
> ... Conscious articulation of a 'black aesthetic'; as it was constructed by African-America artists and critics in the sixties and early seventies, was an effort to forge an unbreakable link between artistic production and revolutionary politics.[38]

By referencing the Black Arts Movement of the 1970s as a critical forbear, hooks questions the ethos of that moment, which called upon African-American artists to imaginatively evoke black nationhood, by recreating bonds with a mythical African past.[39] The movement was meant to be the 'cultural arm of the black revolution', and as a result the black aesthetic movement was, as hooks illuminates, fundamentally essentialist:[40]

> Links between black cultural nationalism and revolutionary politics led ultimately to the subordination of art to politics. Rather than serving as a catalyst promoting diverse artistic expression, the Black Arts Movement began to dismiss all forms of cultural production by African-Americans that did not conform to movement criteria. Often this led to aesthetic judgements that did not allow for recognition of multiple black experiences or the complexity of black life.[41]

The Black Arts Movement is a fitting historical antecedent to post-black, because it is precisely the confining nature of the movement's value systems that has encouraged the post-Civil Rights generation to retreat from black cultural nationalism. While the younger generation mobilizes biting satire, they neither turn their backs on the struggle, nor have they taken on an attitude of apolitical apathy. There are African-Americans who still demand that black art contain a visible link to political struggle – a demand that is as present and fervent as ever. At its most effective, post-black gestures towards artistic expressivity that resists mandates and experiments conceptually. In this regard, hooks correctly suggests that we need to 're-open the creative space that much of the black aesthetic movement closed down'.[42] Further, she proclaims, 'it seems vital for those involved in contemporary black arts to engage in a revitalized discussion of aesthetics'.[43] I believe the *blackness* in post-black does this by reopening debates surrounding African-American visual expressiveness – though I believe the generational redefinition of blackness comprises its most urgent feature. In a dialogue between art historian Huey Copeland, Thelma Golden, and Glenn Ligon, the issue of intra-cultural obligation surfaced quite prominently; in fact, Ligon articulated the shifting relationship to African-American history characteristic of the post-Civil Rights generation:

> For me, the whole discussion of post-black art was really about a notion that there's a generation of artists younger than myself that has a different relationship to images and history than my generation or the generation before me. So the kinds of debates that Thelma and I were deeply engaged in in the era of what we might call High Multiculturalism – the question of negative and positive images, for example – were debates that they felt distant from.[44]

The issue of positive and negative images and the assertion that there is a proper way to represent black people and their history is at the heart of this discussion. One could characterize post-black as an anti-essentialism filled with good intentions: a choice to adopt a kind of creative and intellectual itinerancy, rather than seeking refuge within the fragile comforts of racial belongingness. The 'post' in post-black was always meant to reject restrictive and narrow conceptions of blackness by those who still believe that blackness has an essence, that it contains an authentic experience. Thelma Golden echoes Ligon's sentiment, suggesting that, for her, post-black was an intervention into the historical struggle over racial meanings and the consumption of blackness:

> Post-black was an abbreviation of post-black art, which really referred to our way of talking about a particular kind of practice at a particular moment that engaged with a particular set of issues and a particular ideology. For us, in those conversations of the late 1990s, it was often a way to talk about what we thought was coming next: saying a practice was post-black art was how Glenn would tell me that 'this is an artist who has moved several steps beyond having to work out their relationship to a particular set of issues.' That working out could be a positive or a negative, a wrestling with or an ignoring of, which is why I feel it is necessary to say that post-black was not about a particular artistic strategy, but about what had happened over the last thirty years and how artists were moving beyond a place in history and to the present moment . . .[45]
>
> . . . In fairness, I also found the debate around post-black somewhat fruitful, just because it allowed me to understand how hard it was for some people to imagine that we could have debates in this way and to ask why we couldn't imagine that in this space at this moment, there are different ways we can understand what's happening artistically. I think the notion that there is some singular narrative that we all have to be a part of doesn't seem fruitful for our understanding of contemporary practices. This is something I learned from being within an international context, in which the practices can unfold individually and still be a part of larger dialogue, but are not necessarily tied to one track of ideas.[46]

Golden's commentary suggests something rather significant: that there is a need for critical discussion about the representation of blackness that wrestles free from the shackles of historical obligation.

Ligon's artistic production embodies the polemical and rhetorical slipperiness necessary to resist the ideological expectations imposed upon black artists. There are various ways in which he manages this, most notably the dexterity of his linguistic and textual playfulness. As I articulated earlier, the black male body – as a type of ideologically constructed social fiction – is always present, even if not visually manifested. One of the more extraordinary features of Ligon's engagement with this archetype is the way he manages to convert 'the particularities of racial experience into the generalities of fiction from which he selectively gleans to represent his own experience in a black male body'.[47] It is through a powerfully discursive set of operations that he manages to resist the expectation to essentially stage the black body as a self-conscious spectacle of racial difference, despite the frequent demands of the high cultural forums of the art world. These operations most readily take the form of appropriated textural and visual elements that function as allusions to the canons of literature and art – though these elements, in their references to the particularities of race, gender, and sexuality, should always be read as surrogates for the artist's own subjectivity. In this sense, both Ligon's body and autobiography become fragmented by a series of rhetorically complex linguistic and formal declarations that represent 'not a unitary self, but a dialogic, citational, and wholly subjective being-for-others'.[48]

Ligon's clever rejection of the art world's racial fetishism, while still managing to wrestle with black subjectivity, is a conceptual feat that warrants closer attention. Scholar Lauren DeLand suggests that it is by 'coalescing a legion of voices into an approximation of a unitary speaking subject that Ligon both gestures towards and offers thoughtfully a means of navigating a problem endemic to "black" art since its conception in the early twentieth century'.[49] In this passage, DeLand makes an important point, which is that Ligon's conceptual approach purposefully rejects the transforming of his body into a commoditized object. The formal objectness, the linguistic and literary references to race, and the complex semiotic playfulness, evade pandering to the fetishism of black male bodies as a visual spectacle. As we will see in the following pages, Ligon's conceptual slipperiness has its roots in an ongoing dialogue about the proper form and function of black art production – a polemic wrestling with a history defined by racial obligation and the mandate that African-American art be forever wedded to a political programme of uplift. In its defiant post-blackness, Glenn Ligon's art refuses this stricture and questions the demand that representations of African-American life be central to the project of black enfranchisement.

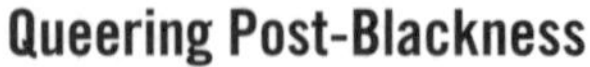

Queering Post-Blackness

As the case of Glenn Ligon illustrates, post-blackness functions neither as an artistic genre nor as an explicit ethos. Instead, it can more aptly be described as an operation that oscillates back and forth between the political and the formal. The slipperiness of post-blackness originates from its ambivalent relationship to the history of black commodification. But within post-blackness lingers a desire to complicate blackness as an ideological signifier – to queer it. As I articulated in the introduction to this book, the queering has a double meaning. It is not simply a means of reading the concerns of queer cultural politics into the work of black artists. On the contrary, I aim to explore how queer subjectivities are at the vanguard of critically and representationally redefining what blackness is and how this queering (as an operation) now extends beyond the politics of debunking the stability of gender and sexual norms. Capitalism's sadomasochistic culture of commodification has always created a rigid ideological lens through which to view black bodies. In the words of Greg Tate, capitalism tends to transform the black body 'from a marketable object, into a magical thing of desire'.[50] In Tate's formulation, blackness is caught between dehumanization and commodity fetishism, a contradictory set of relations that gives people of African descent a kind of representational exchange value, while negating the humanity of actual black people:

> It is my belief that capitalism's original commodity fetish was the Africans auctioned here as slaves, whose reduction from subjects to abstracted objects has made them seem larger than life and less than human at the same time. It is for this reason that the Black body, and subsequently Black culture, has become a hungered-after taboo item and a nightmarish bugbear in the badlands of the American racial imagination.[51]

Tate's consciousness around the objectification and commodification of black bodies comes out of a history of thought that has its roots in Marxism, particularly the notion that commodities are objects that satisfy human needs and wants.[52] This understanding has particular resonance in light of Homi Bhabha's notion of fixity, the grafting of debased stereotypes onto the bodies of the colonized. The stereotype objectifies and strips the marginalized subject of their humanity, locking them into a state of stifling and confining objecthood. However, it is important to remember that this process is not simply meant to degrade individuals; it serves another function as well, which is to satisfy the needs, the fantasies, and the desires of a social system of inequity. Racist fantasies about blackness, like all commodities, are the fundamental units of capitalism and their production and distribution is both ideological and economic. Assessing a commodity's essential usefulness is central to quantifying its intrinsic value – it is therefore able to satisfy the needs and wants of the society that produces and mobilizes it. This quality of usefulness (in Marxist terms) is described as its *use-value* – a quality that all commodities must contain. In her discussion of the commoditized objectification of racialized representations, scholar Alessandra Raengo states that 'blackness has a very intimate relationship with the commodity form, one rooted in slavery of course, but surviving also in the way blackness has continued to circulate in popular and visual culture'.[53] The history of slavery is, as Raengo suggests, inextricably bound to the objectification of black people – what she has termed 'optic black' or 'blackness as phantasmagoria'.[54]

Emerging from the legacy of slavery, there is perhaps no visual form more potent than blackface. The history of racist representations of black people that proliferated during the nineteenth century had a specific social function: the systematic distribution of stereotypes about people of African descent. In addition to their performative envisioning, these stereotypes were also represented and distributed as toys, memorabilia, and as common household objects. In his critical breakdown of racial representation and objecthood, as evidenced in blackface and racist memorabilia, Bill Brown makes a distinction between the two forms, suggesting that, 'whereas the minstrel show animates the stereotype of the "plantation darky," these objects might be said to deanimate it, to arrest the stereotype, to render it in three-dimensional stasis, to fix a demeaning and/or romanticizing racism with the fortitude of solid form'.[55] Blackface has garnered a significant amount of critical attention within studies of theatrical performance history and vaudeville culture (characterizing the commodification that blackface represents as essential to the entertainment industry).[56] Bill Brown's approach diverges somewhat from the existing literature, in that his focus is on the commodity status assigned black bodies – a condition that is a byproduct of a slave economy. This ideological commodity status, particularly within regimes of representation, is the intentional consequence of stripping away personhood and replacing it with a symbolic object. The extraordinary masquerade at the core of this performative gesture, the *blacking-up*, is a very specific kind of racial image, 'one created by the application of a man-made signifier on top of the face . . . it is an image of blackness as an image of race'.[57] What Raengo implies here, is that blackface is not a naturalistic sign, its referent is not black people. On the contrary, it is a symbolic facsimile of race in commodity form, a holdover from the cruel economics of slavery.

The problem at the core of racist representation is the distinction between *humans and things* that plagues cultural understandings of difference. However, what concerns me is the notion that the images of black people (the visual signifiers of race) circulating within the realm of contemporary visual culture are responsible for faithfully and authentically representing them. The challenge posed is that these representations are almost always taken as truth.[58] It is in this regard that Raengo echoes Brown's notion that in representations of blackness – what could be regarded as 'modernity's distinction between human subjects and inanimate objects' – resides the potential to illuminate the messy intricacies of race:[59]

> I am convinced that blackness – a most carnal and at the same time most abstract visual property – can shed light onto the contemporary ontology of the visual; it can teach us something about the way in which we live with, understand, and use, images. Race, in fact, continues to provide the most enduring template for what constitutes a visible sign.[60]

Given its preoccupation with the historical signifiers of race, the artwork of Glenn Ligon is certainly concerned with the aforementioned distinction between *humans and things*. The history of black bodies as commodity objects – in particular the manner in which this history expresses itself in the social imaginary – is arguably Ligon's subject matter. Although, it is important to remind oneself that in his artistic world, blackness can be detachable from black bodies – it can be an abstraction. When thinking about Ligon's work it is imperative to ponder the relationship between the invisibility of black people in America (as a political and cultural reality) versus their hyper-visibility as a commodity sign. His material engagement with blackness is not inherently embodied – meaning it does not always reside in the representation of an actual human body. My aim here is to break from understandings of blackness as bodily matter and to imagine its expressiveness as a more fluid sensorial terrain. Is it even possible to think of blackness as something that exists detached from actual people? Both blackface and racist memorabilia tend to function in this manner, as symbolic distancing – but so does Ligon's semiotic sign system that disallows the fetishization of black corporeality while simultaneously wrestling with its embattled social condition. Many of the artist's works engage this perplexing duality, but they never fully imagine blackness as something coherent and entirely knowable, but rather as a spectral and sensorial presence that fuels fantasies. Therefore, it could be argued that in his multi-media works, it is the integrity of the black subject as an ideological symbol that Ligon assaults, even while its presence shadows our understanding of their meaning.

The manner in which Ligon's images wrestle with the complex intersection between race, materiality, and the sensorial demands further reflection – though when thinking about fetishistic desire, we might also explore the notion of blackness as a kind of adornment. Is it definitely true that with blackness comes a sense of cool? A veneer of hipness representative of some idea of African-American life, yet estranged from it? Cool, according to Harry J. Elam, Jr., is the 'ultimate aspiration of social belonging'[61] and in this regard, blackness is exceedingly attractive. He further intimates that it is therefore entirely possible to 'love black cool and not love black people' – a condition 'where style is much more important than political substance'.[62]

When pondering Glenn Ligon's artistic interventions, it is impossible not to also contemplate the condition of black art as a commoditized object that oozes cool: a fetish that functions as a surrogate for African-American life and as a stand-in for the pleasure of cultural tourists. The appeal of these objects is that they allow spectators the ability to enjoy the liberating sensuality of blackness, the pleasures of black cool – even if at the level of intent, these objects are in fact, dedicated to the causes of black liberation and radical social change. Many African-American artists have wrestled with the quandary of this predicament. The great African-American figurative painter Kerry James Marshall, when asked to discuss why he chose to paint black people as *literally* black in colour, replied:

> I had always heard jokes about blackness, because even in the black community blackness was a state of or condition for derision, a negative state. Back then, calling someone black could get you beat up. There were sayings – don't marry anybody blacker than you – and jokes about people being so dark you can't see them at night unless they're smiling: folk humour and folklore. I was looking for a way to reclaim that image of blackness so that it wasn't negatively valued, but achieved an undeniable majesty.[63]

Figure 6 Kerry James Marshall, *Invisible Man* (1986). Acrylic on canvas, 50 × 38 in. Collection of Paul Winfield, Los Angeles. © Kerry James Marshall/Jack Shainman Gallery

There is something meaningful in Marshall's stated desire to remove the negative value historically assigned to blackness and to give it majesty and a 'mythic beauty and grace'.[64]

In comparison, Ligon's *Prologue Series #2* and *#5*, both produced in 1991, represent forays into abstraction, specifically the rich historical terrain of the black painting. Since the beginning of his career, text and image has been an enduring preoccupation, though the words themselves – as narratively loaded as they tend to be – were not always meant to be legible. I began this chapter with a quote from Ralph Ellison's celebrated novel *Invisible Man*, a book credited as one of the most searing testimonies of the plight of African-Americans in the twentieth century. In the book's prologue, Ellison's narrator, a young college educated black man, reminisces about his invisibility in a racist society that refuses to see his humanity and intelligence. His melancholic testimony speaks of a life in the shadows of intolerance, but most importantly, it communicates, in Marshall's account, a 'powerful psychological and perceptual invisibility – rather than a lack of density'.[65] It is the perceptual invisibility of blackness that motivated Marshall to consider its visual poetics by exploring the boundary between what he describes as a 'flattened-out stereotype, a cartoon, and a fully resonant, complicated authentic representation – a black archetype'.[66] Marshall's *Invisible Man* (1986), a large acrylic on canvas painting, depicts a ghostly black figure set against a stark black background. The figure is barely visible aside from the faintest outline along the borders of its body. To create this perceptual illusion, Marshall slightly changed the colour and temperature of the paint, giving the figure a feeling of warmth that offsets the cool background. At the top right of the composition, at the head of the artist's 'simplified, pure black figure' is a face rendered rather crudely in bright white paint.[67] Aside from the faint outline of the figure, all we can see are bright bulging eyes and a wide toothy grin. The painting alludes to the history of blackface and the coal black countenance of minstrel figures. Marshall's picture is an exercise in minimalism and, in its reductive palette, bears an uncanny semblance to Ligon's *Prologue* paintings. However, the glaring divergence between them is Ligon's choice to use text as image, as opposed to foregrounding the body. Both paintings are based on Ellison's novel, and in each instance the artist meditates on the writer's remarkable description of blackness and the social condition of invisibility. *Prologue Series #2*, similarly to Marshall's *Invisible Man*, presents a ghostlike image, in this instance a barely visible text in tonalities of black, that are set against the flat chalky background. The stencilled words are from the opening passage of Ellison's novel and their slight luminosity renders them barely readable, yet discernable enough to interpret the powerful

Figure 7 Glenn Ligon, *Prologue Series #2* (1991). Oil stick, gouache and graphite on paper, 20 × 16 in. © Glenn Ligon/Regen Projects, Los Angeles

inscription. In *Prologue Series #2*, Ligon uses the same text, but shifts the tonalities and density of the stencilled words just enough to render them gradually illegible. At the top of the composition, Ellison's words are readable, but as the eye follows the text downward, it becomes impossible to do so – descending into a murky, textural mass. The paintings 'achieve a sustained gap between signification and abstraction' that ultimately creates a tension between reading and seeing – a visual

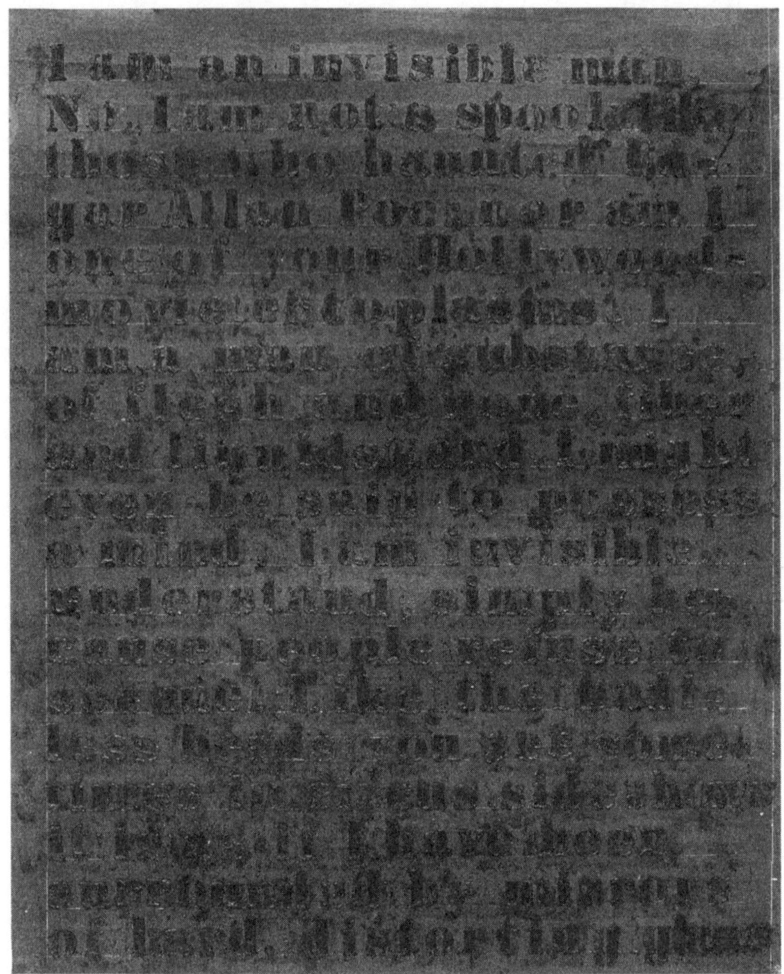

Figure 8 Glenn Ligon, *Prologue Series #5* (1991). Oil stick, gouache and graphite on paper, 20 × 16 in. © Glenn Ligon/Regen Projects, Los Angeles

and textual play that has become a hallmark of Ligon's conceptual approach.[68] The interplay between the overtness and didacticism of the text versus the mythic openness of abstraction creates a sense of anxiety, because as Okwui Enwezor suggests, 'the substance of the subject is the sensuous ground of painting'.[69]

A significant amount of scholarship has been done on Ligon's text-based paintings, exploring the intricacies of their literary references.

The art historian Darby English has discussed in detail Ligon's early forays into Abstract Expressionism, noting the incongruity of his black queerness in an artistic genre defined by an ethos of cultureless neutrality. Ligon's identity as a black queer man was arguably the greatest barrier to his acceptance as an abstract painter, particularly considering that the universality ascribed to abstract painting was traditionally the domain of white heterosexual males. In his textual appropriations, we can see the artist's conceptual preoccupations with race and colour; even sexuality and masculinity are dominant themes that populate his pictures. The embattled masculinity in the *Prologue* paintings is perhaps more subtly rendered than in *Cocaine (Pimps)*, a 1993 text-based painting in brilliant red, with his trademark oil stick letters in a bright yellow-orange. This time the passage was taken from the satirical humour of comedian Richard Pryor. The text reads:

> Niggers be holding them dicks too . . .
> White people go 'Why you guys hold your things?'
> Say 'You done took everything else motherfucker.'

Pryor's off-colour humour has always functioned as a critical send-up of American racism, while playing sardonically with stereotypes about black people. The intersection between race and sexuality takes precedence in *Cocaine (Pimps)*, though what is skewered is a stereotype grounded in a heteronormative logic. Like Ellison's *Invisible Man*, the focus of Pryor's ire is the emasculation of the African-American male, by a society hell-bent on its destruction. One might recall that these classic Pryor witticisms also found their way into Ligon's *Mudbone (Liar)* (1993) – a text-based painting referencing the unusually large size of the black male penis. Ultimately, these quips reveal the social condition of having one's humanity defined as monstrous and lascivious. The Pryor jokes, as irreverent as they are, brought with them a socially codified black male voice – a black cultural distinctiveness that, in its tragic dimensions, is still entirely legible.[70] The choice of text could appear somewhat perplexing, if not for the obvious homoerotic subtext in their fascination with the black man's sex. This narrative element always shadowed Pryor's humour, endowing it with the danger of queer desire, while never fully committing in earnest to a progressive sexual politics. In fact, embedded within Pryor's dick jokes is a lingering anxiety about the feminization of black males by

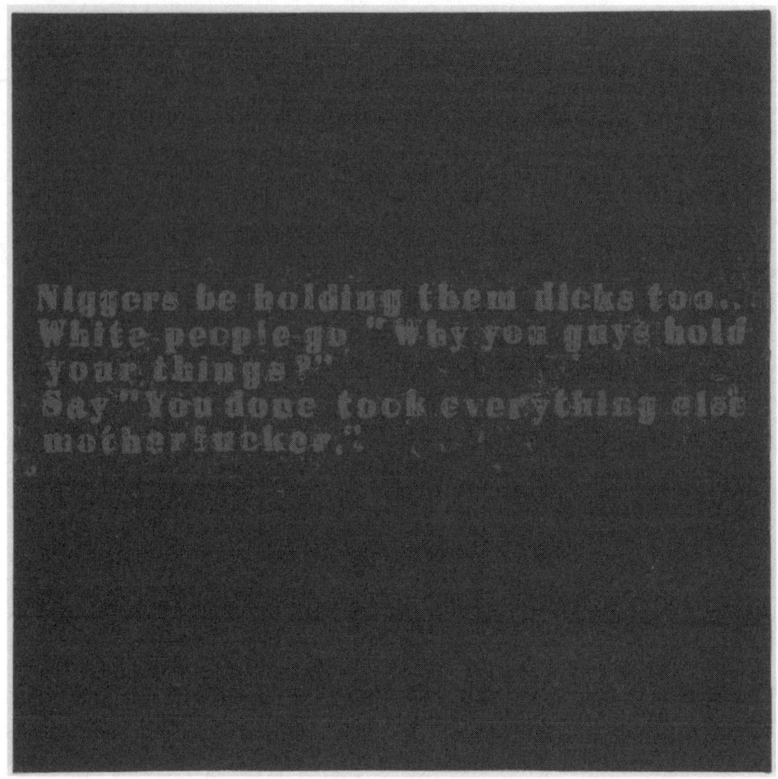

Figure 9 Glenn Ligon, *Cocaine (Pimps)* (1993). Oil stick, synthetic polymer and graphite on linen, 32 × 32 in. Whitney Museum of American Art, New York. © Glenn Ligon/Regen Projects, Los Angeles

a racist society. In the 1970s era of hyper-masculine black power, emasculation was tantamount to queerness. It was a form of abjection meant to be transcended; although Pryor satirically skewered this anxiety, mocking it while comedically eroticizing relations between 'niggers' and 'faggots' – two maligned groups suffering under the indignity of social stigma.

It might be all too easy to regard Ligon's painterly interventions as a type of queering process. To do so would not be incorrect per se, but in his acts of appropriation, he also attacks a sign system that is both heterosexist and homophobic at its core – even if it also expresses an elegiac mournfulness about the psychic effects of racism. The signifiers of African-American masculinity that Pryor's comedy personified do not speak to the experiences of a young gay black man of the post-Civil Rights generation. The words themselves may in fact inflict an ideological violence that is more profound than the racial inequity to which they allude. This reading holds great significance for the notion of post-black, because Ligon cleverly interrogates a set of cultural signs associated with a period of collective uplift and resistance that he may potentially feel estranged from. It would therefore be careless to think of his evocation of authentic blackness as commemorative. On the contrary, they more aptly convey a feeling of intellectual distance, a semiotic deconstructive coldness gesturing towards a contradictory mix of condemnation and understanding.

There is perhaps no better example of this than Ligon's 1988 work *Untitled (I Am a Man)*, a rather rustic looking oil stick on canvas painting. As a racial spectacle, *Untitled* appropriates one of the more notorious signifiers of African-American struggle, a recreation of the iconic sign carried by striking sanitation workers in 1968. The Memphis sanitation strike gained international recognition because it brought attention to the horrendous treatment, rampant discrimination, and preventable work-related deaths faced by black employees. As the conflict escalated, it became a major Civil Rights struggle, attracting the attention of influential leaders and activists including Martin Luther King, Jr., Bayard Rustin and the NAACP. Striking workers, in their efforts to resist exploitation and poverty, famously carried signs saying, '*I Am A Man!*'. The phrase became a unifying and iconic Civil Rights theme. The white painting appears to be a well-preserved sign from the period, when in fact it is a replica of sorts, designed to faithfully resemble the original. On the surface, *Untitled* feels commemorative, like a tribute to a history of struggle. In a sense, it might very well be; but given Ligon's body of work, there is a hint of cynicism and satire brewing beneath its surface. Like so many of his works, the iconicity of reclaimed black masculinity is perhaps more symbolic of estrangement, and alienation, rather than a sentiment of collective belonging.

If we think about Ligon's *Prologue Series* and *Untitled (I Am a Man)* in comparison to Marshall's *Invisible Man*, the issue of satire reemerges. What distinguishes the work of Ligon from that of his elder predecessor is his satirical approach to the visual emblems of African-American identity. The repetition of these symbols in his representational strategy is not meant to be celebratory, or even critical of a history of white racism. I argue that, to the contrary, Ligon

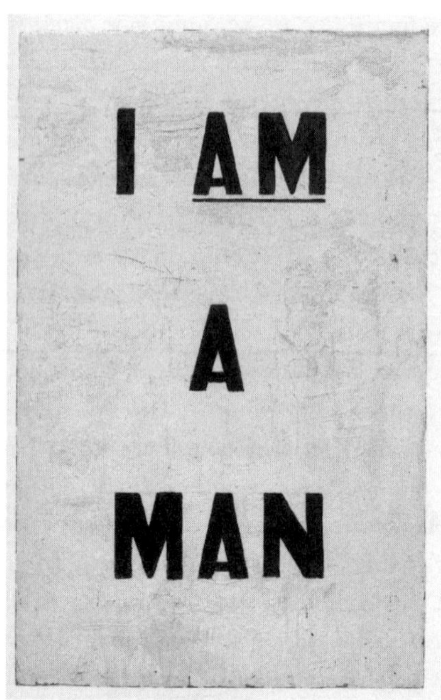

Figure 10 Glenn Ligon, *Untitled (I Am a Man)* (1998). Oil and enamel on canvas, 40 × 25 in. Collection of the artist. © Glenn Ligon/Regen Projects, Los Angeles

ponders a construction of black masculinity in which he cannot, and ultimately refuses, to participate. His critical lens is turned inward and can be more aptly described as an intra-cultural interrogation of the heteronormative value systems that informed the construction of racial pride and belongingness within the black community. This queering gesture renders these symbols foreign and alienating, even while on the surface they appear to celebrate a history of struggle and resistance to American racism. In contrast, Marshall's *Invisible Man* appropriates one of the most powerful and hurtful representations of blackness and repurposes it in the form of critique. Blackface represents the total dehumanization and objectification of black people. It is meant only to degrade and to strip the humanity and dignity away from the subject it represents. Marshall utilizes this iconic image as a means to interrogate white American culture's debasement of black people. It is a critique that turns outward, casting a rather harsh light on a history of intolerance and oppressive power dynamics. While Marshall wields the minstrel image ironically, I wouldn't characterize its usage as satirical in the manner that Ligon approaches similarly loaded cultural symbols. Both artists address states of presence and absence in the historical representation of the black subject, although for Ligon, that absence is embodied in a queer subjectivity that always remains unseen, even by forms of subjecthood designed to confront oppressive structures.

Ligon's satirical queering of blackness found a more literal expression in a series entitled *Coloring*, a suite of drawings and paintings the artist debuted in 2000 at the Walker Art Center in Minneapolis. While participating in a residency at the museum, Ligon conducted art courses with children. During these workshops, the children were given Afrocentric colouring books from the 1960s and 1970s that were originally intended to foster a sense of racial pride and historical awareness of iconic figures such as Harriet Tubman, Frederick Douglass and Malcolm X. Because of the young age and multi-ethnic background of the children, there was little historical knowledge of the subjects they were asked to colour in. The results were ironic and humorous, not least because the students tended to envision these icons in cartoonish ways and definitely not in line with the historical stoicism of commemoration. In certain instances they appeared to be intentionally mocked by the children, for example Fredrick Douglass' eyes were painted blue, afros were rendered in bright orange. As curator Scott Rothkopf recounts, despite the fact that the children 'had yet to be inculcated with the vocabulary of racial stereotypes, some had already learned that flesh was to be coloured a yellowish white'.[71] The most powerful image in the series is *Malcolm X (Version 1) #1* (2000). Ligon's *Malcolm X* is a large silkscreen on canvas reproduction of one of the children's colouring book images. The reductive line drawing of the influential human rights activist had been crudely coloured in with white hair, blue eye shadow, red dots on his cheeks and bright magenta lips. The effect of this transformation is that the Muslim leader appears either clownish, or as intentionally queered. As Rothkopf suggests, 'it's hard not to take this painting as an emasculating send-up of the manly civil rights leader, though it's unlikely that the kid who originally created the image had any clue who Malcolm X was.'[72]

The *Coloring* series, in particular the *Malcolm X* painting, ran the danger of being read as an extremely obvious form of iconoclasm that left

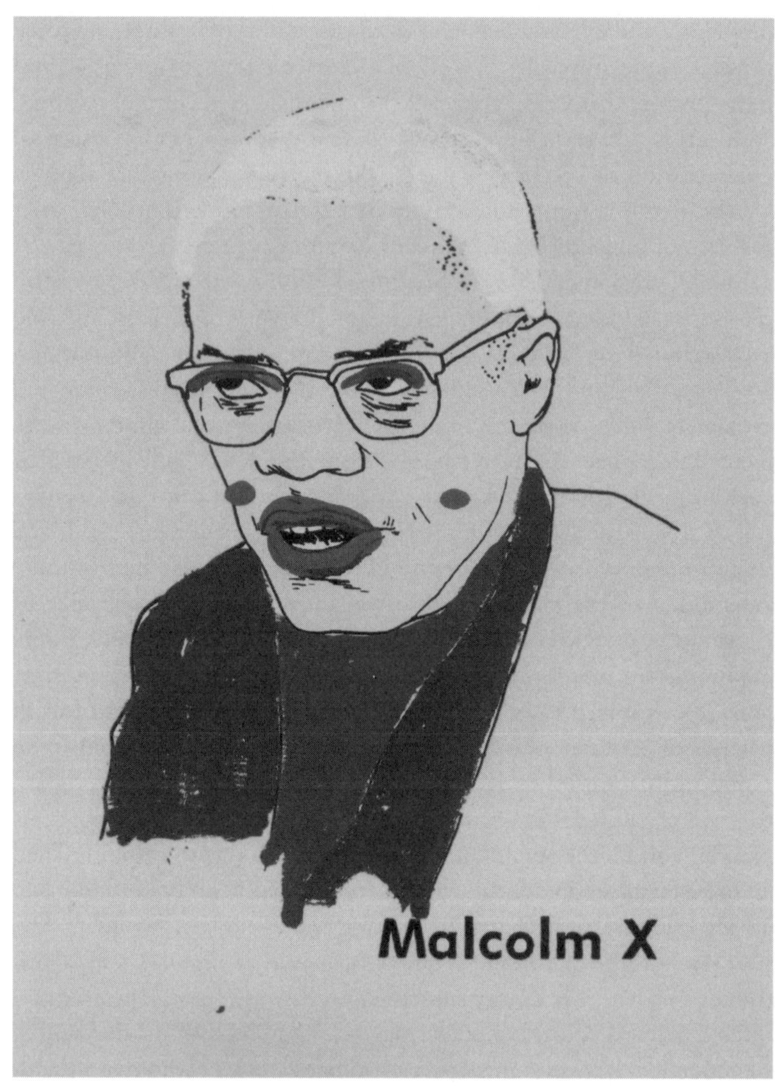

Figure 11 Glenn Ligon, *Malcolm X (Version 1) #1* (2000). Vinyl-based paint, silkscreen ink, and gesso on canvas; 96 × 72 in. Collection of Michael and Lise Evans. © Glenn Ligon/Regen Projects, Los Angeles

little room for interpretive complexity. *Malcolm X* was one of Ligon's few forays into figuration and, like the late painter Andy Warhol, demonstrated the artist's skill as a satirical manipulator of found images. Warhol's silkscreen portraits of celebrities, according to historian Carter

Ratcliff, contained strong overtones of crassness – even vulgarity in the way they ruthlessly exposed the machinery of glamour.[73] There are interesting similarities between Ligon and Warhol: both are queer artists whose dense iconography and quotational style – despite the seemingly endless referentiality of their images – are largely impenetrable. In his explication of Warhol's pictures, Ratcliff believes that viewers are 'drawn by what stays hidden, all the more so because Warhol's Pop imagery seems to veil something basic – perhaps disturbing – about our culture, about us'.[74] Art historians have long debated the intentions behind Warhol's Pop portraits. Was he a politically engaged social commentator using the devices of commercial art to expose the mediocrity and exploitiveness of popular culture?[75] Or were Warhol's Pop portraits simply a celebration of celebrity and a fetishization of fame? Ligon's *Malcolm X* is also deceptively reverential and celebratory, although far less so than Warhol's *Gold Marilyn Monroe* (1962), a large-scale silkscreen portrait of the late actress. A black male artist painting a portrait of Malcolm X comes with certain connotations, despite the whimsical painterly elements. To some it may appear to be ironic, but it still feels like a nostalgic remembrance, or a tribute honouring the slain leader. The rather obvious crudity of Ligon's depiction of Malcolm X is no less blasphemous, despite its having been allegedly rendered by the hands of a child. The feminizing elements in the colouring book image communicate a ridiculing tone, because the iconic figure has become so readily associated with heteronormative resistance and clichéd hyper-masculine blackness. The stereotype of formidable black male virility informs our understanding of Malcolm X's persona. However, the moment of his public prominence was defined by an ethos of both reclaimed and assertive machismo. There is a similar set of clichés that potentially plagues our interpretation of Warhol's *Gold Marilyn*, namely the stereotypical queerness at the root of a gay man's campy celebration of a female Hollywood actress. The stereotype of gay male admiration for glamorous constructions of heteronormative white femininity perhaps leads to scholarly interpretations of Warhol's uncritical embrace of Hollywood shallowness. But perhaps his Pop portraits – which critically reveled in the vulgarity of celebrity culture – made no appeal to modernist refinement or to 'traditions of high pictorial seriousness'.[76]

In keeping with Ratcliff's assessment of Warhol's production, it becomes rather clear that Ligon's satirical post-blackness similarly contains

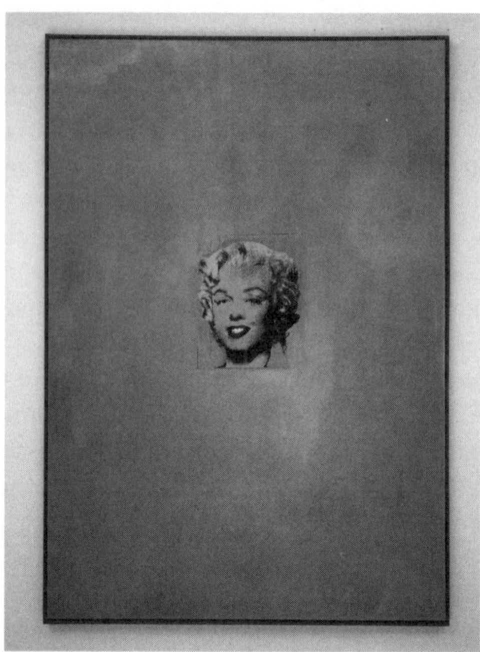

Figure 12 Andy Warhol, *Gold Marilyn Monroe* (1962). Silkscreen ink on synthetic polymer paint on canvas, 6 ft 11¼ in. × 57 in. © Andy Warhol Foundation/Arts Rights Society (ARS)

strong overtones of crassness and vulgarity – and he, too, creates images designed to expose something basic – perhaps disturbing – about our culture. In his often unsettling iconoclasm, Ligon ruthlessly exposes the machinery of racism and homophobia, while simultaneously refusing to critically ignore damaging intra-cultural constructions of blackness that produce their own annihilating logics. The satire in Warhol's *Gold Marilyn*, similarly to Ligon's *Malcolm X*, is conveyed in the violation of a series of taboos, most prominently the deliberate crassness of their colourization. Marilyn's bright yellow hair, her absurdly blue eye shadow and unnaturally deep red lips, convey a cartoonish buffoonery that prefigures Ligon's creation. Ratcliff describes Warhol's rendition of Marilyn as a 'travesty of screen-star make-up and hairdressing, a cluster of flat, garish blocks of colour that don't even correspond very closely to the details of her face'.[77] The controversy at the root of these works is in their perceived outrageousness – a debased, garish rudeness that sets out to queer these iconic larger than life personas.

In visual terms, these are certainly audacious works, yet they also make reference to childhood in their laconic simplicity. *Malcolm X (Version 1) #1* is a return to more overtly queer themes that emerged significantly earlier in the artists career, most notably in a body of work entitled *A Feast of Scraps* (1994–1998). *A Feast of Scraps* is a photo assemblage in which Ligon 'maps the course of his own history and sexuality without ever picturing himself in the work'.[78] The photo archive traces Ligon's family from the 1940s to the 1980s, interspersing images of his relatives with found images of family milestones and the intimate memories of strangers. Placed within the images of domestic life, family reunions, parties, and marriages, were pornographic images of black men. According to Lauren DeLand, some of these images were 'captured with amateurish haste amidst the clutter of private rooms, some deliberately posed in stark outdoor locations or against clusters of trees, reinscribing the set of racialized stereotypes loosely gathered under the term "jungle fever"'.[79] Ligon found the archive of pornographic images in Gay Treasures, a Greenwich Village bookstore. Contained in a box labelled 'Black Men' were scores of photos dating from the 1960s and 1970s. Ligon clearly culled the various snapshots together from various collectors, but their thematic similarity creates a very specific narrative.

A Feast of Scraps is an important work in Ligon's oeuvre because it signals a particular engagement with blackness: one that is resolutely self-critical in its satire. In a sense, Ligon is creating an alternative family album, one where his black queerness is not effaced and excised from the construction of so-called normative heterosexual family life. For many African-Americans, the 1970s was a period defined by a resurgence of patriarchal values, brought about by black men who both asserted and consolidated their roles as fathers, husbands, and leaders of their communities. Like so many of Ligon's works, *A Feast of Scraps* examines the failure of these social constructions of blackness to speak to his own experience of the world. In conversation with DeLand, Ligon stated that the photos of black men in Gay Treasures 'are the photos left out of my family albums'.[80] As a result, *A Feast of Scraps* is a self-portrait of sorts, even as it critiques the ideologically over-determined construction of the black American family. While the visual emblems of blackness pervade his production, they function neither as commemorative nor celebratory, but conflict with a black heteronormative ideal so often evidenced in the constructed narratives

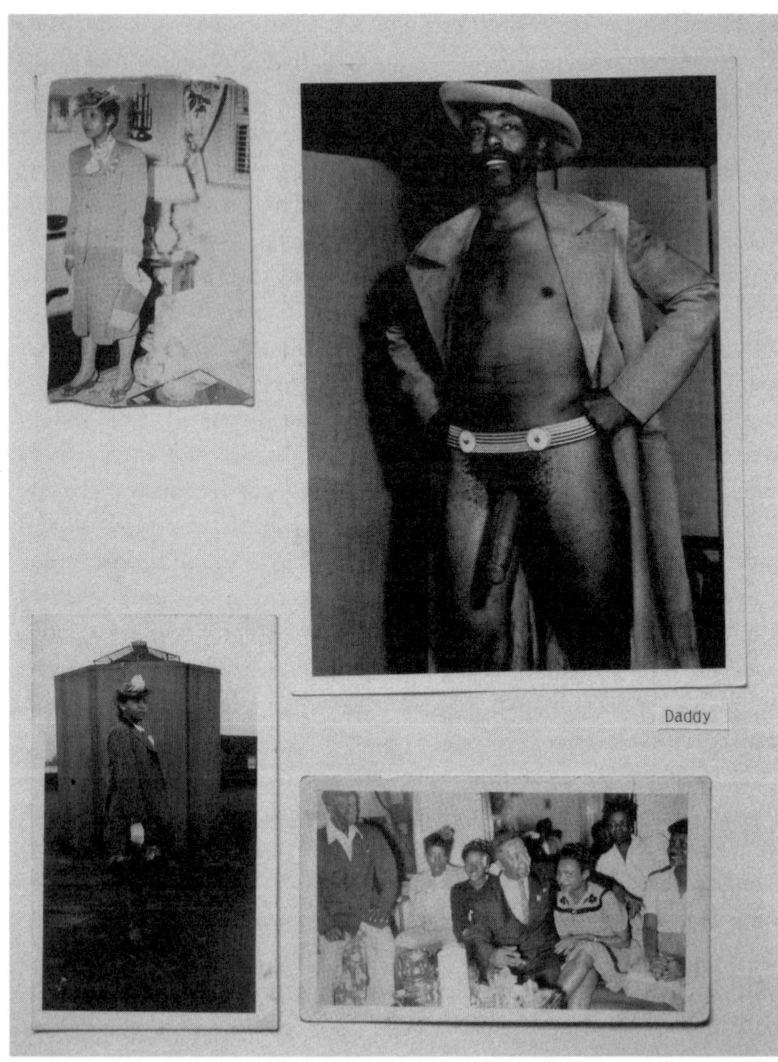

Figure 13 Glenn Ligon, *A Feast of Scraps* (1994–1998). Multi-media installation. © Glenn Ligon/Regen Projects, Los Angeles

of family albums. DeLand makes an important observation about Ligon's *queering of blackness*, stating that he 'catalyzes the process of confrontations, disappointments, and revision of expectations that make up shared family lives through the figure of the black gay man, who remains the most pernicious spectre haunting the black utopias prescribed by thinkers across the political spectrum'.[81] The notion of haunting is perhaps the most apt metaphor for the primary operation at work in the art of Glenn Ligon. Queerness is a ghostly presence in his production, shadowing our understanding of what it means to be African-American. However, it bears remembering that the symbols of blackness are also deeply American. It is in keeping with this sentiment, that Ligon forms a counter-narrative and a corrective to constructions of American identity that erase black queer subjectivities. His elaborate sign system is, in many ways, an alternative family album – and a heretical vision of Americanness that interrogates the profundity of its intolerances and erasures. The psychic and emotional weight of his intervention is embedded within the formal, in a very material and object-oriented aesthetics that repositions blackness within a politics of pleasure. It is, therefore, in his extraordinary and resplendent formalism that we come to a more complex, coherent, and inclusive vision of African-American identity.

2

Kehinde Wiley's Black Utopia: Racial Fetishism and the Queering of Masculinity

> There is nothing about gay people's physiognomy that declares them gay, no equivalents to the biological markers of sex and race. There are signs of gayness, a repertoire of gestures, expressions, stances, clothing, and even environments that bespeak gayness, but these are cultural forms designed to show what the person's person alone does not show: that he or she is gay. Such a repertoire of signs, making visible the invisible, is the basis of any representation of gay people involving visual recognition, the requirement of recognizability in turn entailing that of typicality. Though not indispensable, typification is a near necessity for the representation of gayness, the product of social, political, practical and textural determinations.[1]
>
> – Richard Dyer, *The Matter of Images*

Fantasy, Recognition, and the Queering of Portraiture

The philosopher Slavoj Žižek once said that fantasy is not about an individual creating a scenario in which they get everything they want. On the contrary, an individual's fantasy is about creating a scenario in which 'he or she is desired by others'.[2] When Žižek uttered these words, he was thinking critically about the relationship between ideology and popular cinema. However, his rather playful explication of fantasy continues resonate when I consider the work of Kehinde Wiley. As we will see in the following pages, fantasy plays an important role in both the images Wiley chooses to make, as well as in their appeal. Widely known and celebrated for his heroic scale and beautifully rendered images of black men, Wiley has built an impressive career as arguably the most accomplished portrait painter of his generation. Not since Andy Warhol has an American artist's works so thoroughly captured the attention of the public imagination. There are many points of entry into Wiley's evocative artworks, and my aim is to avoid many of the clichéd approaches to what may appear – on the surface – to be a series of superficial gestures. There is a deceptively frank, even clumsy quality about Wiley's iconography and conceptual approach that plagues its critical interpretation. Despite that challenge, I find something more meaningful and profound in his painterly gestures. Therefore, I endeavour to transcend any previous limitations in favour of constructing a more complex and nuanced interpretive framework.

The fifth of six children, Wiley was raised in South Central Los Angeles by a single mother – an experience that greatly informed his educational and creative choices. On welfare and raising six children while also completing a graduate degree in linguistics, Wiley's mother stressed educational achievement to her kids. The artist described his upbringing as an 'educationally elite but economically impoverished environment'.[3] During his formative years, Wiley attended the Los Angeles County School for the Arts and eventually the San Francisco Art Institute where he received a BFA degree in painting. In 2001 he graduated with an MFA in painting from the Yale School of Art. After graduating from Yale, Wiley was awarded a prestigious and highly coveted artist's residency at the Studio Museum in Harlem. Harlem proved to be a powerful motivator and inspiration for what has become his signature style. Wiley remembers: 'One Hundred Twenty-Fifth Street was so dense and packed with pageantry and peacocking... I wanted to try and get that down in painting.'[4] Harlem's impact on the formation of his aesthetic has become the stuff of legend. Along with a team of assistants, Wiley walked Harlem's streets searching for potential sitters. He would approach black men and recruit them as models, bringing them back to his studio to peruse art history books. His subjects were asked to select a classical painting and a gestural pose in which to be immortalized. Wiley would then take photographs of his subject that functioned as templates for full-size paintings. The results have become infamous.

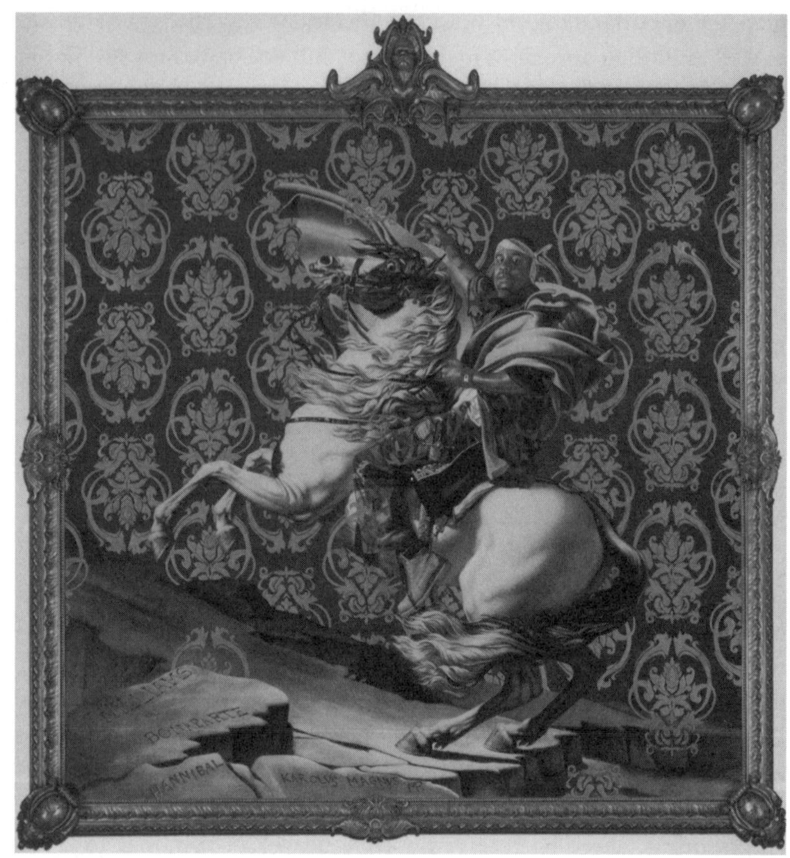

Figure 14 Kehinde Wiley, *Napoleon Leading the Army Over the Alps* (2005). Oil on canvas. 108 × 108 in. (274.3 × 274.3 cm). Collection of Suzi and Andrew B. Cohen. © Kehinde Wiley Studio/Sean Kelly Gallery

A fitting example of his conceptual approach is the painting *Napoleon Leading the Army Over the Alps* (2005), a recreation of French artist Jacques-Louis David's celebrated 1801 painting *Napoleon at the Saint-Bernard Pass*. Considered the preeminent painter of the Neoclassical style, David's particular approach to history painting was perceived to be intellectual and austere for the times. Though perhaps more significantly, he gained infamy as the official court painter for French military and political leader Napoleon Bonaparte. In the wake of Bonaparte's 1799 coup d'état, the then military general commissioned David to create a fitting painterly commemoration of one of his most

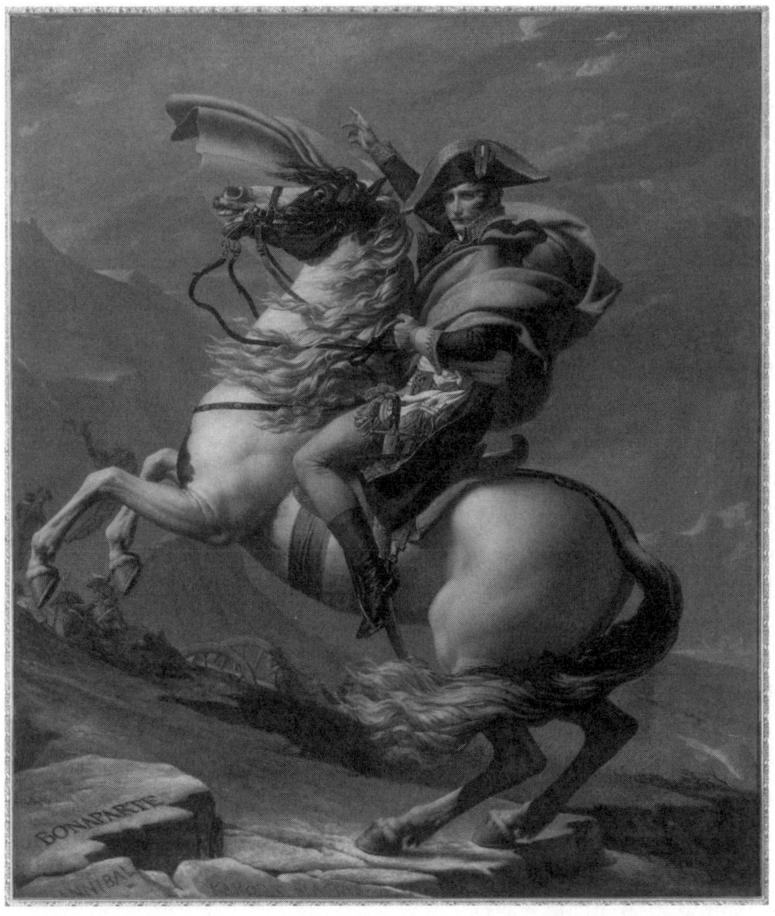

Figure 15 Jacques-Louis David, *Napoleon Crossing the Alps* (1801–1805). Oil on canvas, 8 ft 6 in. × 7 ft 3 in. © Art Resource Inc. (Artres)

glorious victories. The result was a tribute to the Battle of Marengo on 14 June 1800, celebrating Napoleon's successfully leading of the French army across the Saint-Bernard Pass in a surprise victory over the Austrians. One of five versions, David's *Napoleon* was a highly idealized reimagining of Napoleon's great victory, depicting the leader in full military regalia in the role of general. Mounted on a horse as it rears up, the French leader looks towards the viewer as he leads men into battle while his right hand gestures towards mountains in the distance. Wrapped in a large and rather dramatic red cloak while clutching the reins of his steed, Napoleon is pictured regally in a gold-rimmed bicorne hat and a decorative sabre at his side. As the horse rears up, the curly locks of its mane and tail flow forward towards a tumultuous, yet victorious future.

Wiley's version is similar, but diverges in significant ways. Rather than depicting the French historical figure, the young African-American artist has chosen to depict a youthful looking black man in the role of Napoleon. Dressed in what appears to be the standard hip-hop attire commonly worn by men in America's urban centres, Wiley's Napoleon is replete with head-to-toe military camouflage gear, yellow Timberland Chukka boots, red sweatbands on his wrists and a white bandanna tied purposely around his head. Draped over his shoulders is a beautiful and glowing gold cloak and, like the original painting, the young man has an ornate sabre at his side. As the white horse elegantly rears-up, Wiley's hip-hop soldier stares defiantly at the viewer and points into the distance. Not only the choice of subject, but also Wiley's signature decorative background differentiates this work from the stormy, sober skies of David's original painting. Shifting back and forth between the foreground and background, an ornate brocade pattern fills the image – sometimes overwhelming the overall composition. The richly decorative background alludes to embroidered luxury fabrics dating back to the Middle Ages that were popular throughout Europe and Asia. Rendered in luscious oil on canvas, Wiley's version is as tempestuous as the prototype, though it would likely be an understatement to suggest that his chosen subject shifts the meaning in dramatic ways.

Considering his source material, it is clear that Wiley is making a meta-commentary on the relation between portraiture, status, and power. During the Renaissance, it was not uncommon for wealthy aristocrats and powerful patrons of the church to commission portraits as a means to create an enduring visual record of their prominence. Through inserting an anonymous black man into the famous composition, Wiley powerfully re-imagines the form of the classical equestrian portrait while commenting on the historical erasure and marginalization of black people in the tradition of Western painting.

There is some debate around whether Wiley's cheeky recreations represent the redefinition of portraiture, or merely function as cheap knock-offs that ride the coattails of European high culture.

Considering this query, one must frankly acknowledge the reading of his work as a 'sight gag' and a form of ridicule. His paintings, according to writer Christopher Beam, 'appeal to buyers interested in interrogating the social construct of portraiture, those who think it's hilarious to put black dudes in do-rags on horses carrying sceptres'.[5] Part of the striking overtness of his post-black satire is what appears to be a snarky form of queer ridicule, one that lampoons the tragic black masculinity of hip-hop and urban street culture. Beam is right to ask an important question: why should we take seriously the gesture of painting an anonymous black man posing like Napoleon? Does this constitute an act of social justice and radical resistance, and does it 'give African-Americans their rightful place in the Western pantheon'?[6] What Wiley is doing might be a mockery of the pantheon of Western painting itself – or perhaps it is the heterosexual black male that is the butt of the joke. Reading the work as a cheap sight gag, or as a form of ridicule is perhaps too strong, and potentially neglects the critical and intellectual traditions that have informed his creative choices. However, even that understanding does not belie the obvious humour at the heart of his images. It is a rather whimsical experience to witness the careful and detailed insertion of black men into what are already mythical and absurdly bombastic displays of masculinity. In fact, the absurdity of the originals becomes even more apparent through Wiley's iconic substitution. As we ponder this interpretive quandary, it is germane to mention that, when asked to speak publicly about his work, the artist prefers to keep his intentions and motivations ambiguous. In a *New York Magazine* article, Wiley states that: 'As an artist and a student of history, you have to be at once critical and complicit, to take a stance that says, "Yes, I'm in love with this magic, this way of painting, but damn it's fucked up."'[7] Maybe there is something fucked up about the flippant crudity of his symbolism, yet there is also a profundity and sincerity in his self-conscious imaging of America's black male underclass.

As racialized spectacle, ideologically over-determined images of black men continue to haunt popular representation. And as Kobena Mercer suggests, their pathologizing creates a fear/fantasy formulation that operates through the production of images.[8] Mercer highlights the struggles for self-representation that have always occurred within the sphere of black expressive culture, particularly those contending with society's fear and fascination with those dazzling, yet always tragic *niggers*, whose foibles were forever on display in the nightly news. Contending with not just the good, but also with the bad, was a creative and intellectual means to break with what Stuart Hall characterized as the naive and 'innocent notion of the essential black subject'.[9] If Wiley's subjects seemed to lack dignity, it was because the artist's cheeky satire directs a sarcastic wink and a smirk back at those who would demand that he create uncritically devotional and reverential images of black folks. There is no essentialist impulse in Wiley's work, no romantic nostalgia for a mythic black authenticity. But that characteristic does not nullify the importance he places on the recognition and visibility of the black subject.

In this regard, Wiley is in the company of many great black artists, notably figurative painter Kerry James Marshall. The elder Marshall (b. 1955) is known for creating mural size paintings of African-American life. Reminiscent of Renaissance history paintings, the MacArthur 'Genius' award winner's images contain an allegorical allusiveness that, in their iconic expanse, also carry the symbolic weight of a lengthy history of African-American struggle. Marshall has spoken many times about his first encounter with the work of noted Social Realist artist Charles White. The late African-American figurative painter's dignified images of black people greatly impacted Marshall in his youth, giving him a sense of possibility, as well as a fitting subject for his own work. Having relocated to Los Angeles as a child, the now Chicago-based artist recalls visiting the Los Angeles County Museum of Art on a class field trip and being overwhelmed by the classic works of Théodore Géricault, Jacques-Louis David, and Jean-Auguste-Dominique Ingres – though dismayed by the striking absence of black bodies in the history of art:

> When I was growing up, I was bothered by the limited success black artists were able to achieve. I didn't see their work included in general art surveys, but whenever Black History Month rolled around, institutions found the space to show work that wasn't apparently suitable for other occasions. The only time the work of black artists could be thought of as art, it seemed, was when it was made to perform some social or political function.
>
> I wanted to resist that. Some black artists thought that in order to be seen as an artist first, they had to eliminate the black figure from their work and turn to abstraction. That way, you couldn't tell who made the work,

> and it would be judged on equal art terms. But I wanted to find out if there was a way to get respect for my work on aesthetic terms without having to dispose of the black figure. On the contrary, I wanted to make it central to the reception of the work.[10]

Ironically, Wiley similarly muses about the life-altering experience of encountering Marshall's paintings as a child, at the same museum:

> Well my life changed quite radically by seeing a Kerry James Marshall exhibition at the Los Angeles County Museum of Art as a child. There was something about the scale of the work, the fact that it existed on the same scale as a lot of the history paintings I'd seen in that museum, that there were black bodies in public space that way.[11]

Both Marshall's and Wiley's testimonies address their need for recognition and the importance of being represented in the histories of art.

Marshall's famous painting that Wiley encountered as a youth was *De Style* (1993), a 'modern-day genre scene that expresses a sense of community and male bonding'.[12] Massive in scale, Marshall's *De Style* is an acrylic on canvas masterpiece, depicting the everyday goings-on in a black barbershop. The painting is an odd mix of styles, combining the gestural and expressive looseness of Neo-Expressionism with the narrative historicity of Renaissance-era compositional structures. There is even a hint of high modernist abstraction and nineteenth-century American genre painting. The figures are painted in his signature flat black – an allusion to the complex ideological meanings evoked in the cultural imaginary. It is a loaded image, full of history and the kind of folksy cultural distinctiveness that serves as a gateway into the African-American experience. In its figurative allusions to religious iconography in the Western tradition, Marshall endows his subjects with beauty and a saintly air: a dignity and grace that belies the negative associations with the ideological weightiness of their coal black skin. In the world of African-American art, *De Style* was a paradigm-shifting work, influencing many artists to engage critically and formally with the history and aesthetics of European art. The impact of *De Style* on Wiley's conceptual approach is quite evident, even if the younger artist's work moves into more satirical terrain. As a pre-Civil Rights generation artist, Marshall's engagement with blackness is more

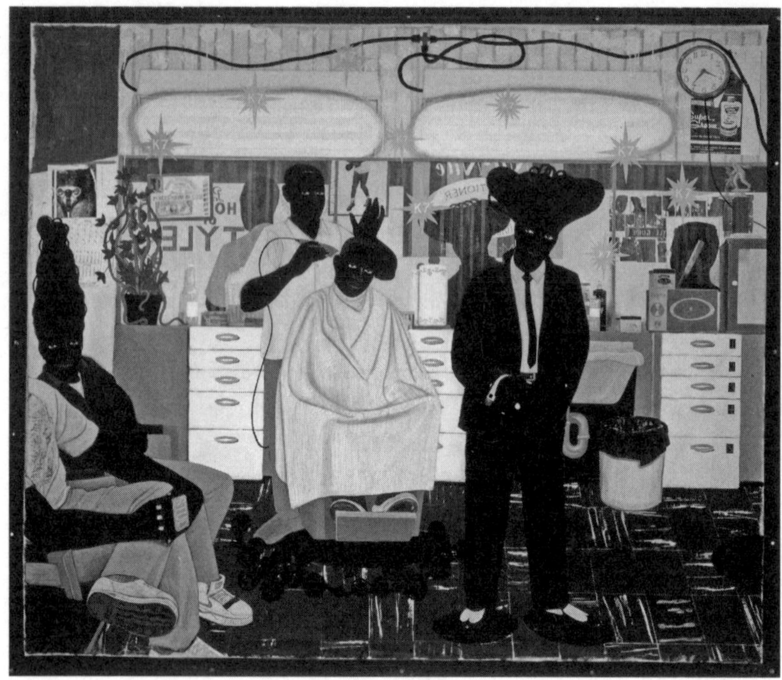

Figure 16 Kerry James Marshall, *De Style* (1993). Acrylic and collage on canvas 104 × 122 in. (264.16 × 309.88 cm). © Kerry James Marshall/Jack Shainman Gallery

recuperative and committed to creating dignified and uplifting images of African-American life, a quality that Wiley has termed a 'politics of redemption'.[13]

Marshall is part of a generation of black cultural producers whose representational politics engaged in a 'mode of resistance that was moralistic in content and communal in character'.[14] As Cornel West suggests, their struggle for 'representation and recognition highlighted moral judgements regarding Black "positive" images over and against White supremacist stereotypes'.[15] In the post-black era of Kehinde Wiley, there is resistance to the mandate that the African-American creative intelligentsia must inherently offer positive images as a counter to racist stereotypes – an ethos that rejects the notion that there is some *real* black community that can be accessed representationally. Both Marshall and Wiley are aware that blackness is a politically and culturally constructed category, but the cynical and satirical dimension of the younger artist's production grates against the recuperative earnestness of Marshall's intentionally uplifting symbolism. We might think of Wiley's politics as a more holistic response to the effects of intolerance – a cyclical form of satire that responds to a history of racist representation while also critiquing the black community's often *essentialist* response to that legacy.

On the other hand, Marshall's iconographic approach is rooted in a cultural politics of difference that always searches for 'positive' images of what could be regarded as a homogeneous community. This striking difference is clearly generational and demarcates pre- and post-Civil Rights sensibilities and political commitments. Wiley's images are undoubtedly committed to contesting racial stereotypes, even as they play with them – though they also seek to demystify power relations within the black community that contain class-based, patriarchal and especially homophobic biases.[16] Wiley definitely recognizes the shift in black art production from a politics of redemption, to a semiotic vulnerability that allows for satirical explorations into the mechanism of racial representation:

> Historically, by and large, we have assumed that the work of black and brown artists had a decidedly political intention. We could spend years trying to define that, but I think it's fair to say that a politics of redemption would be a good approximation of that notion of political artists. And the politics of redemption has been exhausted in many ways visually. I think that in today's visual culture it's a lot more complicated to isolate political intent and social intent and aesthetic intent.
>
> I think that desire for redemption and the desire for a radical presence in the world is clearly visible in my work. At the same time, the work is also self-consciously aware of being a high priced luxury good for wealthy consumers, and it's responding to the aesthetic principles of a very elite social class whose aesthetic references are about exclusion and not inclusion; it's an absolute celebration of decadence and empire. So my work is at once an embrace of Western easel painting, in all of its beautiful and terrible features, and a critique of it as well.[17]

Considering the candid nature of Wiley's self-critical formalism, I am deeply interested in those beautiful and terrible features he speaks of with such frankness. The decadent consumerism of the art world is a phenomenon in which Wiley enthusiastically participates and, perhaps a critique of its garish crudity lingers within his gilded aesthetic. I tend to reject this notion, however, because the artist's self-consciously high-style brand of painting is almost completely devoid of pictorial seriousness. The humorousness of their invention, potentially even contradicts the racial earnestness articulated in the aforementioned quotations. Yet I say this with trepidation, due both to Wiley's intellectual sophistication and knowledge of cultural theory, as well as his dexterity as a provocateur.

Despite the critical depth and aesthetic glamour of his paintings, there is a troubling component that comes across in the quality of his images. When viewed in person and close-up, Wiley's paintings have a cheap plasticity about them, with a formal competence reminiscent of good sign painting. Yet they have none of the surface complexity and dense layering of the masterworks they seek to emulate. Unfortunately – and I say this with the utmost critical seriousness – they look and feel like mass-produced knock-offs of European paintings. The irony of that observation is that Wiley maintains a studio in Beijing, where he presides over a team of assistants, as well as a studio in New York and one in Dakar, Senegal. Wiley is known for using assistants to create his images. As Christopher Beam states, 'There's nothing new about artists using assistants – everyone from Michelangelo to Jeff Koons has employed teams of helpers, with varying degrees of irony and pride.'[18] But according to the *New York Magazine* writer, 'Wiley gets uncomfortable discussing the subject … "I'm sensitive to it," [Wiley] says.'[19] Beam recounts that when visiting the artist's Beijing studio, the assistants had been whisked away and that Wiley instructed him to delete the iPhone snapshots he'd taken of the empty studio space. It's certainly public knowledge that not every brush stroke is his, but Wiley has made it clear that he doesn't want the public to know 'every aspect of where his hand starts and ends'.[20]

I want to make it clear that the lack of material sophistication is not inherently a fault, in fact Wiley's apparent rejection of formalism's loving embrace, is perhaps where the critical force of his work resides. The fact that they look like good illustration, but not good painting, is arguably neither the result of a deficient taste level, nor the failure of a less studied vision – but rather representative of a sophisticated artist entering into a dialogue with kitsch. It goes without saying that the works photograph beautifully, as if they are made more for photographic reproduction than for display in the white cube. My argument here is that Wiley more meaningfully communicates his satire through the formal, rather than in the rather obvious narrative replacement of European bodies with black ones. In other words, the artist's whimsical pictures are not desperately trying to look like European masterworks and failing terribly at doing so. To read them this way is to miss the point. Wiley has always embraced the marketability and commodity fetishism of the black body – and I would argue that he is deeply fascinated with its history of commodification and objectness.

It is in this regard that the sensitive issue of his multiple studios reemerges. Wiley works in the high production factory mode made famous by Andy Warhol, but unlike the late Pop artist, the younger artist's method of manufacture is 'literally producing' black males as objects to be branded and traded as high-priced luxury goods. The multiple studios and atelier of assistants, even the implication that Wiley doesn't paint the works himself, is arguably where the artist makes his critical intervention.

Ever since the dawn of postmodernism, artists have waged war against the hegemony of authorship and the notion of originality. There is nothing new here – but we should consider that it may be necessary for Wiley's images to be mass-produced if they are to have sufficient critical and satirical force. The Beijing studio alone employs up to ten assistants, along with a studio manager: the American artist Ain Cocke, an accomplished painter in his own right.[21] Interestingly, Cocke's illustrative paintings and drawings are eerily similar to Wiley's in style and tone. The Yale School of Art graduate makes paintings that take on themes ranging from the representation of queer desire, to the homosocial bonding of soldiers in war. Situating his masculine subjects in unlikely settings like flowery gardens and lush pastoral backdrops, his painting engenders a kind of swishy queer nostalgia that rests somewhere between the work of artists Pierre et Gilles and Touko Laaksonen (a.k.a. Tom of Finland). The flushed cheeks of soldiers, romantically frolicking in stylized environments with Rococo flourishes self-consciously queers their stereotypically masculine image – much in the same way that Wiley's urban black males pervert our understanding of the classical Western pose. The similarity in their conceptual approach feels like the dawning of a movement, even while the more assured and confident hand in Cocke's painterly gestures calls into question the authorial veracity of his employer's production.

If someone were to proclaim that Wiley creates bad paintings, I wouldn't necessarily disagree with them, yet I think this quality of *badness* is actually its intentionally constructed mode of satirical kitsch: an incendiary send-up of art history's theological adherence to questionable standards of excellence and rigid formalist conventions. In pondering Wiley's pictures, I think of the following quote from the art critic Clement Greenberg's famous essay 'Modernist Painting:'

> Nothing could be further from the authentic art of our time than the idea of a rupture of continuity. Art *is* – among other things – continuity, and unthinkable without it. Lacking the past of art, and the need and compulsion to maintain its standards of excellence, Modernist art would lack both substance and justification.[22]

Greenberg's advocacy of high modernist abstraction was obsessed with continuity, purity, and the mandate that each art form narrow its area of competence. He famously stated that painting should eliminate any and every effect that might conceivably be borrowed from any other art.[23] Therefore, in his self-critical formalism, he believed that every art should strive for purity as a means to guarantee standards of quality.[24] Considering the dogmatic nature of Greenberg's formalism in relation to Wiley's self-conscious engagement with kitsch, it's not a leap to intimate that the young artist playfully vulgarizes the late critic's influential value system – particularly his emphasis on historical continuity and the endeavour for formal and material purity. It is clear that Wiley is a student of history, but the tone of his criticality is suspicious of the vocabulary of power that is so often embedded within formalism. Out of that suspicion, emerges a citational and highly pictorial stubbornness that stridently opposes both continuity and purity – even while his work seems, at least on the surface, to value these properties.

I want to stress that the result of Wiley's manufacturing method is the creation of artworks that look and feel like illustrations: a strategy that self-consciously employs the visual language of consumer culture. His work is not a formal homage and he does not attempt to convey the quality of affective naturalism associated with Renaissance portraiture. In this regard, I think of Wiley as more of a conceptual artist than a painter, as what is being produced is the glamorous and intellectually rich realization of good ideas – and the formal and material vulgarity of the objects he produces are deeply imbricated within them. It's commonly assumed that Wiley's work references a genre of art widely understood to represent the pinnacle of formal mastery. However, I would argue that a cheapening of the hegemony of form resides in Wiley's conceptual cleverness, not merely a critique of the Western tradition's narrative and pictorial pretentiousness.

Black Male, *Black Book*, and Queer Black Subjectivity Imaged

Perhaps, more meaningful than the formal dimension of Wiley's work, is his narrative and conceptual engagement with the black male body. He came of age as an artist in the wake of the 1993 Whitney Biennial, an exhibition widely credited for institutionally legitimating identity politics as a worthy subject for creative intervention. Artists such as Cheryl Dunye, Glenn Ligon, Daniel J. Martinez, Cindy Sherman, Gary Simmons, Lorna Simpson, Pat Ward Williams, Coco Fusco and Fred Wilson, among others, foregrounded critical engagements with race, gender, sexuality, class, and the post-colonial condition – pushing the critical discussions of art into a more self-reflexive terrain.

The controversial 1994 exhibition *Black Male: Representations of Masculinity in Contemporary American Art* emerged in the wake of the biennial. Curated at the Whitney Museum of American Art by African-American curator Thelma Golden (part of the curatorial team that conceived of the 1993 biennial), *Black Male* sought to explore the fraught history of black male representation, unpacking the deepest and most troubling fantasies engendered by the psychopathology of American racism. Arguably the most incendiary and significant intervention advanced in the exhibition was its contestation and troubling of black masculinity – particularly the complex ideological fictions that inform its mythologizing. *Black Male* didn't exactly endeavour to contest the negative images of black masculinity created by Western culture, nor did it attempt to replace the negative representational fictions with more wholesome or idealizing archetypes. On the contrary, Golden's curatorial effort was more satirical in its cyclical critique of the effects of racism on the cultural consciousness – but also its impact on self-perception. While white racism was acknowledged for its complicity in producing the conditions of inequity and stereotype, Golden was also critically skewering patriarchal, homophobic, and regressively masculinist values and identity constructions within the black community.

Kobena Mercer has articulated his belief that 'black male gender identities have been historically and culturally constructed through complex dialectics of power and subordination.'[25] In keeping with that sentiment, *Black Male* proved to be a controversial and polarizing exhibition because it dared to confront the complex and ideologically fraught gender and sexual identities of black men – as opposed to simply engaging in the myth-making enterprise of advancing uplifting and idealizing representations.

Black Male presented several significant interventions into black queer representation, most notably the inclusion of selections from Robert Mapplethorpe's 1986 photographic series *Black Males*, which were eventually published in the book entitled, *The Black Book*. Mapplethorpe's series drew criticism from black queer communities for what was perceived to be objectifying and stereotypical representations of black men. Scholars ranging from Kobena Mercer and Stuart Hall to David Marriott have written passionately about the violence of these images and the manner in which they traffic in stereotypes around the sexual depravity and aggressiveness of black males – as well as the mythologized archetype of the freakishly endowed 'Superstud'. As I discussed in the last chapter, Glenn Ligon responded to Mapplethorpe's problematic series with a work entitled *Notes on the Margin of the Black Book* (1991–1993) that sharply questioned many of the more troubling racial and sexual dimensions of Mapplethorpe's series. In addition to images from *The Black Book*, the exhibition included the work of gay African-American artist Lyle Aston Harris, a photographer whose production was in direct confrontational dialogue with Mapplethorpe's photographic series. In critical response to *The Black Book*, scholar bell hooks opined that 'it is so obvious as to almost be unworthy of note, and certainly not of prolonged debate, that racist/sexist iconography of the black male body is reaffirmed and celebrated by much of Mapplethorpe's work'.[26] According to hooks, the work of Lyle Ashton Harris served as a necessary intervention into the visual hegemony of Mapplethorpe's 'non-progressive white male-produced images of the black male body and the historical racist/sexist iconography they mirror'.[27] In this regard, Harris was said to break from the 'ruling hegemony that has a hold on images of the black body'.[28] Curator Thelma Golden, in response to Harris' photography, suggested that 'in the wake of Mapplethorpe's work, there was an entire project in

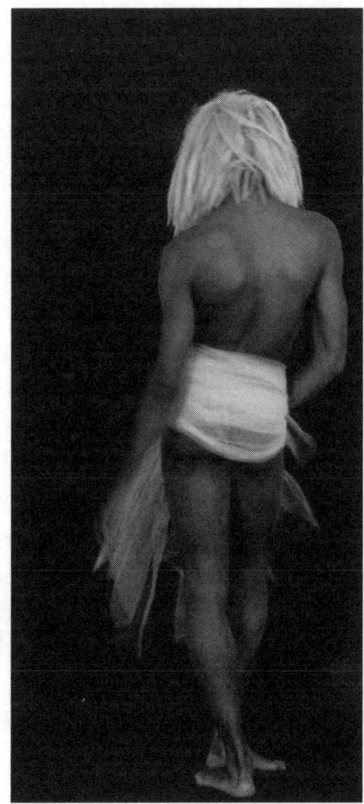

Figure 17 Lyle Ashton Harris, *Constructs #11* (1989). Black & white photograph. © Lyle Ashton Harris Studio

visual art, film, and literature to detach compulsive heterosexuality from black masculinity'.[29] Golden further states that this intervention was 'of course a battle against both rampant homophobia and (hetero) sexual stereotypes'.[30] As she points out, Harris' artwork, particularly his 1989 self-portrait series entitled *Constructs*, both rejects and counters Mapplethorpe's objectifying and sexually demeaning images. In *Constructs*, Harris images his own queer black subjectivity, affording himself the subjecthood that Mapplethorpe often denied his sitters.[31] When asked about his conceptual approach, Harris stated: 'I see myself involved in a project of resuscitation – giving life back to the black male body.'[32] As a response to Mapplethorpe, Harris' brand of self-portraiture created a forum wherein black men could be visually self-identified as gay and in such a manner that went against the grain of both normative heterosexual blackness, as well as racist fantasies about the black male body.

For the sake of context, it is worth mentioning that the *Black Males* exhibition emerged in the shadow of the 'Discussions in Contemporary Culture' series, a forum that produced the conference and subsequent book entitled *Black Popular Culture*.[33] The event took the form of a three-day conference held at the Studio Museum in Harlem and the Dia Center for the Arts on 8–10 December 1991. Organized by scholars Michele Wallace and Gina Dent, *Black Popular Culture* was a landmark event that inaugurated a critical approach to black visual culture that sought to break from the myths of authenticity, nostalgia, essentialisms, and the troubling hetero-patriarchal values that plague the black community. Among the critical interventions made in the conference was the inclusion of radical queer voices such as those of filmmakers Thomas Allen Harris, Marlon T. Riggs, and Isaac Julien. Their presence signalled a shift in critical race discourse toward a more self-reflexive and inclusive engagement with black identity. However, this trend emerged amidst the contentious identity debates of the late 1980s to the early 1990s, a period that produced its own art world controversies – most notably the 1989 political assault on the National Endowment for the Arts. Led by then Senator Jesse Helms, Congress took action against the government's funding of contemporary art – a move motivated by discontent around Robert Mapplethorpe's retrospective exhibition *The Perfect Moment*. Held at the Corcoran Gallery of Art in Washington, D.C. *The Perfect Moment* featured homoerotic and sadomasochistic images that were deemed too offensive and inappropriate to warrant government support. Out of the culture wars emerged a renewed commitment to interrogating the hegemony of representation, and a more rapacious consciousness around the impact and force that images have in shaping social norms. Feminist and queer artists and intellectuals emerged as a newly radicalized force against the institutional forces of inequality.[34]

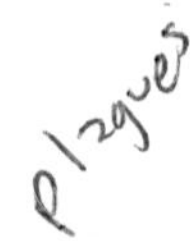

In black queer discourse, the voices of the aforementioned filmmakers Thomas Allen Harris, Marlon T. Riggs, and Isaac Julien; the poet/activist Essex Hemphill; and the Nigerian-born photographer Rotimi Fani-Kayode explored the problem of cultural constructions of black masculinity, along with themes ranging from sexuality, racism, colonialism, and homophobia. The emergence of black queer studies during this intense period represented a crucial response to the institutional rise of what was variously named Black Studies, Afro-American Studies, or Africana Studies – a disciplinary formation that emerged in the 1960s to early 1970s period of post-Civil Rights political activism.[35] According to scholar E. Patrick Johnson, this period of scholarship and political action manifested a distinct gender-sex hierarchy that foregrounded and sought to elevate the heterosexual black male and either ignored entirely or relegated women and gay men to the shadows:

> Given the status of women (and class not lagging too far behind) within Black Studies, it is not surprising that sexuality, and especially homosexuality, became not only a repressed site of study within the field, but also one with which the discourse was paradoxically preoccupied, if only to deny and disavow its place in the discursive sphere of Black Studies. On the one hand, the category of (homo)sexuality, like those of gender and class, remained necessarily subordinated to that of race in the discourse of Black Studies, due principally to an identitarian politics aimed at forging a unified front under racialized blackness. On the other hand, the privileging of a racist discourse demanded the deployment of a sexist and homophobic rhetoric in order to mark, by contrast, the priority of race.[36]

The intervention made by queer scholars in the 1980s–1990s, particularly within the discourse of Black Studies, was to challenge the complete erasure of homosexuality. As Johnson states, within black intellectual thought, homosexuality was 'theorized' as a 'white disease' that had 'infected' the black community.[37]

Kehinde Wiley's work emerges out of this legacy of radical thought, what Roderick Ferguson termed 'queer of colour critique': a mode of inquiry that acknowledges how, in the USA, racism is most often viewed through the lens of gender and sexual conformity – that 'racist practice articulates itself generally as gender and sexual regulation'.[38] Within the sphere of representation, the importance of challenging a racial politics that excised sexual difference became a major preoccupation and motivator for a new brand of intellectual and creative work – as well as the catalyst for revisionist scholarship throughout the humanities and social sciences. Scholar Aliyyah I. Abdur-Rahman's exploration of transgressive sexualities in literary production, considers whether the presence of these narratives holds the potential to undergird an emancipatory political project – an inquiry that has been reiterated by the scholarship of radical feminist and queer art historians engaged in either revisionist or recuperative critical and historical projects.[39] The writing of historians Douglas Crimp, Richard Meyer and the late performance studies scholar José Esteban Muñoz have done landmark work in the areas of art history and visual studies, pushing the imperative of comparative research that explores the intersection of race and homosexuality – and the history of censorship and AIDS activism – in American art and popular representation.[40] As I mentioned previously, this legacy greatly informs Kehinde Wiley's artistic practice, and I argue that the critical urgency of his production in many ways affirms Abdur-Rahman's query about the emancipatory potential of imaging transgressive sexualities.

Henry Louis Gates once wrote that homophobia was rampant among the ideologues, authors, and major leaders of the Black Nationalist movement. Black Power and the aesthetic it engendered mobilized what he called a curious subterraneous connection between homophobia and nationalism.[41] Gates' admission about the history of nationalism among African-Americans represents a major intellectual shift in black critical thought that emerged in the 1980s–1990s, but it also deeply impacted the representational strategies of cultural producers. Out of that paradigm shift emerged one of the movement's most urgent interventions: the critique of heteronormative black masculinity. In Gates' breakdown of the link between homophobia and nationalism, he offers Afro-British filmmaker Isaac Julien's celebrated work *Looking For Langston*, as an exemplar for a newly transcendent black cinema that disrupts the traditional way that black men have been hypersexualized.[42] Although Julien's 1989 film received acclaim for its celebration of black gay identity, one of its most salient features was the way it represented the black male body as soft and vulnerable – a contrast to the visual order of the hardened convention of representation, most readily associated with the cinematic depiction of black men.[43] In the tradition of *Looking for Langston*, the art of Wiley is able to 'respond to the hurtfully exclusionary obsessions of the black nationalist movement' by constructing a counter-narrative and a counter-image that embraces the ambiguity and ambivalence of queerness.[44]

At the beginning of this chapter I mentioned Slavoj Žižek's assertion that fantasy represents, above all things, a desire to be desired by others. In keeping with that sentiment, what Wiley presents to us should perhaps be read as an illustration of that desire: a means of creating a framework within which a queer black subject can be desired and valued. This psychological reading of the work suggests that Wiley makes less a sweeping and recuperative form of image-maintenance for heterosexual black men than he, more accurately, thinks about a queer subjectivity vis-à-vis the racist fictions that inform its historical representation. The effect of inserting black men into the framework of classical painting creates a strange alchemy that achieves the softness and vulnerability that Gates talks about in relation to the films of Isaac Julien: a contrast to the hardened convention of representing black men that the scholar speaks of. Wiley's softened black men, imaged within the stylistic tropes and signifiers of Western power, create a contradictory dialectic in which to ponder the relation between power and fantasy (a psychosocial dynamic that all black men, including Wiley, are entangled within). As Stuart Hall has pointed out, this relation greatly informs how black masculinity is represented within a racialized regime of representation. Citing the writings of art historian Kobena Mercer and Afro-British artist Isaac Julien, Hall suggests that the dominating forces of slavery, colonialism and imperialism have shaped image-making practices around black masculinity:[45]

> ...A central strand of the 'racial' power exercised by the white male slave master was the denial of certain masculine attributes to black male slaves, such as authority, familial responsibility, and the ownership of property. Through such collective, historical experiences black men have adopted certain patriarchal values such as physical strength, sexual prowess, and being in control as a means of survival against the repressive and violent system of subordination to which they have been subjected.
>
> The incorporation of a code of 'macho' behaviour is thus intelligible as a means of recuperating some degree of power over the condition of powerlessness and dependency in relation to the white master subject... The prevailing stereotype (in contemporary Britain) projects an image of black male youth as 'mugger' or 'rioter'...But this regime of representation is reproduced and maintained in hegemony because black men have had to resort to 'toughness' as a defensive response to the prior aggression and violence that characterizes the way black communities are policed... This cycle between reality and representation makes the ideological fictions of racism empirically 'true' – or rather, there is a struggle over the definition, understanding and construction of meanings around black masculinity within the dominant regime of truth.[46]

In Mercer's well-regarded treatise on black masculinity, he suggests that as black men, '*we look, but do not always find the images we want to see*'.[47] In this sense, black men are implicated in a 'landscape of stereotypes which is dominated and organized around the needs, demands, and desires of white males'.[48] The result is that black men are both reduced and confined to a 'narrow repertoire of "types" – the supersexual stud and the sexual "savage" on one hand, or the delicate, fragile exotic "oriental" on the other'.[49] In regards to Wiley, what I find most salient about Mercer's critical formulation is that the young artist's iconography dialogues with a lengthy and rather problematic history of black male representation. As an openly gay artist, Wiley's work is in keeping with trends in radical queer subcultures (particularly in music and performance) that skewer very *straight* signifiers of black masculinity.

Blurring the lines between the threatening symbolism of the inner city black male and the petulant swishiness of the queen, Wiley's inimitable pictures of black men echo the performance styles of multi-gendered poet, musician and cross-dresser Mykki Blanco (a.k.a. Michael David Quattlebaum, Jr.) and Jonte' Demarcus Moaning, the notorious choreographer/performer for pop sensation Beyoncé. Both Blanco and Jonte' use gender bending as a lynchpin of their performative strategy – slipping between the masculine and the feminine with such ease and dexterity that they shatter the hegemony of both identifications. *Vogue* magazine writer Yomi Abiola proclaimed that Jonte' is 'beautiful like a woman and a man at the same time'.[50] The California-born Quattlebaum, who studied at the Art Institute of Chicago, 'defines himself as embodying both female and male spirits', but he does not want people to think of Blanco as just some drag alter ego: 'People have a hard time understanding that there is no difference between Mykki and Michael.'[51] The performative eroticism at the core of Blanco and Jonte's style in many respects depends upon stereotypes surrounding masculine power, as well as expressions of heteronormative femininity. Though it is important to remember that these designations, and the representational strategies they engender, are always associated with (and motivated by) the hegemony of white masculinity. I argue that the black gay men's political consciousness, in which Wiley, Blanco, and Jonte's work participates, critically converses with both fantasy and the stereotypical conventions of racial and sexual representation.

If we contemplate the intervention made by these artists in wider cultural terms, the presence of hip-hop emerges as increasingly significant. In Wiley's early, Harlem-inspired works, the aesthetic of hip-hop culture was ever present. And like the performance-based work of Blanco and Jonte', his pictures always engage critically with the hyper-masculine pose of hip-hop – revelling in its majesty while exposing the fragility and vulnerability at the heart of its artifice. The moment when Wiley's star began to rise in the New York art world coincided with the bling-bling era of hip-hop's mainstreaming and material excesses. The rise of rap stars as household names and business moguls, transformed the economic and cultural life of New York City. Hip-hop's nouveau riche quickly became the new glitterati, and with their presence, emerged a rapacious brand of decadence and conspicuous materialism. Hip-hop flourished within the milieu of New York's larger economic excesses. All of this indulgence led, of course, to the epic fall of Lehman Brothers and the 2008 financial crisis that almost brought down the world's financial systems. It's hard not to think about the massive crippling of the world economy when pondering the decadence that Wiley's hip-hop aesthetic gleefully celebrates.[52] The kind of cheap, kitschy glamour of hip-hop's new money aesthetic personifies Wiley's aesthetic choices, most notably the iconic branding of black male bodies within the dubious logics of multinational capitalism. I have written before about Wiley's branding of 'hip-hop's street nigger archetype', transforming it into an economic symbol akin to the Nike swoosh.[53] I admit, that assessment is rather strong, although as a polemical device, it gets to the core of the potentially bad taste that hovers awkwardly around the artist's work and career. Wiley is known for his embrace of marketing, extending his reach into design: he worked with Puma to design shoes for the South Africa World Cup.[54] And in 2005, he was commissioned by VH1 to create portraits of rap artists for its programme *Hip-Hop Honors*.

In an interview with painter Peter Halley, Wiley said the following about hip-hop:

> I think it's very hard to wrap your arms around the nature of hip-hop as a cultural phenomenon, but it's very hard to define it. It certainly exists musically, and I think we can say that it exists in fashion. And it exists as an oppositional style of political engagement. We can even say that it exists

> in literature as well. But I think to isolate those forms is to miss the point. By and large, hip-hop is about survival – it's about adjusting to change and creating patterns that give rise to new patterns. Hip-hop's essentially an attitude, a state of mind. This can be said about jazz as well. I think that type of radical contingency is one of the central features of the African-American experience. And it goes very much to the heart of what it means to survive in a hostile environment.[55]

The notion of African-American survival that hip-hop represents is affirmed by the cool pose of machismo and masculine prowess adopted by the movement's followers and practitioners – as well as in the visual culture it produced. So, it is therefore notable that Wiley has chosen to celebrate the beauty of that survival, while commenting upon the stereotypical aggressiveness and pathology that haunts popular representation of black men.

Wiley's 2005 series entitled *Rumors of War*, a suite of paintings inspired by equestrian portraiture, takes head on the problematic nature of hip-hop's tragic machismo, in such a manner that seems to awkwardly oscillate between recuperation and satirical mockery. A fitting example is *Equestrian Portrait of the Count-Duke Olivares* (2005), a reimagining of Diego Velázquez's 1634 painting, *Count-Duke of Olivares*. Similar in style and tone to his Napoleon portrait, Wiley's version presents a youthful black man in what is coded as street attire, perched upon a majestic white horse as it rears up. In this humorous update, Count-Duke Olivares wears a bright red 'hoodie-style' sweatshirt, with a commemorative *Negro League* logo on its back. Wiley's urban equestrian is adorned in baggy grey silken sweatpants and black Nike high-top sneakers. The reference to Negro League baseball feels rather curious and slightly sarcastic because of its allusion to African-American nostalgia and a longing for an authentic historical past. The logo forms a compelling contrast to Velázquez's original, which immortalizes Spanish politician Gaspar de Guzmán, whose travails as prime minister were marked by a dramatic mix of perseverance and failure. It would appear that Wiley is thinking about histories of struggle as much as the construction of patriarchal power and the performance of masculinity. A lot is conveyed in Gaspar de Guzmán's gaze as he peers backwards defiantly at the viewer. However, Wiley's figuration arguably possesses greater narrative power because

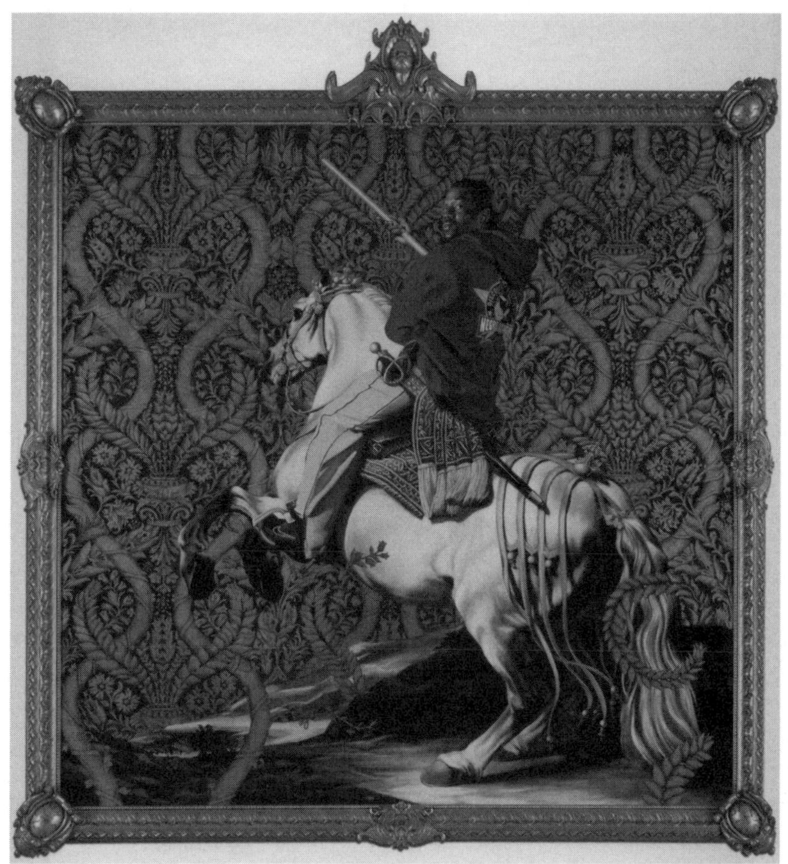

Figure 18 Kehinde Wiley. *Equestrian Portrait of Count Duke Olivares* (2005). Oil on canvas. 108 × 108 in. Courtesy of CAC & Rubell Family Collection. © Kehinde Wiley Studio/Sean Kelly Gallery

of the rhetorical and confrontational force of a young black man in the act of returning the gaze. His processed and slicked-back hair, close-cropped goatee, and defiant countenance represent distinctively black countercultural codes of street style, elegance, and swagger. Wiley always chooses to situate his figures against decorative backgrounds, in this instance an ornate brocade tapestry pattern in detailed black and gold. He resists the urge to recreate the pastoral scenes and stormy skies of his source materials, in favour of something more self-consciously decadent and vulgar – though a no less idealized envisioning of an elaborate fiction.

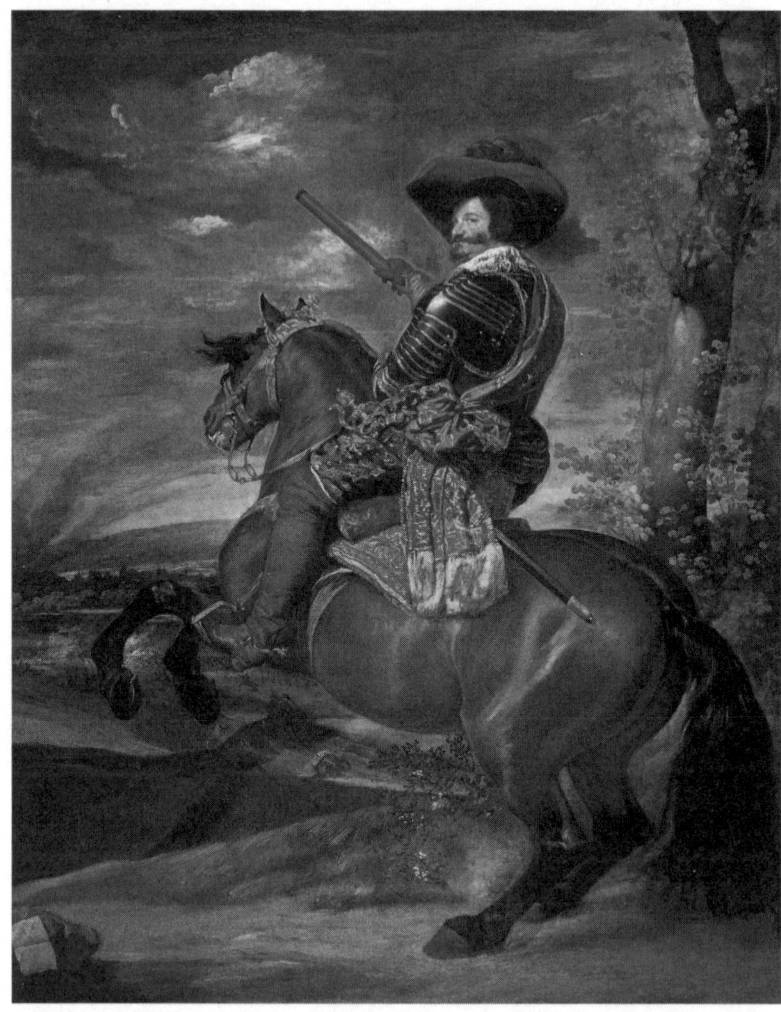

Figure 19 Diego Velázquez, *Count-Duke of Olivares* (1634–1635). Oil on canvas, $50^1/_4 \times 41$ in. (127.6×104.1 cm). © Art Resource Inc. (Artres)

Fantasias/Fantasies of Queer Black Masculinity in Film

When I examine the iconography of Wiley's paintings, the rather pervasive, albeit fraught history of black gay men in popular film comes to mind. In his writing on the representational emergence of black gay men in the cinema, Phillip Brian Harper discusses this as a phenomenon fixated on the black man as both subject and object. As an exemplar Harper mentions the highly politicized moment of the late 1980s, which reached its pinnacle with Senator Jesse Helms' Congress-led assault on the art of Robert Mapplethorpe. Controversies around Mapplethorpe's exhibition *The Perfect Moment*, as Harper illuminates, 'stemmed largely from the intensely conflicted issues of race, power, and sexuality raised by the photographer's aestheticized images of black male faces, bodies, and genitalia'.[56] The result of this set of frictions was the rise of the queer black male subject in popular representation, an archetype that gained a remarkable visibility in several notable instances. As examples of significant antecedents and critical responses, Harper mentions Isaac Julien's *Looking for Langston* (1989), the censorship of Marlon Rigg's celebrated film *Tongues Untied* (1989), Jennie Livingston's *Paris Is Burning* (1990), Shirley Clark's 1967 documentary *Portrait of Jason* and the mainstream films *The Boys in the Band* (1970), *Next Stop, Greenwich Village* (1976), and *Car Wash* (1976). Considering these examples, Harper goes on to state that 'it would be easy to conclude that homosexuality among black men is not just a highly social and politically charged phenomenon, but that its representation in U.S. culture became crucial only amid a general preoccupation with racial and sexual difference, multiculturalism, and political correctness that seemed destined to characterize the period'.[57] What is perhaps most fascinating about this moment, and the ensuing controversies, is that Mapplethorpe's images of black men proved to be the catalyst for the emergence of a highly-political black queer visual culture that sought to contest the presence of stereotypes – while also taking control of and asserting creative agency over its imaging.

If we think about the rise and eventual mainstreaming of black queer visualities in the wake of Mapplethorpe's controversies, artists and performers like Kehinde Wiley, Glenn Ligon, Jonte', and Blanco reemerge as important figures. In particular, Jonte' who is pop sensation Beyoncé's choreographer, has designed the singer's hybrid sex kitten/Amazonian super bitch personae, an embodiment that is less emblematic of black female sexuality – but is more accurately, a black gay man's constructed fantasy of the super-empowered black feminine ideal. The significance of Jonte's influence is that when we behold Beyoncé's sexualized gyrations, what actually seduces us is the erotic power of the queer black male. In his memoir/biography of his relationship with Robert Mapplethorpe, Jack Fritscher talks candidly

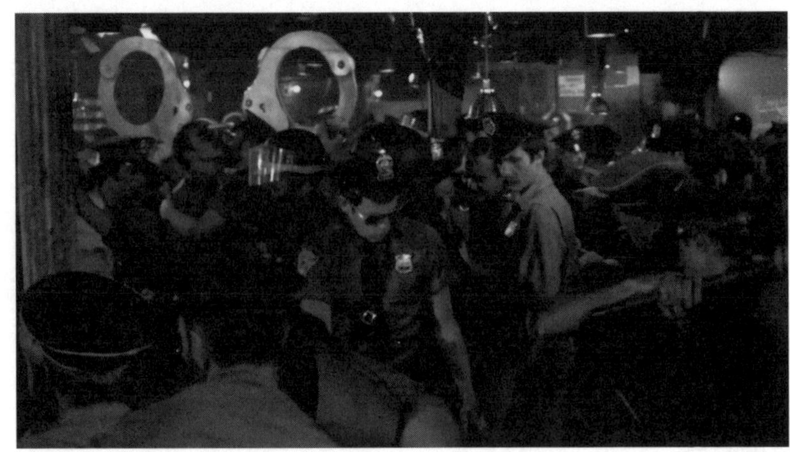

Figure 20 William Friedkin, (1980) *Cruising* screen shot by author [bar scene]

about the late photographer's obsession with race (especially black male sexuality) – a fascination that captured his imagination 'as much as sex and more than gender.'[58] According to Fritscher, it was the artist's contact with William Friedkin's controversial film *Cruising* (1980) that inspired him to take head-on the issue of race: 'In 1979, Robert sat bolt upright, startled erotically, by William Friedkin's searing screenplay, *Cruising*, which captured precisely the dangers and excitement of leathersex in the New York nightlife that was Robert's milieu.'[59] *Cruising* was director Friedkin's return to queer subject matter after the gay-themed *The Boys in the Band* (1970), the mainstream Hollywood hits *The French Connection* (1971), and horror classic *The Exorcist* (1973). The film – a police procedural – is loosely based on the novel *Cruising* by *New York Times* reporter Gerald Walker – a detailed and gruesome account of a serial killer targeting gay men in New York's underground S&M scene.

Critical response to the film was extremely negative, bolstered by the protests of gay rights activists who attempted to obstruct its production. As scholar David Greven highlights, *Cruising* has not been given its critical due because of its characterization as a deeply homophobic film. Most notable queer scholars and cultural commentators share this perspective – although as time has passed, the mood has softened somewhat.[60] In fact, Greven argues that *Cruising* is: 'far from being a homophobic work … the film critiques homophobia by pursuing the

Hitchcockian play of male doubles in its representation of straight and queer masculinities'.[61] As Greven further suggests:

> [*Cruising*] is as determinedly non-mimetic – non-realistic – as it is self-consciously realistic. To take it as an attempt at a realistic representation of gay life is to ignore the film's much broader exploration of the psychosexual dimensions and foundations of American masculinity. None of this is to say that *Cruising* presents an attractive or nuanced vision of gay life. But within its often negative portrayal lies something more challenging: a provocation to contemplate queer male desire in unfettered forms within a larger homophobic culture.[62]

Greven's critical reassessment of *Cruising* echoes many of Jack Fritscher's memories and reflections on the influence Friedkin's film had on Mapplethorpe – that it 'shocked him to a new crystalline vision: the erotic power of the black male'.[63] In Fritscher's account, despite the protests by more conservative constituencies in the gay community at the time, Friedkin's film, what the author calls a 'virtual documentary', 'caught the fear of violence quite accurately, because there were always instances of leathermen killing other leathermen'.[64] He states: 'many gay men were victims of killers from their own kind during the seventies'.[65] According to Fritscher, this rather morbid phenomenon apparently consumed Mapplethorpe's creative and intellectual interests:

> [Mapplethorpe] was very aware that in San Francisco, shades of *Cruising*, several murdered leathermen had been last seen in the S&M bars South of Market. For a period in 1978–1979 (coincidentally, the time of Robert's first spending time in San Francisco), a canny murderer cruised the bars where leathermen, surrendering to play S&M games, got themselves into what Tennessee Williams called, in *Night of the Iguana*, 'tied up situations.'[66]

Considering the hateful backlash to Friedkin's film, Fritscher's perspective is quite intriguing. The author characterized the film as the best cinema vérité take on the queer 'masculine-identified' leather subculture of the 1970s that Mapplethorpe ultimately 'cleaned up for museum consumption'.[67]

There is no doubt that *Cruising* is an inflammatory film, not least because of its depiction of killing driven by homosexual self-loathing – which was not the message the gay community wanted to send mainstream audiences in the homophobic 1970s and 1980s. At the beginning of the film, we see an anonymous man dressed in black jeans, a leather motorcycle jacket, and dark aviator glasses as he descends into an underground club in New York's meatpacking district. Once inside we see a rather surreal, bacchanalian scene of gay men dancing, drinking, doing drugs, and having anonymous sex. As the camera pans through the club, a voyeuristic gaze is established: one that is often read as judgemental and ideologically distant from the decadence that unfolds in the field of vision. The reading of the camera's movement and gaze as having a condemnatory tone has a narrative significance, because the perspective of the camera is meant to double as the hateful and sadistic gaze of the killer – an individual who preys upon and butchers gay men.

Several scenes in the film take viewers into what the filmmaker seems to present as an illicit world of moral depravity and sexual irresponsibility. Viewing it in the present, the devastating spectre of AIDS that ravaged the gay community haunts these representations. Ironically, the film was produced in a moment of sexual liberation, just prior to the disease's explosion and the social consciousness that came with it. However, the film feels like an extremely cynical and condemning portrait of a social scourge, even if that was not the director's intent. More accurately, *Cruising* is a kind of psychological horror film, an irrational narrative of closeted desires in a climate of extreme repression and intolerance. As Al Pacino's Steve Burns cruises the various clubs, the scenes of sexual excess and drug use become more extreme and immersive, implying that the undercover cop is becoming a reluctant participant in a seductive world he finds repulsive, yet is struggling to understand.

On a close viewing of the film, structural, though intentional inconsistencies appear in the narrative. For example, characters that were killed reappear as murderers, and voices are dubbed over multiple characters – which disrupts the film's narrative cohesion. For example, in one scene, a murder suspect converses with his father in a park. But disturbingly, in this scene the father's voice is the same one dubbed over the faces of the various anonymous perpetrators in the film. Ultimately these structural devices effectively function as an articulation of a pathology that infects a community forced into the shadows – while simultaneously conveying a rather brutal consciousness about a form of repression that expresses itself through violence. On the level of form, the effect of these elements causes greater narrative confusion, while creating an affect that is incredibly disturbing – not least because of the unfiltered sentiment of moral scrutiny and damnation they convey.

What is arguably most evocative after multiple viewings, however, is the racial coding that hovers quietly over the images, complicating its ideological depiction of alterity. In the opening sequence, as we descend into Friedkin's infernal underworld, the camera follows its anonymous protagonist as funk music plays. The song *Lump*, by the band Mutiny, is from the 1979 album *Mutiny on the Mamship*, by former Parliament-Funkadelic drummer Jerome Brailey. In tandem with the music, men dance and move rhythmically through the space, eyeing each other and cruising in search of the next sexual encounter. At times the camera panned low, focusing on the sweaty naked buttocks of men in chaps and jock straps as they jiggle to the music. In this sequence, like all of the club scenes, the men are always white, yet these filmic moments seem as suggestive of a kind of masculine cool, as much as they present an image of alterity and abjection. In various states of undress, the club's participants pantomime a facsimile of ideal hyper-masculinity as a kind of drag, but as we learn, this is a world defined by racial exclusivity and privilege. The effect of Brailey's funk is that it encourages and intensifies the racially coded swagger of the club's inhabitants. Everything about this world reflects the breaking down of social mores, the embodiment and performance of unbridled male lust and desire, all taboos in a society where repression, power, control, and sexual inhibition define masculinity. Kobena Mercer has articulated that 'prevailing definitions of masculinity imply power, control, and authority, attributes that have been historically denied to black men since slavery'.[68] Mercer's argument suggests that in gay subcultural style, there has been a trend towards the adoption of 'straight' signifiers of masculinity, as means to challenge stereotypes of the swishy queen or 'poof'.[69] According to Mercer what developed was a:

> ...stylistic flirtation with S/M imagery, leather gear, quasi-military uniforms, and skinhead styles. Politically, these elements project highly ambivalent meanings and messages, but it seemed that the racist and fascist connotations of these new 'macho' styles escaped gay consciousness, as those who embraced the 'threatening' symbolism of the tough-guy look were really only interested in the eroticization of masculinity.[70]

Mercer makes a strong case that the performance of these styles largely depends on connotations of masculine power, but they also convey a kind of aggressive masculinity associated with the alterity of blackness – even while these environments are often racially homogeneous. What we see in *Cruising* is not a form of gendered power usually associated with white masculinity; rather one that derives its sense of difference and excitement from an ethnic presence that is erased from view. The irony of that fact is that, as Mercer reminds us, the origins of the modern gay rights movement were directly intertwined with the black liberation movement – in fact the African-American Civil Rights movement became the prototype for all new movements.[71] What Mercer articulates here is that, while white gays derived symbolic inspiration from the black liberation movement and from black ways of being, there was no reciprocity or equal exchange between racial and sexual politics during the 1970s.[72]

The notion of inspiration gains significance when considering the cultural and symbolic influence of blackness on white American culture – while the issue of racism was marginalized and excised from the gay liberation movement. The history of relations between black and queer communities, specifically the highly politicized moment of the 1970s, provides some context to understand why specific stylistic tropes emerged in the gay underground. While some of these styles took the form of a black-identified brand of racial masquerade, Mercer points out that others seemed to embrace a series of white-signified archetypes: nativist, outlaw biker, or even a skinhead aesthetic – modes of being that have potentially racist connotations, even if the intention behind their adoption was not intolerant and these models were appropriated as a means to resist harmful anti-gay stereotypes. What is significant about these, and all, identifications of hyper-masculinity; is that they each represent states of marginality, outsiderness, and disenfranchisement.

In the film, we see various performative modes of masculinity, including the pantomiming of what could be described as a black male swagger – which, in its embodiment, functioned as a form of play and a means to achieve an alterity and libidinal freedom denied in most aspects of life. The filmmakers appear to be quite aware of this contradiction and the tension it engenders. A powerful and slightly perplexing scene occurs early in the film, in which several detectives interrogate a murder suspect at the police precinct. The suspect, a

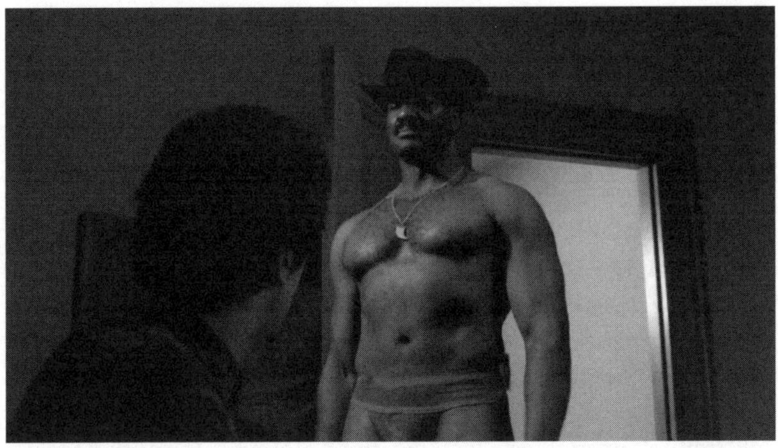

Figure 21 William Friedkin, (1980) *Cruising* screen shot by author [Interrogation scene]

young white gay man in his 20s, who is presented earlier in the film as a type of tough guy, is shaken down and interrogated aggressively by the detectives. In the middle of the interrogation, a large black man, nude with the exception of a tiny jock strap and cowboy hat, enters the room and violently slaps the suspect in the face. In this moment the young man's tough exterior completely dissipates as he is reduced to a shivering and whimpering mess. The violence is repeated, further disorienting and dismantling the suspect's fragile facade.

It is a bizarre scene and one that abruptly introduces the notion of race into a narrative in which, until then, it appears only symbolically. The African-American interrogator, who never speaks, dresses similarly to many of the white gay inhabitants of the underground clubs. But when faced with the presence of an actual black man (an identity that is only mimicked and performed) fear overcomes the suspect. It is definitely intriguing that the police would, as a form of intimidation, use the personification of a subjectivity that (in the American cultural consciousness) is both feared and fantasized about as a means of breaking down its gay suspects. In this strange sequence, there appears to be awareness on the part of the police that a tendency exists within this beleaguered (cinematically constructed) subculture to conceive of and perform a very specific (and racially coded) notion of alterity, while keeping actual forms of difference outside of its socially privileged spaces and value systems. This is why the abrupt and violent insertion of that difference (in this instance the black male) would disturb the fantasy and thoroughly cut through the fictionally constructed veneer of masculine toughness. And as Jack Fritscher points out in his memoir, it was this uncanny scene that greatly impacted Mapplethorpe, unlocking a representational obsession with the erotic potential of the black male.

Wiley's artwork – while certainly emerging out of the black queer critiques of *The Black Book*, is indirectly engaged with a rich history of queer representation, of which Friedkin's *Cruising* serves as a vital filmic example. Wiley's artwork emerges from a series of erasures: namely, the excision of queer men of colour from normative American hetero-patriarchal value systems, from mainstream gay life, further still from alternative gay life, and finally through the pathologizing of black gay men from African-American liberation struggles. Robert Mapplethorpe's *The Perfect Moment* exhibition, and the controversies surrounding his inflammatory images of black men inspired by *Cruising*, had a profound effect on black artists, encouraging them to radically self-image. I find something germane in the relation between sex and death in the subcultural dimensions of gay life that permeate the visual obsessions of Friedkin and Mapplethorpe. Both artists were fixated, for better or for worse, on the shadowy presence of a queer underground – a community closeted and contending with contradictory identifications of radicalism and shame. Even if the queer underground regarded itself as politically subversive, the absence of racial difference – especially within the conditions of homophobia and illness – calls into question the veracity of its sense of radical alterity. Wiley's artistic production equally concerns itself with the sex/death relation, but also with the invisibility of race that has all too often dominated popular representations of gay life. In all of the artist's portraits, the stereotyped and fetishized hypersexual masculinity of black men grates against the spectre of pathology and violence that informs dominant understandings of African-American existence. In contrast to the fantasias of Mapplethorpe and Friedkin, Wiley rescues the black male imago from its state of erasure and neglect – from its unfortunate social function as an unknowable symbolic to be eroticized, yet socially maligned.

Struggle and survivorship are important components of the visually resplendent spectacle of sex, death, and race that Wiley's pictures often convey. But rather than position black men in a mythical state of embattled subcultural grace, his portraits foreground their beauty and complexity as an expression of power and dominance. We see this set of qualities throughout his vast body of work, but perhaps most dramatically in a suite of portraits entitled *DOWN* (2008). Inspired by Hans Holbein's *The Body of the Dead Christ in the Tomb* (1520–22), *DOWN* comprises a series of heroically scaled paintings of prone figures, all young black men in the throes of death. Wiley has stated that history paintings of fallen soldiers in the ravages of war have also greatly influenced this series. Arguably his most ambitious series, *DOWN* marks Wiley's rather triumphant foray into the genre of monumental portraiture. Among the more disturbing and evocative paintings in the artist's oeuvre, the works unsettle in their more overt allusions to violence, death, and sex. Wiley conveys the softening and queering of black men in the disarming sensuality of their quietude. But these figures also have a vulnerability that belies the aggressiveness usually associated with the inner city black male – a quality that is rather unnerving, because the images invite the viewer to voyeuristically consume these men in their state of vulnerability. The contradictory relation Wiley's paintings set up alludes to the manner in which the fear/fantasy matrix of American racism preys upon black men, even though the images simultaneously convey the euphoria of sexual ecstasy. Extending upwards of 30 feet in length, the portraits in *DOWN* have a more palpable heroism that emanates forcefully from the presence of an aggressively queered brand of masculinity. The title of the series is especially poignant because it alludes, in its literal dimension, to the dramatic physical state of his subjects, although it also makes reference to the black vernacular expression of *being down* – to being complicit with and in agreement with the group, or simply be willing to participate in collective action. The notion of *being down* is significant to Wiley's unique expression of post-blackness, in that his images articulate defiance to the politics of redemption demanded of African-American artists: the mandate to be authentically black. In that defiance is a refusal of the tribalism and rapacious group belongingness that is often based upon a sense of collective victimization. When queried about the issue of intra-cultural obligation, Wiley spoke about the importance of resisting collective identities:

> It feels good to all be down with one another. This notion of being authentically black is comforting. To be down is to be with it, to be with your people, to be part of the collective. But I think it's time to grow out

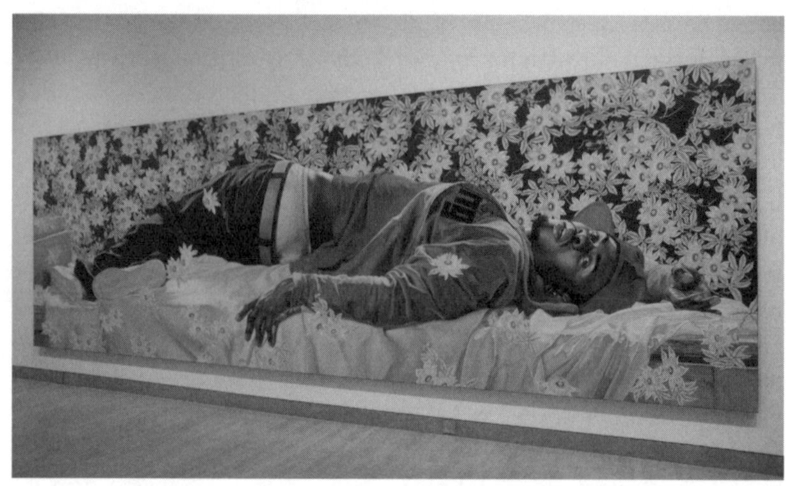

Figure 22 Kehinde Wiley, *Femme Piquée par un Serpent* (2008). Oil on canvas, 102 × 300 in. (259.08 × 762 cm). © Garrett Ziegler/Flickr

> of that. The cult of the individual is something that is going to be a rescuing point for black people. I think in order to do good for your community you have to do good for yourself and you have to stop thinking about being down.[73]

Resistant in their defiant serenity, the subjects in Wiley's *DOWN* series refuse the collective masculinity of authentic blackness, in favour of something more individual: an expressiveness that, in its sensuousness and sensitivity, conveys a humanity that transcends the artifice of toughness and armament, the *down-ness*, that black men so often project.

A fitting example is Wiley's *Femme Piquée par un Serpent*, a 2008 reimagining of Auguste Clésinger's 1847 marble sculpture of the same name. Clésinger's original is based upon the notorious French courtesan and artist's muse Apollonie Sabatier. When exhibited at the Paris Salon of 1847, the sexually suggestive sculpture caused a scandal, due in part to Sabatier's reputation as the mistress of French poet Charles Baudelaire. In Wiley's painterly version, the *femme* is a 20-something black man in contemporary clothing: blue jeans that sag slightly on the buttocks, exposing grey Hanes underwear, a red t-shirt that is hiked up just enough to reveal his sitter's bare midriff, a bright green sweat jacket, red baseball hat, and gold Adidas tennis

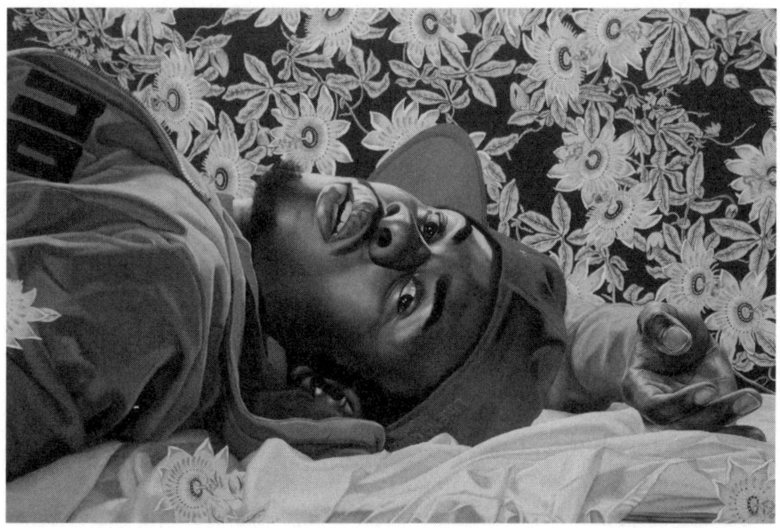

Figure 23 Kehinde Wiley, *Femme Piquée par un Serpent* (2008) [DETAIL]. Oil on canvas, 102 × 300 in. (259.08 × 762 cm). © Garrett Ziegler/ Flickr

shoes. The sensuously posed figure reclines seductively on his back, one arm to his side, while the other drapes dramatically behind his head, as he gazes dispassionately at the viewer. Narratively, the painting conveys contrasting themes that rest uncomfortably between sexual suggestiveness and the slow agony of an untimely death. But it nonetheless invites us to find a voyeuristic pleasure in its spectacle and to contemplate the intimacy and eroticism of black masculinity disarmed and devoid of its tragic ideological dimension. Surrounding Wiley's dying man is a bevvy of orange-yellow flowers that decorate the background like wallpaper, while others seem to fall ever so gracefully around the subject. Every inch of *Femme Piquée* conveys a feeling of overt sexuality and gratuitous decadence, which perhaps is its strength. Although, like the original; its dares to be provocative and slightly scandalous in the brazen sexualizing and queering of a black man adorned in the signifiers of hyper-masculinity. It is an image of subversive grace, especially when reflecting upon the racial fetishism of Mapplethorpe's *The Black Book* series. As Kobena Mercer forcefully stated in relation to the late photographers pictures, the series functions as 'cultural artifacts that say something about certain ways in which white people "look" at black people and how, in this way of looking, black male sexuality is perceived as something different, excessive, Other'.[74]

In the context of Mercer's critical reading, Mapplethorpe's black men were trapped within a condition of abject 'thinghood' that 'conveyed certain racial and sexual fantasies about the black male body'.[75] Numerous scholars contend that in Mapplethorpe's phallocentric fantasy, black men are 'confined and defined in their very *being* as sexual and nothing but sexual, hence hypersexual'.[76] Mercer is indeed correct in his assessment of *Black Book*, but in many respects all of Mapplethorpe's images of gay men create that quality of thinghood – even the more active S&M pictures. Mapplethorpe's radical queerness was tinged with a sentiment of shame and ambivalence that fixated on a subcultural gayness – one that existed in the darkness, and on the margins of a deeply homophobic society. Friedkin's offensive opus polarizes critics because it simultaneously captures the radicalism and shame, the excitement of unbridled sexuality, and the pathology of repression. Whether or not it is a homophobic vision is up for debate, but it nonetheless traps the queer male body in a hegemonic system of visual representation that demeans and objectifies, even despite the fact that black men are largely invisible. Inspired in many ways by Friedkin, the fetishistic logic that governs Mapplethorpe's depictions of black men was also about mastery and control of these sitters as 'objects' and not as fully realized human beings.[77] Kehinde Wiley's images function as a corrective to the fetishistic logic, the thinghood, and the racist erasure of black queer men from the field of representation. There is no doubt that his images of black men are sexualizing, though I argue there is a distinct difference between how he plays with these conditions and the aestheticizing of stereotype that Mapplethorpe's images indulge so carelessly. As a response to the racial and sexual fantasies about black men that lock them into a state of inherent inferiority, Wiley's subjects, in their aestheticization of power and masculinity, convey a powerful and unrepentant heroism in the face of death.

3

Loving Aberrance: Mickalene Thomas and the Queering of Black Female Desire

> Black women's bodies continue to bear the gross insult and burden of spectacular (representational) exploitation in transatlantic culture. Systematically overdetermined and mythically configured, the iconography of the black female body remains the central ur-text of alienation in transatlantic culture . . . Yet there are ways to read for the viability of black women making use of their own materiality within narratives in which they are the subjects.[1]
>
> – Daphne Brooks, *Bodies in Dissent*

New York-based artist Mickalene Thomas (b. 1971) is known for her large-scale paintings of black women in decorative and highly staged settings. Reminiscent of classical odalisque poses, Thomas' portraits take on a range of themes from gender and sexuality to race, femininity, and power. A 2002 graduate of Yale University, Thomas has built an impressive career as one of the most celebrated artists of her generation. There is something extremely perplexing about Thomas' pictures, an unsettling quality that distinguishes them from the work of her contemporaries. In many respects, her artwork conveys a striking sense of familiarity, in what appears on the surface to be a self-consciously citational style of visual appropriation. Anyone with knowledge of art history will recognize the artist's rather overt allusions to Western art – and of course, she also nods to Blaxploitation aesthetics of the

1970s and the hyper-stylized *mise-en-scène* of African photography. What stands out most strikingly, however, is how Thomas foregrounds the black female body, an artistic subject with a rather lengthy history of representation – but primarily as a debased presence. Her iconographic approach to its representation reveals a consciousness of this history, from Orientalist exoticization in the Western tradition, to black feminist portraiture of the 1980s–1990s. The complexities of identity take centre stage in Thomas' art, although arguably, she concerns herself most with the 'dominant meanings' constructed about women in historical and popular representations – meanings that have most often reinforced their marginalization and subordination. Thomas has doubtlessly been influenced by a vast and distinguished canon of artists and scholars from various historical periods. However, in the following pages, I will explore some key connections in terms of their revolutionary contributions to the representation of black women.

In her writings on the conceptual strategies of black women artists, scholar bell hooks suggests that in a racially discriminatory and hetero-patriarchal society, 'we mostly see images of black folks that reinforce and perpetuate the accepted, desired subjugation of black bodies . . . and that we look at these images with suspicion and distrust'.[2] This realization has produced an entire genre of artistic production that could be read as corrective – as a politics of the periphery that sets out to redress the historical debasement of marginalized bodies in the field of representation. Thomas' artwork emerges from this tradition, most notably from revisionist scholarship that interrogated the hegemony of the Western canon – most remarkably, its racial and sexual exclusivity.

As Griselda Pollock has brought to our attention, the very notion of canon formation has been steeped in ideological values that are enshrined not just in the choice of preferred texts and works of art, but also in the methods of their interpretation.[3] Pollock's feminist revisionism criticizes value systems in which women and people of colour are voiceless and faceless – and in their marginalization are therefore unable to contest the demeaning and objectifying stereotypes that have been uncritically canonized.[4] Pollock has done groundbreaking work to reveal how the phallocentric underpinnings of institutionally dominant art history 'negated femininity in order to secure the supremacy of masculinity within the sphere of creativity', a critical approach that has been taken up by other notable feminist art historians, namely Linda Nochlin.[5] It is nearly impossible to contemplate the work of Mickalene

Thomas and not think about Pollock's feminist unpacking of Edward Said's notion of Orientalism, a critical model that explores the West's construction of its centrality and dominance through the presentation of non-Western cultures as primitive, exotic, and inferior.[6] The Orientalizing of women in the history of Western painting, as Pollock points out, is particularly egregious, presenting women of colour as a 'form of gross physicality, indecency, and indolence: coded signs of an unharnessed sexuality . . . confirming yet again that race and gender are complexly interwoven in the Western imaginary'.[7] We see this kind of representation in the work of celebrated painters throughout the history of art, but it is important to remember that the depictions of non-Western women, in their Oriental otherness, functioned as 'a dangerous antithesis to Western ideologies of male dominance'.[8] This representational legacy has positioned the black female body as an 'excessive body:' a condition that visually characterizes black womanhood as aberrant.[9] In the wake of this legacy, is it even possible to reimagine black female subjectivity beyond its historical overdetermination?

I pose this question because I believe it is a query that Thomas has taken up quite remarkably and successfully. Many notable female artists have endeavoured to disrupt the problematic history of female objectification, but few have intervened into this phantasmagoric space with Thomas' inventive dexterity. While her stunning pictures appear to merely cite a history of feminist representational politics, I argue that she manages to assert something innovative that inspires a renewed sense of curiosity and aesthetic decipherment.

A post-modern strategy of evoking the past bristles from within Thomas' historical consciousness, while denying the nostalgic impulse that tends to shadow it. This approach has dominated feminist oppositional strategies since the culture wars of the 1980s. Ever since the 1993 Whitney Biennial exhibition, there has been a backlash against identity politics in visual arts. A special disdain has been reserved for the type of institutional critique that satirically sends-up the hegemonies, biases, and foibles of the historical canon. Artworks functioning in this manner have an activist-oriented oppositional politics that often take the form of appropriation and the reimagining of great masterworks. Art historian Donald Kuspit characterizes this approach as 'postart' or, in other words, the 'defamatory banalization of great traditional art'.[10] Part of Kuspit's displeasure issues from feminist appropriation art that takes an intentionally blasphemous approach to the artworks of great white males, skewering every dimension of these works that bask in the visual mythologizing of masculine power and dominance. Feminist oppositional strategies that critically take on white patriarchal systems in the history of art intervene into a fiercely protected theology: a dangerous and risky move that has received its fair share of venom. In his characterization of 'postart,' Kuspit critiques the work of various artists, including Mary Beth Edelson, Brazilian photographer Vic Muniz, Keith Tyson, Annie Sprinkle, and Rachel Lachowicz, among others:

> Mary Beth Edelson's 'revision' of Leonardo's *Last Supper*, in which photographs of the heads of trendy feminist artists replace those of apostles, is the classic example. In a similar vein, but without feminist intention and much more nihilistically, if with the same heavy-handed irony, Vik Muniz re-does masterpieces – Caravaggio's *Medusa* and Gericault's *Raft of the Medusa* among them (suggesting that Muniz has a problem with the phallic woman as well as with high art) – in chocolate or spaghetti, among everyday edible materials. He democratizes the masterpieces by turning them into cheap junk food, high caloric but with little nutritional value, and very tasty, literally. But the subtle tastefulness of the masterpieces has completely disappeared . . .
>
> . . . Crudely copying several of Rubens' paintings of women, a craftless feminist postpainter added male hands around their voluptuous bodies, suggesting Rubens' lechery. This is explained in an accompanying text, which hypes the paintings as a telling revelation of Rubens' all too male psyche. The long-winded text is a telling example of the pseudo-profound theorizing that has become *de rigueur* in postart. Indeed, such texts – which are usually less interesting than the objects they pretend to enlighten us about (if there is any reason to choose between their banality) – have become essential weapons in the armory of ideological didacticism that supports postart . . . [11]

I quote Kuspit at length because, in the forcefulness of his language, lies a dismissal of a range of artists' attempts to interrogate the structures of inequality – and their effort to bring awareness to a complex array of erasures, debasements, and pernicious forms of myth-making. Mary Beth Edelson's *Some Living American Women Artists/Last Supper* (1972), a work acquired by New York's Museum of Modern Art (MoMA), is one of the most iconic works of the feminist movement and the inspiration for future generations of women artists. Kuspit's ill-tempered criticisms, especially his disdain for the discourses of identity, suggest that these discussions (and the so-called 'postart; works they illuminate) are in fact a-historical. This a-historical quality, that Kuspit bemoans, issues from intellectual debates viewed as extraneous to the materiality of art, discourses such as queer theory, feminist activism, post-colonial studies, and critical race theory.[12] The issue of didactic materials accompanying the display of activist artworks emerged quite prominently in the response to the 1993 Biennial. Respected art historian Rosalind Krauss questioned whether historical awareness is of any importance to understanding the exhibited works. Describing the didactic support materials as 'arrogant', Krauss questioned (in a roundtable discussion in the journal *October*) the theoretical rigour of works dedicated to discussing racial politics and the visualization of blackness, inquiring if the 'idea of black rage' is more difficult than what she described as her enlightened and intellectually complex formal experience with works of art.[13] In a similar line of thought, art historian Hal Foster suggested that cultural and art world fascination with trauma – what he rather cynically terms 'an envy with abjection', was driven by a range of crises, namely despair over poverty, crime, a broken welfare state, and the stubborn persistence of AIDS.[14] In his formulation, this fixation with trauma creates a binary that situates us in two distinct camps 'the abjector' and the 'abjected': a condition that he vehemently rejects for it demands identification with the trauma narratives of identity, unless one wants to find his/herself 'counted among sexists and racists'.[15]

The 1993 Whitney Biennial inaugurated the institutional legitimation of an identity-based artistic movement that claimed the body as a site for political struggle. This paradigm shift was mobilized around various social and cultural inequities, not the least of which included the marginalization of difference from the histories and canons of art. It was in these transformative conceptual vocabularies that new artistic and intellectual approaches emerged, giving birth to a rapacious theoretical and political aesthetic that was intersectional in its comparative engagement with issues of identity, such as the complexities of the mechanisms and operations of race, gender, and sexuality. These issues are always considered the *simple* stuff that vulgarizes and distracts from the more heady concerns of form: characteristics that are ideologically constructed and uncritically assigned (as scholars like Griselda Pollock have suggested) to the work of white male artists. However, the concerns of social inequity, identity, and inequality comprise one of the most intellectually challenging, the most perplexing, and the most politically and culturally urgent phenomena in which intellectuals and artists are constantly entangled.

Mickalene Thomas' artwork can only be fully understood in its articulation of this legacy. However, her post-black futurity contains a conceptual restlessness that extends beyond an interest in punishing the abuses that Western culture has inflicted upon black bodies. To the contrary, Thomas advances something perhaps more incendiary, a queer feminist desiring gaze; a powerfully defiant and aggressively sexual representation of black womanhood that bears the *power of the look*. In her reference to art history's lasciviously Orientalist fixation with women's bodies, Thomas advances an aesthetic, or a scopic practice, that engages in what could be described as self-surveillance: a radical and boldly empowered re-inscription of black female corporeality within the sphere of visual culture.[16] The artist's playful allusions to sex images of the 1970s gestures towards a self-consciously queer eroticism that cleverly takes ownership over the imaging of black female desire: a bold move that breaks from a history of feminist representational politics that denies the inherent convergence of sexuality and womanhood.

A fitting example of Thomas' signature aesthetic is *Baby I Am Ready Now* (2007), a diptych in heroic scale, made of acrylic, rhinestones, enamel, and wood. Thomas' paintings have the kind of unworldly quality that straddles the line between historical consciousness, nostalgic longing, and what could be characterized as a post-black futurity. Perhaps even more so than Glenn Ligon or Kehinde Wiley, Thomas' images gesture towards the creation of something new: a vision even less corrective and less entangled in an embattled relationship with the past. *Baby I Am Ready Now* is a visually striking and slightly overwhelming painting, depicting a black woman with ample Afro sitting on a sofa as she gazes dispassionately at the viewer. There is something defiant in her stance. She sits with her legs open, one hand on her face and the other resting between her legs. Her expression conveys a mix of boredom and judgement, but is also devoid of pathos. Thomas renders the figure's skin in flat brown, with little articulation or painterly rendering to convey three-dimensionality. The background is a collage-like patchwork of densely organized and

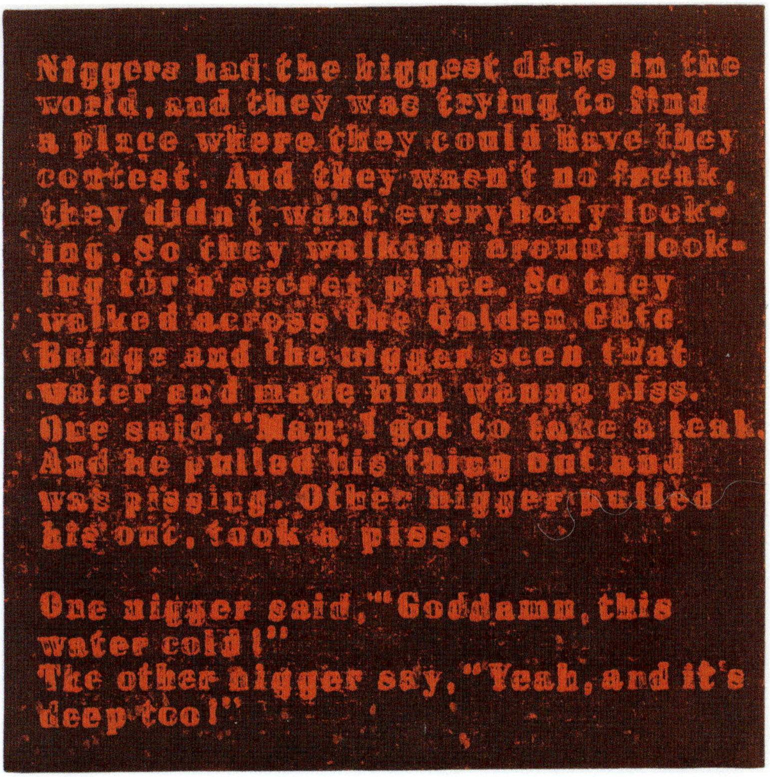

Plate 1 Glenn Ligon, *Mudbone Liar* (1993). Oil stick, synthetic polymer and graphite, 81.3 × 81.3 cm. © Glenn Ligon/Regen Projects, Los Angeles

Plate 2 Glenn Ligon, *Prologue Series #2* (1991). Oil stick, gouache and graphite on paper, 20 × 16 in. © Glenn Ligon/Regen Projects, Los Angeles

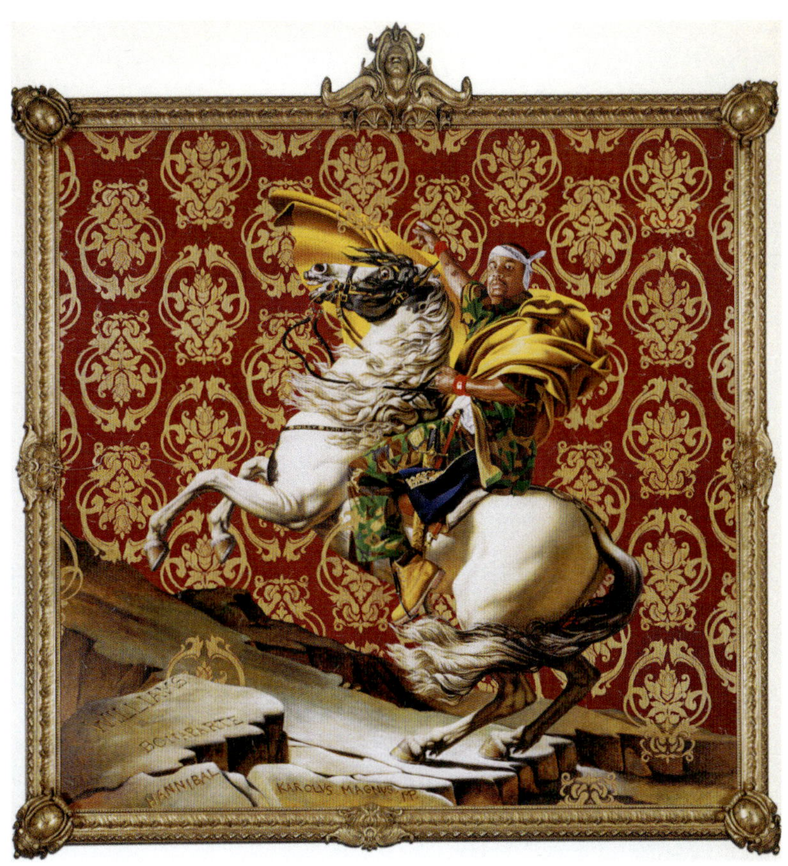

Plate 3 Kehinde Wiley, *Napoleon Leading the Army Over the Alps* (2005). Oil on canvas. 108 × 108 in. (274.3 × 274.3 cm). Collection of Suzi and Andrew B. Cohen. © Kehinde Wiley Studio/Sean Kelly Gallery

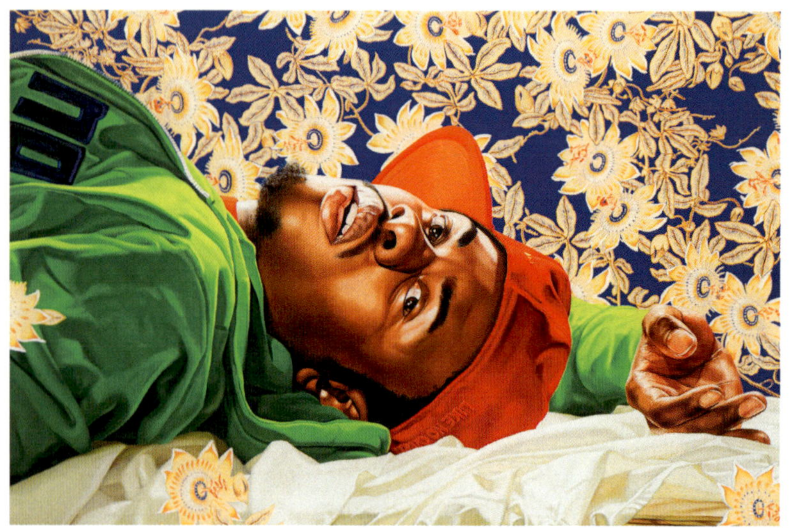

Plate 4 Kehinde Wiley, *Femme Piquee Par Un Serpent* (2008) [DETAIL]. Oil on canvas, 102 × 300 in. (259.08 × 762 cm). © Garrett Ziegler/Flickr

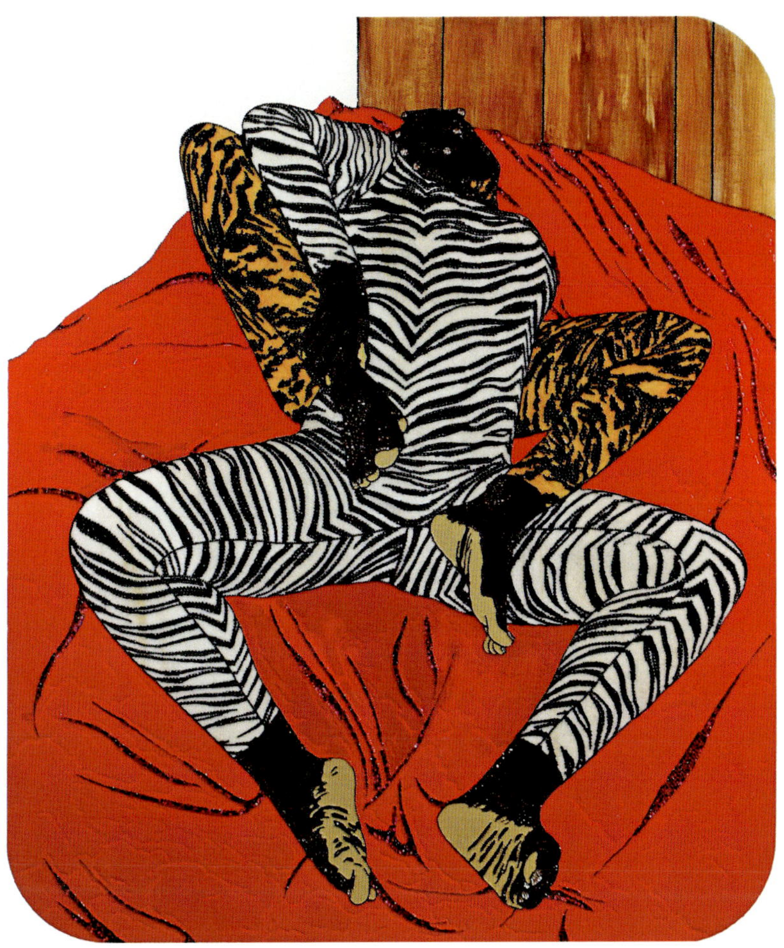

Plate 5 Mickalene Thomas, *I Still Love You* (*You Still Love Me*) (2007). Rhinestones, acrylic, enamel on wood panel, 72 × 60 in. © Mickalene Thomas Studio/Lehman Maupin Gallery, New York

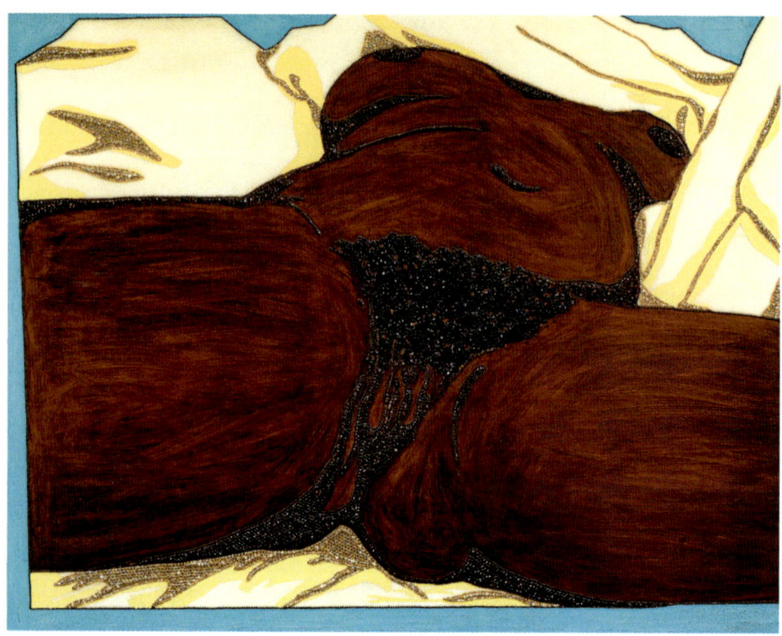

Plate 6 Mickalene Thomas, *Origin of the Universe* (2012). Rhinestones, acrylic, oil, and enamel on wood panel, 48 × 60 in. © Mickalene Thomas Studio/Lehman Maupin Gallery, New York

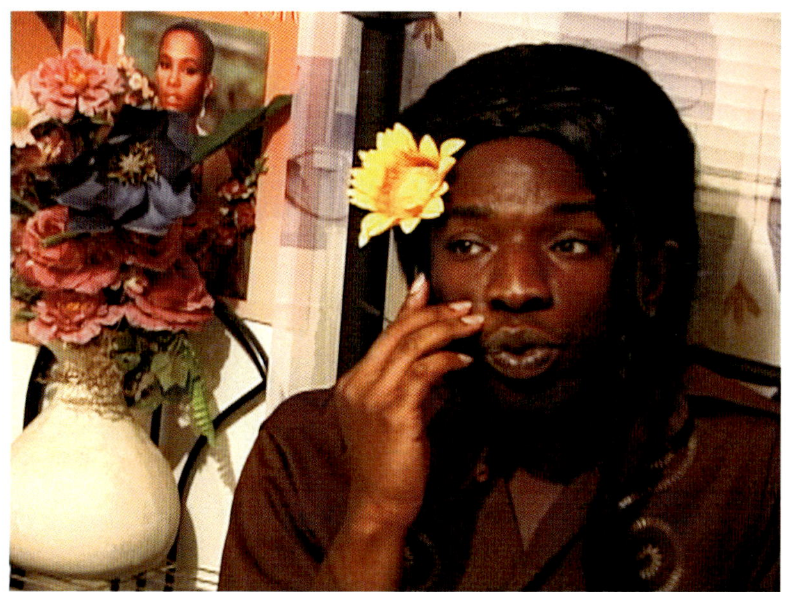

Plate 7 Kalup Linzy, *Conversations Wit De Churen II: All My Churen* (2003). *Radical Presence: Black Performance in Contemporary Art*. Digital video, colour, sound, 29:14 minutes. © Contemporary Arts Museum Houston. Reproduced by permission of Contemporary Arts Museum Houston

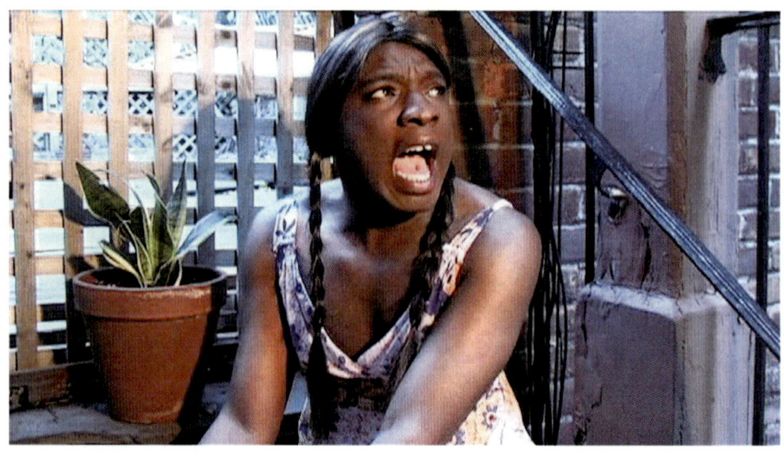

Plate 8 Kalup Linzy, *Melody Set Me Free* (2007). Video, 15:16 min, colour, sound [Production Still #1]. © Kalup Linzy/Electronic Arts Intermix, NY

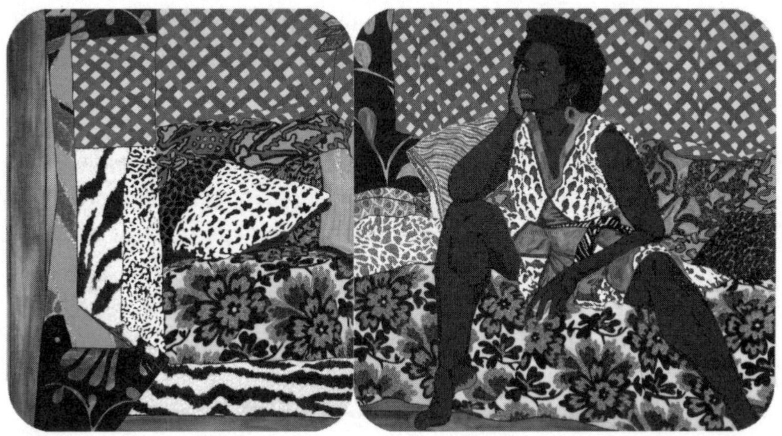

Figure 24 Mickalene Thomas, *Baby I Am Ready Now* (2007). Acrylic, rhinestone and enamel on wooden panel, diptych, 72 × 132 in. overall. Rubell Family Collection. © Mickalene Thomas Studio/Lehman Maupin Gallery, New York

complexly arranged colours and patterns. This multi-coloured element serves as a pleasing contrast to the bright green dress and brown skin of the subject. However, the *mise-en-scène* tends to intentionally engulf and overwhelm the sitter, competing with the figure's phantasmagoric appeal. The lushness of the patterning, the gold and browns, and the vast array of bright colours creates a textural density that oozes decadence and excess – creating a kind of orgiastic formalism that is distinctly about pleasure.

In her writings on the history of African-American photography, specifically the relationship between blackness and beauty, art historian Deborah Willis asks, 'What is beauty? Is it tangible? How is the notion of [black] beauty idealized and exploited in the media?'[17] Stating that she has always 'struggled with the continuing challenges surrounding visual images of black people', Willis suggests that, central to her own work, is an 'ongoing critique on how the display of the black body affects how we see the world and how the world sees us'.[18] The issue of beauty that Willis raises is significant to the historical representation of black people, and Thomas' *Baby I Am Ready Now* presents an intervention into a lineage of black images that were either debased, or wielded for their symbolic ideological meanings. Blackness and beauty, within the realm of representation, have never been truly synonymous and Thomas seems intent to imagine an image of blackness that is overtly communicative of beauty, pleasure and formal/material decadence.

If we think about Thomas' defiant subject in *Baby I Am Ready Now* in terms of art history, there is the obvious reference to Orientalism, which is communicated in the female subject's exotic and opulent staging, her lush and sensuous skin, and beckoning pose – all signifiers for a specific and lengthy pictorial history of exoticizing representations of African and Asian women in Western painting. However, in the presentation of Thomas' resistant subject is a consciousness around a history of black representation in the history of American genre painting – a rather expansive repertoire of images that present African-American identity in a condition of servitude. An exemplar is William Sidney Mount's 1845 painting *Eel Spearing at Setauket*, a beautifully rendered image of a robust and proud looking black woman in a boat in the act of spearing an eel. Sitting in the back of the small fishing vessel is a young Caucasian boy in white shirt, black vest, and a black and red trimmed hat. As the boy mans the oars, the black slave woman is portrayed in the act of labour. Mount presents her heroically at the top of the composition, as a striking and imposing presence that ultimately dominates the scene. It is an image of slavery, although one designed as a defence of a violent institution at a time when the abolition debates were gathering momentum.[19] Mount's soothing image of noble servitude situates its two figures within a stunning pastoral scene: a lush tree-lined prairie rendered in greens, oranges, and beautiful ochre yellows that extends down to the placid and reflective water's edge. Nearby, quaint cottages sit nestled within carefully manicured trees. It is an image of beauty and harmony, of a rustic, yet peaceful existence.

Response to Mount's humanistic images of slaves were often met with condemnation and *Eel Spearing at Setauket* was critiqued for imaging a white male child being apprenticed by a black slave woman: an interaction that, while rooted in historical truth, upset the delicate power dynamics of Long Island plantation life of the period.[20] Art historian Albert Boime has discussed Mount's creative impatience with the institution of slavery, particularly the demand placed upon him to produce images that defend its values. According to Boime, Mount's resistance took the form of humanistic portrayals that countered the crudely rendered caricatures that dominated the period. However,

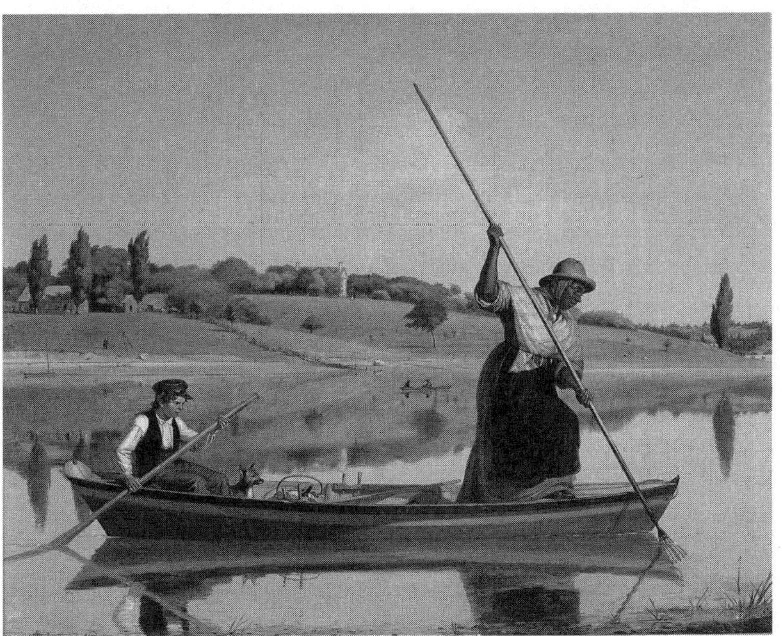

Figure 25 William Sidney Mount, *Eel Spearing at Setauket* (1845). Oil on canvas, 28½ in., Width: 36 in., Framed: H: 33¼ in., W: 40½ in. D: 3 in., Framed: 33⅜ in. H. × 40⅝ in. W. × 2⅞ in. D. © Art Resource Inc. (Artres)

Boime's *Eel Spearing at Setauket* dared to image a black woman in a position of strength and dominance, a depiction that would not have been accepted if the subject were a black man. To make this point, Boime references a selection of celebrated works by Mount and artist Winslow Homer as examples of black male representation where the figure is presented as lazy, docile, or in a state of narrative inaction. In contrast, the slave woman in *Eel Spearing at Setauket*, while presented in a noble fashion, also subscribes to the mammy stereotypes of the period. Her ample frame, long and tattered floor-length dress, black apron, red bandanna, and large-brimmed hat complement her strong, uncovered and muscular forearms. She is an image of asexuality; a woman bearing the signifiers of masculinity denied black men, yet still an image of degradation. Boime suggests that this protective and maternal black female held a symbolic function that alleviated anxieties around sexuality and race. According to Boime:

> The supposed total devotion of the mammy to white children and her benign sexuality pacified guilty fears of miscegenation and of women's emasculating sexual powers. Mount's mammy attains transcendent status as symbol while black women were actually at the very bottom of the social scale . . .
>
> . . . Finally however, *Eel Spearing at Setauket* is about human dominance over natural contingencies . . . the black woman, in her identification with the ebb and flow of nature's cyclical and therefore ultimately changeless time, is portrayed as the key to the white man's survival.[21]

The notion of survival is key to the historical representation of black people, not least because their representation is always a form symbolism meant to convey something about culture, or the complexities of social relations. The very human dimensions of black life, the folly of survivorship, is rarely imaged and in its place, is a facsimile of blackness – a commodified imago designed to assuage the fears and anxieties of a culture in the midst of great social, political, and economic change.

Mickalene Thomas' *Baby I Am Ready Now* employs some the same compositional elements, most notably the prominently displayed black female figure set against a lush background. However, in the younger artist's revisionism, the subject stands alone, impudent and disobedient. Yet she is presented not in servitude, but rather in the posture of leisure. The pleasure and beauty that Deborah Willis speaks of emerges quite prominently in Thomas' painting and conjures an eerie narrative allusion between the decadent optimism of *Baby I Am Ready Now* and Winslow Homer's 1899 painting *Gulf Stream*, an image depicting a tumultuous sea during a storm, as a lone black male figure in a small dilapidated boat attempts to stay afloat while hungry sharks circle around. Homer's image, as Boime attests, glorifies the 'noble savage' while also focusing on the perennial dilemma that blacks face in a racist world.[22] The turbulence of *Gulf Stream*'s allegorical symbolism, in many ways, personifies the historical representation of African-Americans as caught between fetishism, racial stereotype, political symbolism, and the violence of subjugation. *Baby I Am Ready Now* offers a corrective stance against this visual history, one that also images a lone black figure engulfed by a chaotic *mise-en-scène*, yet in Thomas' opus the black female subject is in a state of relaxation and ease, surrounded by the trappings of beauty and opulence. Her

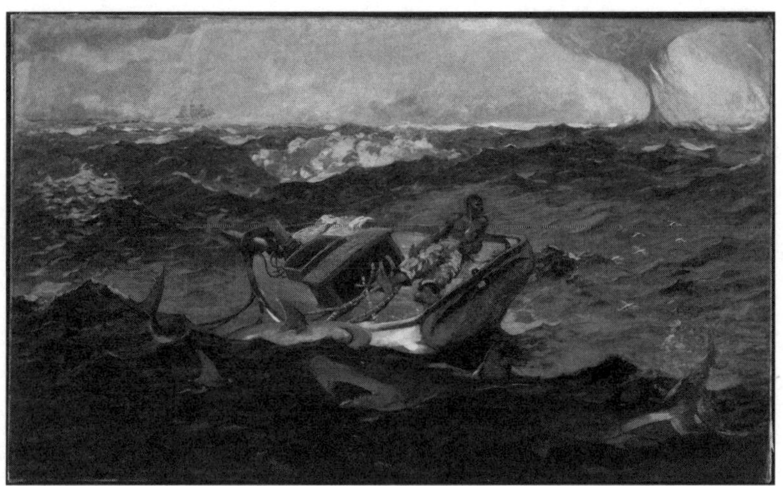

Figure 26 Winslow Homer, *The Gulf Stream* (1899). Oil on canvas, 28 1/8 × 49 1/8 in. (71.4 × 124.8 cm.). © Art Resource Inc. (Artres)

leisure contrasts the stranded sailor, who reclines in seeming calm in the face of an imminent and violent death. Everything about *Baby I Am Ready Now* is seductive, yet the figure is rendered in a manner that is not designed for the male gaze or for the titillation of an assumed masculine viewer. Unlike the tradition of Orientalist representations of women, the figure is fully clothed, her breasts, midsection, and hips are concealed. Only her legs are partially revealed and the assertiveness of her pose coveys a defiant agency that contrasts with the feminine softness of her surroundings.

I argue that, in the painting's seductive beauty, lies a homoerotic attraction that emerges from a queer feminist perspective. It is an adoring image, one that self-consciously conveys beauty and strength, while not negating the erotic potential of the black female body. The figure is feminine, yet denies the clichéd forms of sexually suggestive positioning that all too often accompany painterly depictions of women. The obstinate proudness conveyed in *Baby I Am Ready Now* stands in contrast to the extensive history of courtesans, prostitutes, and female servants – images personified by two iconic works by painter Édouard Manet (1832–1883), *La Négresse (The Negro Woman)* 1862 and *Olympia* from 1863. According to Denise Murrell, Manet rather curiously referred to Laure, the subject in *La Négresse* as 'Laure, une très belle négresse (Laure, a very beautiful black woman)'.[23] A frontal portrait, *La Négresse* is a lovingly rendered image of Laure in a white dress with shoulders exposed and her hair concealed under a red, yellow, and green wrap. Her pleasant expression has a softness that compliments her pearlescent earrings and necklace. In its gestural expressiveness and sensitive attention to the subtleties of colour, the image conveys adoration and just a hint of sexuality, while serving as a contrast to the overtly Orientalizing sexuality of *Olympia* – an oil on canvas painting depicting a nude reclining woman on a decorative bed as a black servant brings her flowers. The fair-skinned prostitute's confrontational gaze was the cause of controversy when the painting was first exhibited at the 1865 Paris Salon, and some art patrons characterized the work as obscene and vulgar, though the presence of the black maid (imaged with a calm equanimity in proximity to the defiant courtesan) has also polarized and perplexed art historians.[24]

The colourful staging and the flatness of the figurative rendering in *Baby I Am Ready Now* recalls several key antecedents, namely Henri Matisse's Fauvist portraits painted in the neo-expressionist style – but perhaps the most striking comparison can be found in the celebrated work of the late African-American artist Romare Bearden (1911–1988). His 1970 collage entitled *Patchwork Quilt* images a nude female figure composed of flat blacks and browns, set against a highly decorative, quilted duvet, with contrasting and brightly coloured patterns in stripes and polka dots. Rendered in cut-and-pasted cloth and paper, Bearden's composition bears a direct similarity to Thomas' chosen aesthetic, though the black female figure in *Baby I Am Ready Now* breaks from the stylistic conventions of the female nude and portrays a more confrontational female presence, while embracing femininity in the stylized and densely patterned backdrop.

The nudes of Romare Bearden, as art historian Judith Wilson attests, are rather remarkable because they represent a shift in African-American artistic production to an engagement with sexuality and erotic subject matter – a phenomenon that only emerged after 1960 in the USA.[25] According to Wilson, 'the black nude only becomes a permissible subject for black artists in the twentieth century' and its absence represents a central problem in the history of African-American art.[26] In her essay 'Getting Down to Get Over', Wilson discusses Bearden's use of pornography in his collage-based work, although by pornography, she means 'the entire spectrum of representations that fetishize the body and objectify desire for public consumption'.[27] In her critical assessment, Bearden was able to transcend a historical taboo within black visual culture: the stigmatization of black sexuality. According to Wilson, '[h]e was able to recuperate the nude black female body, wrestling it from the clutches of white purveyors of erotic fantasies about exotic Others, and reposition it in relation to black vernacular culture'.[28] Wilson is correct that the nude has been an enduring taboo in the history of African-American art, a condition that was motivated by a desire to forgo the fetishization and objectification of black bodies: a remnant of the ravages of slavery. One of few examples of a pre-1960s nude by a black American artist is William H. Johnson's *Nude* (1939). In Johnson's expressionistic naive style of painting, we can see shades of Thomas' formal and conceptual proclivities: reductively rendered figures in simple shades of brown, ornately patterned décor in brightly configured complimentary colours and delicately composed stripes. There is an unabashed quality to Johnson's nude – a boldness in his choice to proclaim the beauty of the black nude, while 'rejecting the inflammatory myths so often attributed to black sexuality'.[29] Wilson, in her revisionist take on the art of Romare Bearden, uncovers something rather important in African-American art that has often gone unnoticed. In her reading of the late artist's evocative iconographic choices, the utilization of pornography is certainly problematic in its voyeurism and romanticizing of sex work – however it also represents resistance to a taboo and a refusal to deny black beauty, sexual desire, and eroticism.[30]

Given this historical taboo, it is all the more remarkable that Mickalene Thomas has chosen to foreground sexual desire in her work, a creative and intellectual gesture that challenges the history of black representation while also intervening into similar resistances within feminist representational politics. Like Bearden, Thomas wields the photographic image for its ideological baggage, making explicit reference to popular sex images that, in their obscenity, communicate the insidiously objectifying logics of America's hetero-patriarchal brand of racism. According to the artist, 'I think the photograph defines my practice. It provides a connection between all the works. There's something about a photograph that I can never get in a painting.'[31] The visual and ideological rhetoric of the photograph is eerily present across

Thomas' expansive body of work, which is evidenced most noticeably in her allusions to the crass eroticism of pornography – even if she ultimately flips its meaning away from the history of fetishism that has defined its social function.

Feminist art historian Amelia Jones suggests that the photographic image, because of its 'collusive role in reinforcing patriarchal structures of gender and sexual identity', has been the 'primary site of feminist intervention in the postmodernist art practices that rely on strategies of appropriation'.[32] It is significant that Thomas mentions the centrality of the photographic image to her painting practice, because since the 1970s, there has been what art historian George Baker has described as the photographic turn in contemporary art:

> Everywhere one looks today in the world of contemporary art, the photographic object seems to be an object in crisis, or at least in severe transformation. Surely it has been a long time now since reformulating the history and theory of photography has seemed a vital intellectual necessity, an art historical project born rather of the new importance of the photograph in the art practice of the 1970s and '80s. As theorized then, postmodernism could almost be described as a photographic event, as a series of artistic practices were reorganized around the parameters of photography.[33]

We have seen the effects of this turn most prominently in the pioneering work of feminist artists – exemplified most strikingly in the early photographic self-portraits of Cindy Sherman. The artist's acclaimed series 'Untitled Film Stills' consists of photographs of Sherman posing in highly constructed settings, meant to function as recreations of cinematic scenes.

According to Laura Mulvey, 'each photograph has its own *mise-en-scène*, evoking a style of filmmaking that is highly connotative but elusive'.[34] Referencing the underground films of 1950s, the New Wave Cinema, Neo-Realism, and the Hollywood productions of Alfred Hitchcock, Sherman's film stills make reference to an extensive history of female representation in both moving and static images that, in their 'claims to truth, have most obediently served consumerist, patriarchal, and heterosexist directives'.[35] Amelia Jones refers here to the feminist critique of pop cultural images of women, representations that – in their demeaning and objectifying logic – coerce women into an enduring struggle to 'conform to a façade of desirability': what amounts to a complex conglomeration of cultural norms that are regressively patriarchal.[36] Jones expresses an awareness around the specific violence caused by hetero-sexist and patriarchal regimes of representation and, perhaps more specifically, the iconography of misogyny. She states: 'Through the photographic image, femininity is constructed as a locus of male desire and pleasure, embedded in the photographed and commodified female body via a system of fetishistic visual codes.'[37] In keeping with the oppositional nature of feminist representational politics, African-American women artists, who came into prominence in the 1980s and '90s, appropriated the photographic image as site of political antagonism – taking on the historical representation of black female subjectivity. Artists Lorna Simpson and Carrie Mae Weems exemplify a post-modern conceptualism that wielded the photographic image as a form of radical opposition, speaking back to its origins in colonizing logics and imperial expansion.[38]

Simpson's iconic portraits of black women, like *Waterbearer* (1986), inaugurated a new visual vocabulary into the extensive history of black representation, but in their feminism, they resist its history of racial and sexual fetishism. In these early portraits, Simpson chose to present the black female body in an act of defiance: back to the viewer, 'rejecting any familiarity' in a manner that 'did not appear to be the customary vessel of beauty and sensuality onto which we could project our fantasies'.[39] The denial of racial and sexual fetishism is seen in *Waterbearer*, a large black and white portrait of a dark skinned woman elegantly posed with her back to the viewer. Her arms extend outwards to each side as she pours water from two pitchers. The black woman, with dishevelled hair and head slightly cocked to the left side, wears a simple white dress that reveals her bare arms, upper back, and neck. Kellie Jones describes the subject's pose as delicate and graceful and the vessels – 'one silver and the other plastic – seem to mark the endpoints of the economic spectrum... Women of all classes, it appears, face regulations and impediments to expression and power.'[40] *Waterbearer* signalled an important shift in African-American art towards a more aggressively resistant form of conceptualism. The notion of power, or more specifically the gesture to claim it in the representational field, began to take precedence over the more passive approach of bemoaning the condition of victimization. We see this strategy at play once again in the work of black female artist Carrie Mae Weems. A recipient of the prestigious MacArthur Foundation

Fellowship, Weems is most known for *Kitchen Table Series* (1990) a powerful collection of photographic works that was inspired by the writings of influential feminist scholar Laura Mulvey.[41] Situating herself at the centre of each composition, Weems directs narrative attention towards the modern black woman, an often-overlooked subject, and in the process meditates on the complexities and perils of African-American women's lives.

As we have seen, the move to recover black female identity has many precedents and marks a decisive evolution in the political strategies of African-American women artists. In many ways, Mickalene Thomas is the beneficiary of a rich legacy of creative practice. Although her work pays tribute to her historical forbears, she also innovates, pushing the visually expressive possibilities of black representation into new and uncharted territory. To a large degree, this quality of newness emanates from a much bolder and more incendiary expression of sexuality: one that takes head-on greater sensitivities around the representation of queer sexualities. Even the oppositional boldness of Simpson and Weems' work still adopts a more conventionally heteronormative exploration of the visual rhetorics of black female subjectivities. Residing in the whimsical historical allusions and the lush *mise-en-scène* of Thomas' playful compositions is a political mischievousness that plays with a very specific expression of desire – one that has never really been represented in the history of art, or in popular representation for that matter. To put the force of Thomas' intervention into context, it is necessary to consider a history of intellectual thought around the taboo issue of black woman's sexuality. According to Evelynn Hammonds, 'black women's sexuality is often described in metaphors of speechlessness ... an empty space that is simultaneously ever-visible (exposed) and invisible'.[42] In response to this history, as Hammonds attests, 'black women have been silent' ... largely because of their lack of access to positions of power.[43]

On Spectral Black Female Sexualities

The condition of black female invisibility, particularly around discussions of sexuality, has it roots in the rise of Black Studies. In previous chapters, I discussed the hetero-patriarchal bias in the black liberation movement, which ultimately impacted the formation of African-American Studies and its related disciplines. Within the scholarship of Black Studies, as Patricia Hill Collins has noted, 'black women's sexuality is either ignored or included primarily in relation to African-American men's issues'.[44] Collins rightly suggests that black women's historical silence around the issue of sexuality has its roots in the notion of solidarity, specifically the need to exhibit allegiances with black men in the fight against racism: a strategy that, in its cooperation with anti-racist struggle, fails to implicate black men's complicity in a lengthy and ongoing battle against misogyny and sexual abuse.[45] The necessity therefore is to forge a discourse in which black women's sexuality can be examined, while acknowledging the limitations of a 'race discourse that has historically privileged the experiences of African-American men'.[46] Collins sees the suppression of black female sexuality as part of a larger system of regulation. This marginalization benefited the dictates of anti-racist agendas, but the consequence was that black women's forms of self-definition were publicly silenced. For Collins, this silencing (disabling black women from speaking about their sexuality) seemed the logical counter to a culture that has routinely and historically accused them of being sexually promiscuous and immoral.[47]

In gauging the force of Thomas' contribution, lies an understanding of the contributions that black lesbians have made to discussions of sexuality and race. Since the 1980s, black lesbian theorists and activists have waged war against homophobia and the consequences it enacts upon the lives of black women. Even within black feminist thought, homosexuality has largely been ignored and there has been no serious or committed analysis of homophobia within African-American communities.[48] Collins has stated that black feminists, as a group primarily consisting of heterosexual African-American women, 'have been strangely silent on the issue of black lesbianism'.[49] The result is that black women's sexuality is caught between a complex historical condition of domination and control: a system of power that marks black women's bodies with demeaning and ultimately confining social meanings. Mickalene Thomas intervenes precisely into the violence of these social meanings. These ideologically and culturally constructed notions result from the pathologizing logics of heterosexuality that characterize queerness as a kind of 'deviant' and abnormal sexuality. We can begin to see the larger impact of Thomas' visual and intellectual choices by acknowledging this troubling historical trend. In many instances, she has chosen to make reference to the cheap artificiality of pornography, even while creating images of black femininity designed to transgress racial and sexual boundaries.

Implicit within mainstream pornography is an implied violence that positions women as sex objects for male desire: a relation indicating that women are inherently available for men's sexual proclivities. However, in a larger sense, the more insidious understanding of female *passivity* lingers – the ideologically accepted and repugnant notion that '*women have things done to them* [my emphasis] . . . a theme repeated over and over in contemporary pornography'.[50] The mythologizing of female passivity in pornography is, in many respects, where the titillation resides: in the visualization and performing of a gendered and sexual domination that women are subject to, but not activated by. As Laura Mulvey has instructed, this representational inequity is the product of a society ordered by sexual imbalance. In her formulation, 'pleasure in looking has been split between active/male and passive/female . . . the determining male gaze projects its fantasy on to the female figure', which is stuck in an objectifying condition that Mulvey rather cynically characterizes as *to-be-looked-at-ness*.[51] Thomas' queer-feminist intervention contests the condition of black female passivity, creating an active/female representational space, even while embracing the voyeuristic pleasures embedded within the *to-be-looked-at-ness* that Mulvey cautiously theorizes against.

Thomas' irreverent active/female, passive/male aesthetic is personified in the painting *Feel Like Makin' Love* (2006); a multimedia work depicting the conjoined bodies of two women engaged in an ambiguous form of play. Both subjects are clad in opposing tiger print jumpsuits: one in brown and white, the other primarily in yellow. The more discernable of the two figures, a brown-skinned woman with a close-cropped Afro, appears to be the aggressor – although the women's laboured contortions simultaneously recall a kind of ritualistic foreplay. Ensnared in a playful grip, the dominant subject looks directly at the viewer, while her partner's head is obscured and curiously hidden from view. The title is an allusion to the 1975 song of the same name by the British pop group Bad Company – however, the track was covered by the African-American R&B/soul singer Millie Jackson, a fiery stage performer whose often raunchy compositions advanced a rather explicit approach to sexuality. Jackson's bawdy and brash feminism, created new possibilities for black female expression,

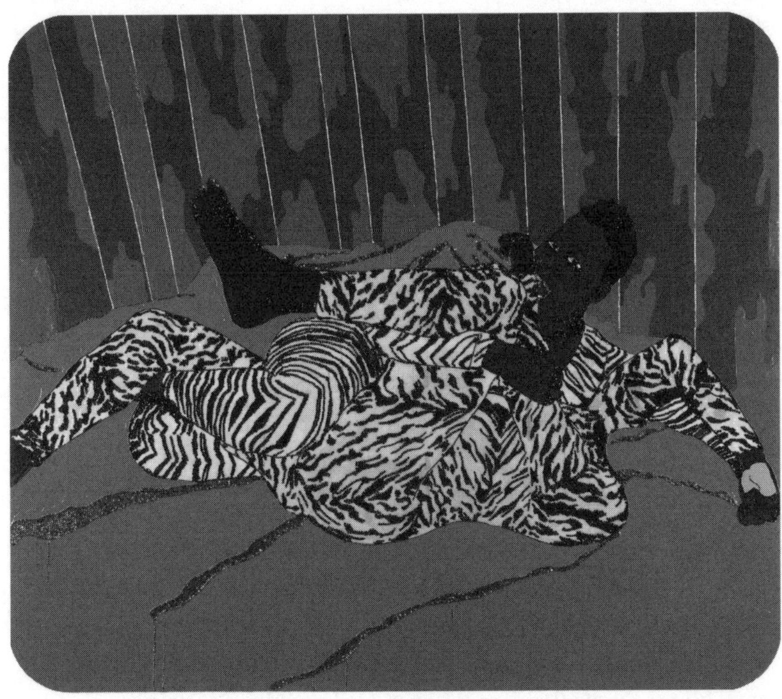

Figure 27 Mickalene Thomas, *Feel Like Makin' Love* (2006). Mickalene Thomas, Feel Like Makin' Love, 2006, Acrylic, rhinestone and enamel on wooden panel, 84 × 96 in. (213.4 × 243.8 cm). © Mickalene Thomas Studio/Lehman Maupin Gallery, New York

influencing future generations of performers in music, comedy, and theatrical performance.

Thomas has referenced Jackson's musical odes to liberated sexuality before, most notably in the work titled *A Little Taste Outside of Love* (2007), a play on the notorious singer's track 'A Little Taste of Outside Love' (1977). *Feel Like Makin' Love* is in many ways a visualization of Jackson's sexual forcefulness, although it presents two black women in a loving tussle of sorts – an erotic dance that unapologetically asserts a queer feminist desiring gaze. In its imaginative and petulant crassness, Thomas plays with the dictates of good taste, situating her entangled figures in a setting reminiscent of a makeshift 1970s porn set. The tacky brown walls and crudely rendered red bedding have a raw frankness that flies in the face of a history of negation and

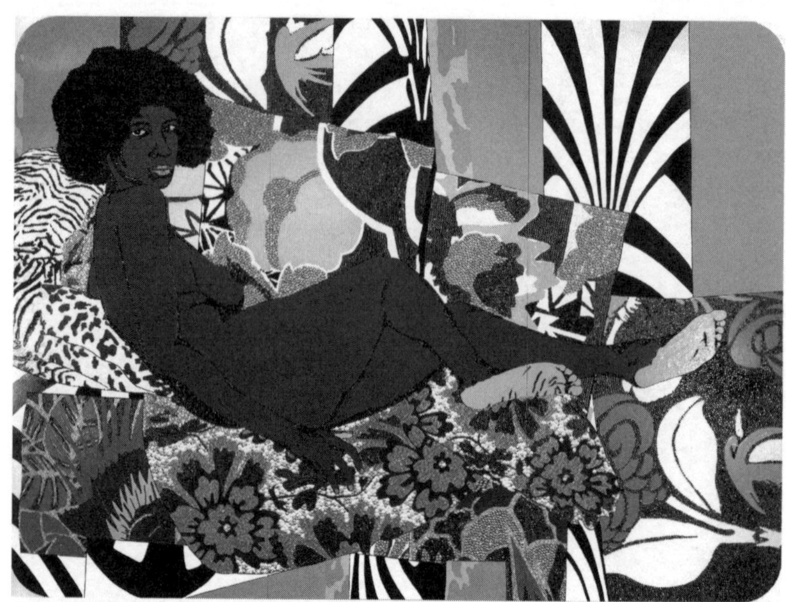

Figure 28 Mickalene Thomas, *A Little Taste Outside of Love* (2007). Acrylic, enamel and rhinestones on wood panel, 108 × 144 in. © Mickalene Thomas Studio/Lehman Maupin Gallery, New York

invisibility. This is repeated in her 2007 painting *I Still Love You, (You Still Love Me)*, a Millie Jackson inspired composition similar to *Feel Like Makin' Love* that images two figures reminiscent of those in the earlier work. Dressed in the same patterned jumpsuits, the contorted bodies are twisted in a manner that gives them a slightly unworldly, or inhuman quality: heads completely obscured from view, hands clasped, and legs that bent in awkward directions. In their distorted knottiness, Thomas' subjects are positioned in a manner that seems to defy what is physically possible. With its figures staged in a rapturous missionary-style embrace, the image (in its quality of ungainly clumsiness) conveys the awkward violence of sexual intimacy – a riposte to the male-constructed sex images that, in their objectifying active male/passive female logics, have often reduced black women to a debased and racially abject spectacle. In the aforementioned works, I want to assert that Thomas has created a new form of visual representation – an oppositional worldview that radically asserts the power of female sexuality, albeit one where the desires of a black queer subject can exist with an uninhibited and unapologetic force.

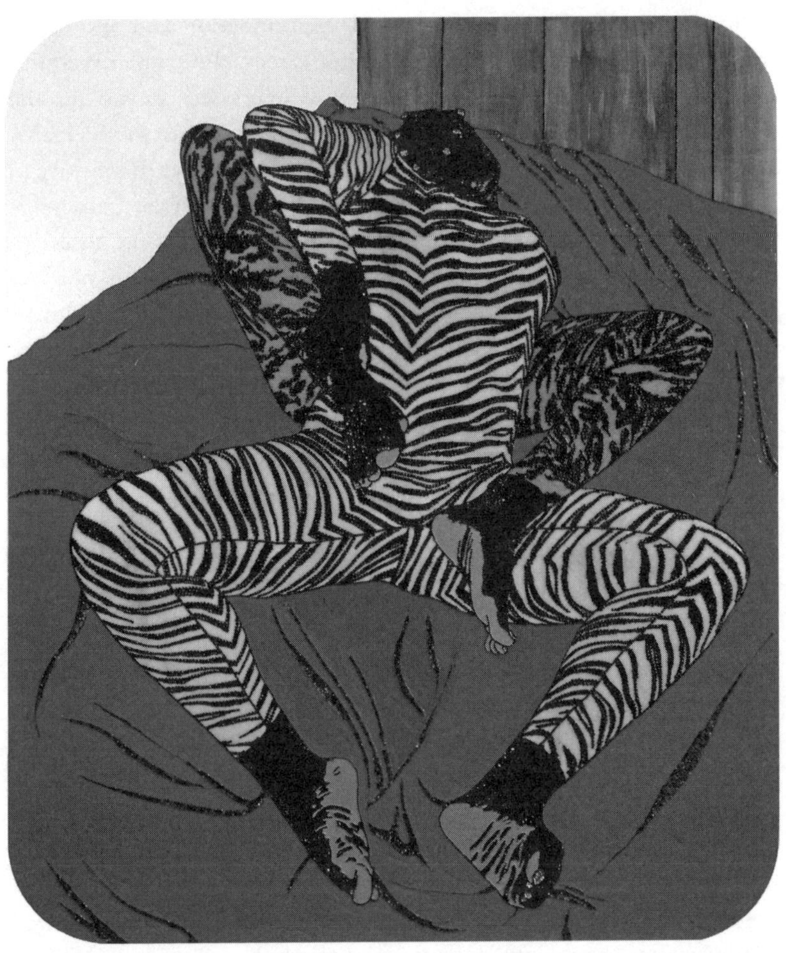

Figure 29 Mickalene Thomas, *I Still Love You (You Still Love Me)* (2007). Rhinestones, acrylic, enamel on wood panel, 72 × 60 in. © Mickalene Thomas Studio/Lehman Maupin Gallery, New York

In her essay on the politics of radical black subjectivity, bell hooks asks, 'how do we create an oppositional worldview, a consciousness, an identity, a standpoint that exists not only as that struggle which also opposes dehumanization but as that movement which enables creative, expansive self-actualization?'[52] For hooks, there is a great necessity in oppositional politics to *become*... to make oneself anew. To make oneself anew is its own rebellion in the larger struggle for freedom and self-actualization – a realization that informs hooks' reformist feminist politics in the face of persistent racial discrimination and sexism. In her recollections on the beginning of her career, the scholar recounts her encounters with white feminists who expressed disdain for the work of black male writers – characterizing them as irredeemably sexist and misogynistic. While hooks acknowledges that the history of black liberation struggle in the USA insisted on regressively patriarchal values, 'equating black liberation with black men gaining access to male privilege', she also admits, rather forcefully, that this need to assert power over black women 'was one of the most significant forces undermining radical struggle'.[53] But despite that historical challenge within the embattled auspices of black liberation, contemporary feminist movements have, as hooks recounts, not meaningfully impacted black political thinking: a problem that has equally undermined the integrity of radical feminist struggle.[54]

In many respects this is due to the sidelining of black women's concerns, even while the movement claims to speak on behalf of all women. An important component of hooks' radical politics is to challenge conventional thinking that pits the political needs of oppressed groups against one another – fostering a spirit of collectivity that re-envisions black subjectivity in a manner that refuses to ignore the centrality of black female identity. I tend to agree with hooks that forms of resistance need not necessitate antagonism towards the political aims of other constituencies and this aversion should not become the justification for an essentialism that passes judgement on the cultural production of those endeavouring to resist the forces of dehumanization. When hooks recounts the condemnation and dismissiveness of some white feminists towards the expressivity of black male thinkers, she equates these experiences with the censure she encountered early in her career – mostly at the hands of other more established black feminists, who were threatened by the younger scholar's radical vision. hooks' rather progressive critique of the mainstream feminist movement's racism and sexism was viewed as too incendiary and too dissident to be acceptable – a sentiment that echoes the judgements she encountered by white feminists who were more than willing to 'pass judgement on black male writers when it is rare to hear such condemnation of white male writers'.[55] She elaborates: 'Within literary studies racism often shapes this response. White women who cannot imagine excluding Chaucer, Shakespeare, or Joyce from their reading list (even though their works reflect sexism and racism) easily use this criterion to defend ignorance of writing by black men.'[56] Even in the face of such sentiments, hooks advocates an intellectual rigour and openness that accepts diverse ideas and perspectives, an ethos based upon reciprocity and mutuality.

Being caught between the ideological limitations and essentialisms of both black and feminist liberation struggles, hooks came to a consciousness around the importance of resisting forms of solidarity that are rooted in an exclusionary logic. Her notion of *becoming* – of making oneself *anew* – finds an increasing resonance in this regard. We might envision this notion in the form representational politics, but it also has meaning in how we intellectually approach our struggles for recognition and equality.

I refer to hooks' writing because it has greatly influenced my critical approach to the study of art and visual culture – a self-conscious revisionism in which I have sought to resist the masculinist exclusionary frameworks that continue to dominate critical and historical analysis of African-American art. To do so has been an enduring challenge, particularly because of the manner in which black liberation struggle has been codified in such patriarchal terms. I am compelled to envision new strategies to discuss black subjectivity that no longer antagonize or negate black women, but also aggressively resist the persistence of sexist norms. Discussing blackness in terms of gender is a tricky endeavour because of a history of animus between the competing aims of a very masculinist struggle for black liberation and a feminist movement often hostile to the radical voices of black men. hooks sums up this friction as an impasse between perceived black male sexism and the rise of dissident black female voices that oppose them. She acknowledges that black men express legitimate concerns around feminists attempts to silence their voices, while also giving credence to black women's resistance to constructions of oppositional politics that equate black resistance only with male uplift.

In the previous chapter I spoke about the rise of Black Studies in the 1960s and 1970s, a period that was defined in extremely patriarchal terms and in a manner that was hostile to black women and especially to feminist thinking. This history of negation greatly informs my thinking about African-American art, in particular the politically expressive work of black women artists. I admit, in a similar ein as hooks articulates, that I too feel somewhat caught between radically opposing forces: on one side an authentic blackness too rooted in black male thought, and on the other side, an art historical canon that has always relegated difference to the margins of its value systems. Even progressive feminist art historical scholarship has not adequately elevated the voices and subjective concerns of black women to such a degree that we see substantive change. In response to that predicament, I have endeavoured to create a new methodology that is post-disciplinary, but one that also strips away the essentialisms and antagonisms between duelling identities that inhibit progressive forms of resistance.

My approach to breaking down the barriers erected by essentialism, as well as a turning away from the perniciousness of restrictive solidarities, has been informed by the writings of Slavoj Žižek. The retreat into the bosom of collectivity and solidarity, which mars so many resistance movements, is in many ways the performative expression of *culture* that merely masquerades as political action. I want to make it clear that a black political struggle that negates black women is as ineffective as a feminist movement that sidelines and subordinates racial difference. These types of resistances merely perform an *aesthetic of oppositionality*, while not taking any substantive action against the forces of oppression – because to do so would necessitate abandoning the exclusionary logic of essentialist thought. Žižek has termed this problematic the 'culturalization of politics': a tendency within liberal multiculturalism towards a political inaction steeped in a sentiment of tolerance that is disingenuous:

> Why are today so many problems perceived as problems of intolerance, not as problems of inequality, exploitation, injustice? Why is the proposed remedy tolerance, not emancipation; political struggle, even armed struggle? The immediate answer is the liberal multiculturalist's basic ideological operation: the 'culturalization of politics' – political differences, differences conditioned by political inequality, economic exploitation, etc., are naturalized/neutralized into 'cultural' differences, different 'ways of life,' which are something given, something that cannot be overcome, but merely 'tolerated.'[57]

Žižek's characterization of liberalism's tendency towards the 'culturalization of politics' (the superficial engagement with what could be characterized as an aesthetics of resistance) suggests that this value system preaches tolerance between cultures, while maintaining the status quo of division.[58]

I find this notion to be extremely meaningful when thinking critically about feminist aesthetics and the history of women artists. In the 1970s, as Laura Mulvey has pointed out, women artists contributed greatly to an emergent discourse in which many cultural producers and scholars argued for a cultural politics of the margins.[59] In the culture wars of the period, and most prominently within the feminist movement, the body emerged as a key site of political struggle. In the women's movement this shift was mobilized around abortion rights and agitation over medical marginalization and sexual regulations as a site of women's oppression.[60] Therefore, 'a politics of the body led logically to a politics of representation of the body'.[61] In her reflections on the feminist movement of the 1970s, Mulvey recalls the shift away from political action, in terms of policy fights – to what she terms a political aesthetic: a notion based upon the idea that 'images contributed to women's alienation from their bodies and from their sexuality'.[62] The focus on cultural production by feminists in the 1970s is widely known and the movement generated some truly remarkable and groundbreaking creative and intellectual forms. Yet as hooks addressed, we must consider the absence of black women within this moment of political action – particularly their efforts to seek recognition within the mainstream feminist movement and to question the presence of racism within it. The struggle for black female recognition was particularly frustrating in the 1970s because, while the Civil Rights and Black Power movements served as exemplars for resistance, black female subjectivity was ultimately negated from their calls to political action – as was also the case with mainstream feminism. Therefore, it may be necessary to interrogate the radical feminism that Mulvey is nostalgic for, if its deconstruction of gender-based ideologies failed to acknowledge black female subjectivity.

In a similar vein, hooks sites noted black feminist scholar Michele Wallace who suggests that within mainstream feminism, African-American culture was seen as the starting point for white self-criticism, but there was ultimately no room for women of colour to assert new and different feminist narratives.[63] Within art historical study there is some focus on the historical representation of black female subjectivity, most notably by feminist art historian Griselda Pollock's investigation of Orientalist aesthetics in the history of Western painting.[64] However, with a few notable exceptions, there was very little work being done by black women scholars that received prominence and widespread critical attention.[65] Interventions by black female scholars and curators in the arena of visual arts such as hooks, Wallace, Debra Willis, Kellie Jones, Cherise Smith, Gwendolyn DuBois Shaw, Sharon E. Patton, Samella Lewis, Valerie Cassel Oliver, Leslie King-Hammond, and Lowery Stokes Sims have been a persistent presence, even despite the continued marginalization of black female contributions.[66]

Transgressive Black Female Sexualities, Progressive Historical Interventions

In certain respects, Thomas wears the dual hat of producer/scholar, formally innovating while advancing a progressive historical consciousness that both educates and challenges. An engagement with the Western tradition emanates from her better-known works that mirror the intellectual commitments of her post-black contemporary, Kehinde Wiley. We see this tendency in two works entitled *Le Déjeuner sur l'Herbe: Les Trois Femmes Noires* (2010). Both pieces (one photographic, the other a mixed media painting) reconceptualize Édouard Manet's *The Luncheon on the Grass* (*Le Déjeuner sur l'Herbe*) from 1863. Manet's scandalous painting, a cheeky nod to bourgeois excesses, is a slightly surreal and Impressionist pastoral image of four picnickers. Imaging two fully clothed men engaged in conversation, while a fully nude woman sits awkwardly among them in the foreground, Manet's opus was initially ridiculed for its narrative whimsy and formal absurdities. Behind the three figures and nestled within the lushness of the bucolic scene, is a fourth figure, a partially clothed woman bathing herself in a shallow stream.

Despite its mixed reception, Manet's controversial painting cemented the artist's reputation as the father of modernism. However, in the 1990s, feminist scholars, most notably art historian Griselda Pollock, advanced a revisionist assessment of the French painter's problematically gendered conceptual intentions. Citing feminist writer Angela Carter's analysis of *Le Déjeuner sur l'Herbe*, Pollock echoes Laura Mulvey's notion of active/male–passive/female, suggesting that in the painting 'man does and is dressed so to do. Woman is; and is therefore, fully dressed in no clothes at all, her skin is common

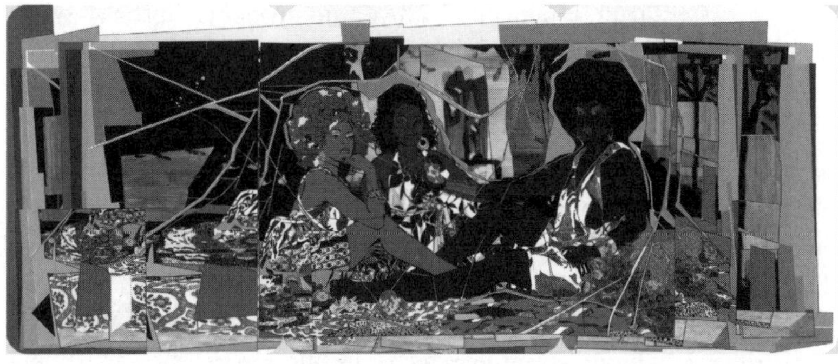

Figure 30 Mickalene Thomas, *Le Déjeuner sur l'Herbe: Les Trois Femmes Noires* (2010) rhinestone, acrylic and enamel on panel 120 × 288 × 2 in. (304.8 × 731.5 × 5.1 cm). © Mickalene Thomas Studio/Lehman Maupin Gallery, New York

property'.[67] Along these lines, Pollock further elaborates: 'We take it for granted that women's breasts must be seen . . . The nude is the commodity which allows its owner – or now, its collective surrogate owners – rights to look and appraise a fictive woman's sexual allure and purposes. The looking is normally done dressed; the looked-at wears only art's nudity.'[68] In Thomas' painterly reimagining of Manet's provocative masterpiece, three beautiful black women occupy the pastoral scene, each staged in poses reminiscent of the original – but in the younger artist's conceptual inversion, the subject's gaze confrontationally at the assumed viewer. Replete in African-inspired floral-print dresses, the women strike regal poses, projecting an air of defiance and forcefulness – rejecting the narratively constructed passivity that dominates Manet's problematic original.

Thomas' *Le Déjeuner sur l'Herbe: Les Trois Femmes Noires* is a formal masterpiece. Mural-sized at roughly 24 feet in length, the work feels like a pastiche of painterly approaches: from the fragmentary aesthetics of Cubism, the self-consciously naive styles of Romare Bearden and Jacob Lawrence, Abstract Expressionism's heroic gestures, to the chaotic neo-expressionism of Jean-Michel Basquiat. It is a style that art historian Richard J. Powell would call a 'pictorial gumbo,' a 'fractured, cubistic approach to art and representation'.[69] The bright colours and layered patterning recall African aesthetics, but the women themselves, are a tribute to the heroines of the Black Power era. The two subjects in the foreground wear voluminous Afros and bright theatrical makeup (one wears brilliant blue eye shadow and magenta lipstick) while the third looks distinctly contemporary with more processed-looking hair. In contrast to Manet's image, Thomas' subjects sit on what appears to be a colourful and ornately African-patterned tapestry, with a mix of flowers strewn about. Rather than a rustic landscape, the three black women occupy a highly fictionalized and artificially lit mise-en-scène. The women are clothed yet, in keeping with many of Thomas' portraits, possess a sensual quality that is more celebratory than beckoning.

In their rebellious countenances is an allusion to the iconic, yet often overlooked women of the Black Power and Blaxploitation eras, such as singer and model Marsha Hunt and most recognizably, actress Pam Grier and American political activist and scholar Angela Davis. Thomas' tribute salutes a period of black female resistance and strength that defined an era – yet ultimately remained in the shadows and played a support role in the African-American liberation movement's reclamation of black masculinity. *Le Déjeuner sur l'Herbe: Les Trois Femmes Noires* repeats a similar gesture made by artist Carrie Mae Weems in her video work entitled *Afro-Chic* (2009). Set to Marvin Gaye's posthumously released 1985 song 'Sanctified Lady', the video is a document of a staged fashion show, with a series of black and white women strutting the catwalk in fake Afros and 70s-inspired fashions. Projecting a fierce and rebellious brand of sexuality – Weems' Afro-Chic superwomen swagger down the runway with unapologetic fervour, while images of Black Panther members and activist/scholar Angela Davis are projected in the background.

We have seen this iconography wielded before, exemplified in the heroically scaled, constructed narrative photographs of artist Renée Cox. In *Cousins at Pussy Pond* (2001), another famous reimagining of Manet's *The Luncheon on the Grass*, Cox images herself nude in a bucolic scene very reminiscent of the French painter's polarizing composition. Situating her unclothed Jamaican-American body in the exact position of Manet's fictionalized female nude, Cox appears to reject feminism's ideological abhorrence to the sexualizing of femininity – presenting herself as a powerfully sexual being: a kind of Afro-futurist warrior princess. Gazing directly into the camera with stern force, the artist is flanked by two muscular black men with spears, who wear orange loincloths. Presented as her protectors, the men are objectified, yet also presented with strength. In Cox's expression, dreadlocked hair, and middle-aged nude body, is a boldness and agency that claims the force of black female sexuality, rather than negating it – while also denying the voyeuristic fantasy of fetishistic womanhood that mars Manet's original. Thomas' version exudes this quality as well, yet similarly to the French painter's petulant and intentionally provocative envisioning of sexuality, the young feminist artist's work also intends to provoke – albeit by advancing a queer feminist eroticism that is ambivalent to the desires of men. In this important gesture, lies the acknowledgement that: 'In the U.S. cultural imaginary it is quite nearly impossible to separate ideas about race from ideas about sexuality.'[70] In this quotation, scholar Aliyyah I. Abdur-Rahman suggests that the representation of so-called deviant sexualities holds the potential to support an 'emancipatory political project' – in this instance, the advancing of a distinctly queer-feminist brand of political resistance.[71]

Thomas is aware of the representational potential of transgressive black sexualities, particularly the stereotypes of pathology that subtend their cultural meanings. In this regard, she makes reference to a history of sex images containing an erotic frankness that flies in the face of mainstream black feminist scholarship that has, in many respects, taken an unwaveringly prohibitive stance against pornographic representations of African-American women. According to Jennifer C. Nash, black feminists are concerned with pornography's effect on African-American women 'precisely because it has been imagined to make explicit the exploitation that representation already inflicts on black women'. She further elaborates: 'If dominant visual culture objectifies black female bodies, racialized pornography is imagined to be particularly demanding in its incessant exposure of black female flesh and its insistence on black female sexual excess and alterity.'[72] Nash is part of an emergent and rather daring generation of feminist scholars of colour advancing what could be termed as a sex-positive engagement with the sexualities of black and brown women. Along with writers Mireille Miller-Young, Jillian Hernandez and Ariane Cruz, Nash recovers these sexual expressions from a type feminism based upon 'woundedness' and 'away from the production and enforcement of a 'protectionist' reading of representation'.[73] Central to this exciting and urgent intellectual movement is an effort to validate black women's sexual agency and to support their claims to desire and erotic pleasure in such a way that does not inherently position them as social victims.

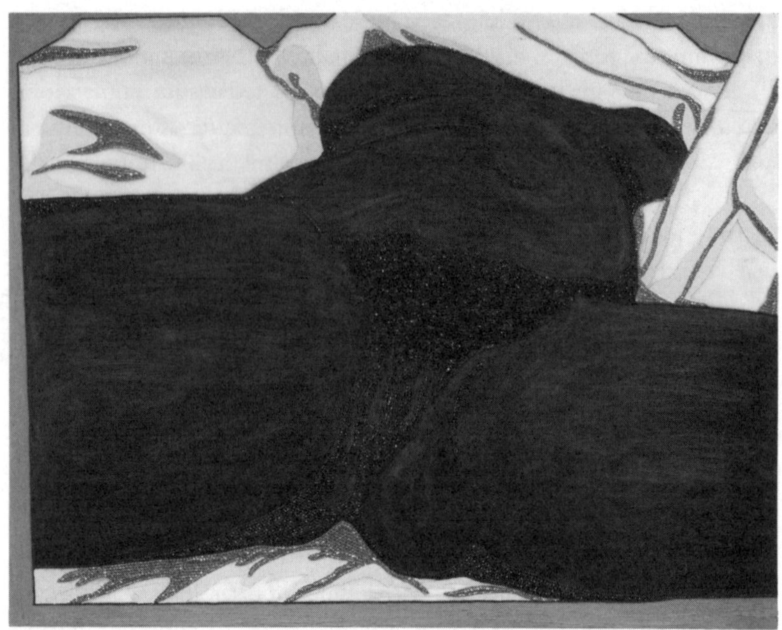

Figure 31 Mickalene Thomas, *Origin of the Universe* (2012). Rhinstones, acrylic, oil, and enamel on wood panel, 48 × 60 in. © Mickalene Thomas Studio/Lehman Maupin Gallery, New York

Nash in particular explores black women's sexuality in terms of varied and multiple pleasures: pleasures in looking, pleasures in being looked at, and pleasures in performing racial fictions.[74] I would say that Mickalene Thomas' art operates on all of these registers, advancing a sex-positive feminism that is unabashed in its erotic forcefulness. It does this in spite of the historic apprehensiveness of black female scholars who are wary of further pathologizing the lives and bodies of African-American women.

I see this sentiment expressed most saliently in Thomas' whimsical 2012 painting *Origin of the Universe*, a satirical send-up of French painter Gustave Courbet's *The Origin of the World* (*L'Origine du monde*) of 1866. Beautifully rendered in oil-on-canvas, Courbet's provocative work is a close-up view of the genitals and torso of a nude woman. Lying on her back, the subject's head and limbs are cropped away and obscured from view, further highlighting the sexually explicit nature of the image. Continually subject to censorship, *L'Origine du monde* has gone on to symbolize Courbet's desire to challenge the repressive sexual norms of

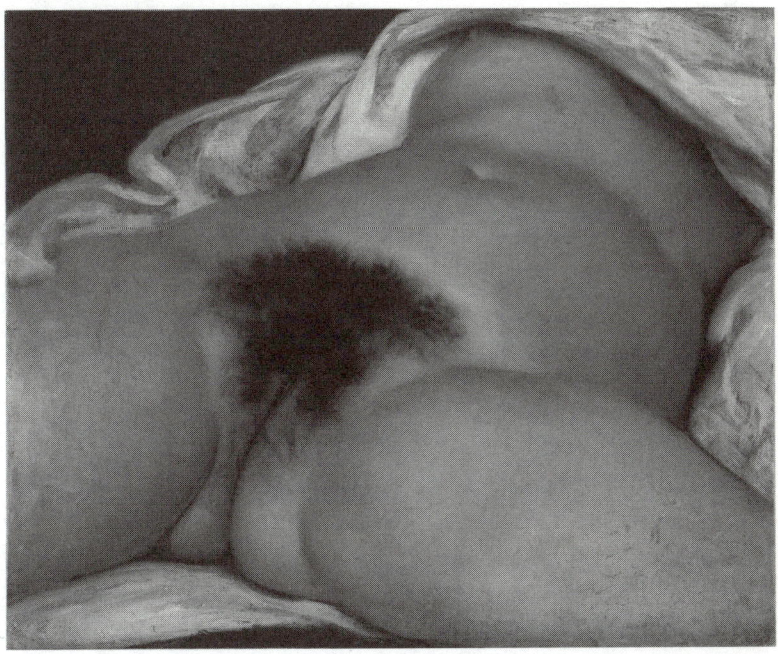

Figure 32 Gustave Courbet's *The Origin of the World* (*L'Origine du monde*) (1866). Oil on canvas, Oil on canvas, H. 46; W. 55 cm. © Art Resource Inc. (Artres)

the period – advancing a realism and graphic eroticism meant to shock and vulgarize artistic convention. Thomas' recreation is eerily similar to the original, albeit in her signature painterly style. There is none of the hyperrealism, nor do we see a romance with the lush affect of oil paint. On the contrary, what we see is a crudely imaged black female figure, painted in thin layers of brown. Her legs are splayed, revealing a facsimile of the artist's own genitalia, rendered in glistening black rhinestones. Like Courbet's original, the figure's torso and breasts are exposed, but the head and limbs are hidden from view.

When asked why she took on one of Courbet's most notorious images, Thomas' retort was: 'I made two: one of my partner and one of myself... Any depiction of woman as "beginning" is philosophical, spiritual, and powerful. With my work, I'm the beginning. So, I'm giving myself completely to the world. I'm relinquishing and revealing my most intimate self. There's no fear!'[75] Emanating from Thomas' striking fearlessness is what Antke Engel calls a '*queer* potentiality':

an insistence that '*queer* is not primarily about sexuality, but is about challenging power relations that that can never be separated out in relation to gender, sexuality, race, ethnicity, or class'.[76] In Thomas' art is a politics of black female pleasure: a bold assertion of self-empowerment that claims access to erotic power through artistic expression. But it is in her resplendent queering of black female desire that Thomas forces us to reassess and reimagine the expressive possibilities of African-American identity.

4

We're All Kalup's Churen

> I always marvel at the ways in which non-white children survive a white supremacist U.S. culture that preys on them. I am equally in awe of the ways in which queer children navigate a homophobic public sphere that would rather they did not exist. The survival of children who are both queerly and racially identified is nothing short of staggering.[1]
>
> – José Esteban Muñoz, *Pop Out*

Neither Revisionist, Nor Recuperative

The art of Kalup Linzy is somewhat of an enigma. In so many ways his creative approach deviates from that of his post-black peers, yet in other respects he is the most fitting exemplar of the movement's political and representational strategies. It is for this reason that I have chosen to close this volume with his creative output. If we think about post-blackness as a gesture towards a type of futurity, the oddness of Linzy's genre-defying performances and videos personifies the effort to stretch the limits of blackness as a visually expressive form.

Unlike the other talented artists discussed in this book, Linzy's production is less overtly entangled with history. For that reason, his work possesses a boldness that transcends the baggage of the past and gestures towards something that is perhaps more incendiary in its post-blackness. His approach is neither revisionist, nor recuperative, even as it manages to provoke our consciousness around the invisibility and marginality of black queer subjects. Linzy was born in Claremont, Florida in 1977 and was raised in a working class family in Stuckey,

Florida – a small rural community. After having been awarded a residency at the prestigious Skowhegan School of Painting and Sculpture in Maine, he went on to complete an MFA degree at the University of South Florida in 2003. In the same year, the artist relocated to New York to pursue a career. And it was in 2005, in the midst of two pivotal exhibitions, that Linzy's career began its rather unlikely upsurge. Having encountered the Southern artist's production in the Studio Museum in Harlem's group show *African Queen*, New York Times critic Holland Cotter enthusiastically proclaimed that: 'A star is born.'[2] At the same time as the Studio Museum show, Linzy had his first solo exhibition at New York's Taxter and Spengemann gallery. And in the same year, he was selected to participate in the well-received exhibition *Frequency* at the Studio Museum in Harlem (curated by Thelma Golden and Christine Kim). In the wake of his debut, Linzy has won a series of highly coveted awards, namely the Louis Comfort Tiffany Foundation, the John Simon Guggenheim Memorial Foundation fellowship, Creative Capital Foundation grant, a Jerome Foundation Fellowship, and an Art Matters Grant.

The work that garnered Cotter's attention was *All My Churen* (2003), a video that exemplifies the uncanny aesthetic that made Linzy an instant art world darling. The title is a satirical play on the enduring and much-beloved soap opera *All My Children*. The video tells the embattled tale of the Braswells, a familial clan embroiled in life's everyday dramas and tragedies. Despite the cheapness of its production, the video feels like an authentic soap opera, in that it contains the stilted and artificial dialogue, the hollowed-out emotions, and the reductive mise-en-scène that defines the genre. There is always something slightly embarrassing about the soap opera form: an awkwardness in its low culture pandering that would appear to grate against the intellectually elitist pretension of the visual arts. *Churen* is so overtly farcical and outrageous that it is initially quite jarring to view, even if its self-conscious hilarity conceals a more politically urgent agenda.

The video's narrative revolves around the trials and tribulations of Nucuavia, a young woman dealing with the drive-by shooting death of her lover JoJo. Consisting of a series of phone conversations, *Churen* is full of melodrama and intrigue, as it follows Nucuavia's attempts to share her tragic news with her colourful family. In the process, we meet a cast of characters whose working-class banality belies the phony

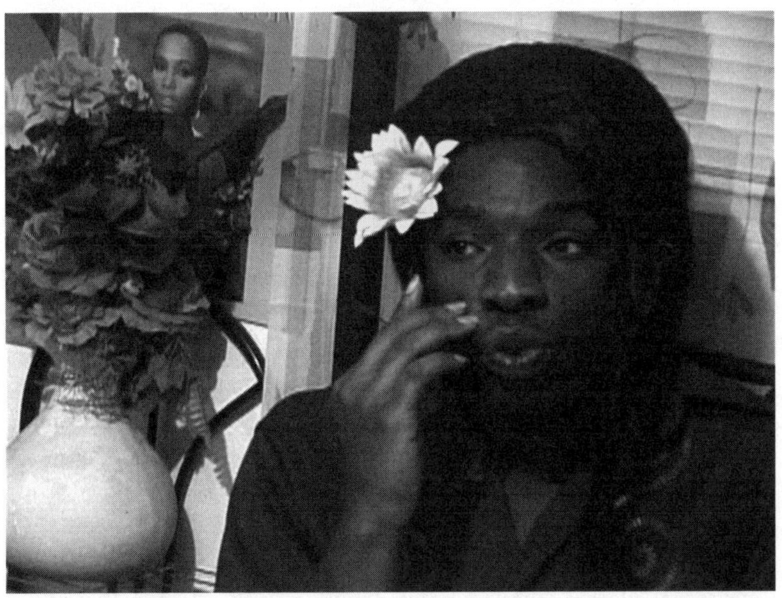

Figure 33 Kalup Linzy, *Conversations Wit De Churen II: All My Churen* (2003). *Radical Presence: Black Performance in Contemporary Art*. Digital video, colour, sound, 29:14 minutes. © Contemporary Arts Museum Houston. Reproduced by permission of Contemporary Arts Museum Houston

glamour most readily associated with the soap opera genre. In her attempts to arrange a memorial service, Nucuavia struggles to garner the sympathies of her mother, sister, and good-for-nothing brother, Taiwan. It is a simple narrative, but one that bristles with humour, most notably because Linzy convincingly plays all of the characters. The artist dubs digitally-altered voices over the various characters to create a makeshift aesthetic that effectively blurs the lines between race, gender, and sexuality. An adept and skillful performer, Linzy's gestures and gesticulations submerge the artist's masculine features into a series of personas that very quickly become convincing. At first glance, the effect appears like a sight gag because of the artist's crude, intentionally facile attempts at drag. Dressed in shoddy costumes like fake wigs and cheap dresses, Linzy seems to perform the roles effortlessly. Several times throughout the video, Nucuavia either directly addresses, or is asked about the state of her *churen* – in this instance, a Southern twang reference for children, a word that is repeated with creative dexterity in subsequent video projects.

We see it used again, albeit in a petulantly sexual way, in the artist's subsequent episodic work *Conversations Wit De Churen IV: Play Wit De Churen* (2005), a video focusing on the plight of Katonya, an employee at KK Queens Survey (a powerful art survey company), as she struggles to balance the pressures of work with an increasingly complex romantic life. At one point in the video Katonya – confiding to a friend on the phone – brags about the sexual merits of her new lover, proclaiming: *'Guuurl, he tongue-kissed me, I am on cloud nine . . . he really took the time and played with the churen!' Play Wit De Churen* is an evolution of sorts, because Linzy works with a diverse cast of white and black actors, dubbing male voices on female actors and vice versa. However, in its gender-bending playfulness, the artist chooses to digitally graft black-sounding voices over the bodies of white characters. The use of black vernacular speech, with a specifically Southern-style intonation, further blurs the lines between prescribed identities. For example, in one instance, the female mixed-media artist Mickalene Thomas (see Chapter 3) plays Katonya's butch lover, a burly black man with a comically deep and masculine voice. In an extended bedroom scene, we see the couple in the throes of wild sex, as our protagonist (replete with a blonde wig) gyrates in ecstasy while her lover irreverently slaps her behind. Adding to the sex scene's comedic absurdity is the overlaid musical track 'What Is Love' (1993) by the American pop group En Vogue.

The silliness of Linzy's videos gives them a populist accessibility that fits quite neatly into the world of social media and reality television; phenomena that, in their democratizing potential, have allowed greater access to the realm of representation. In many ways, this echoes Andy Warhol's famous and prophetic line, 'In the future everybody will be world famous for fifteen minutes.'[3] Linzy's lowbrow aesthetics were literally made for the internet where they can be easily distributed and shared – a stark contrast to the elitist dictates of the Western art market, where high-priced objects are traded, yet are largely inaccessible to the masses. Even by the standards of today's technology, Linzy's videos are shoddily made, betraying an anti-elitist intent that embraces a mass media form that is ubiquitous. The anti-aesthetic dimension of his work is, in many ways, where the humour resides: the excessive cheapness of the settings, the bad wigs, the chest and facial hair on male characters who are in drag, and of course, the bizarreness of the dubbed voices. The sheer comic absurdity lies in the satirical sending-up of everything

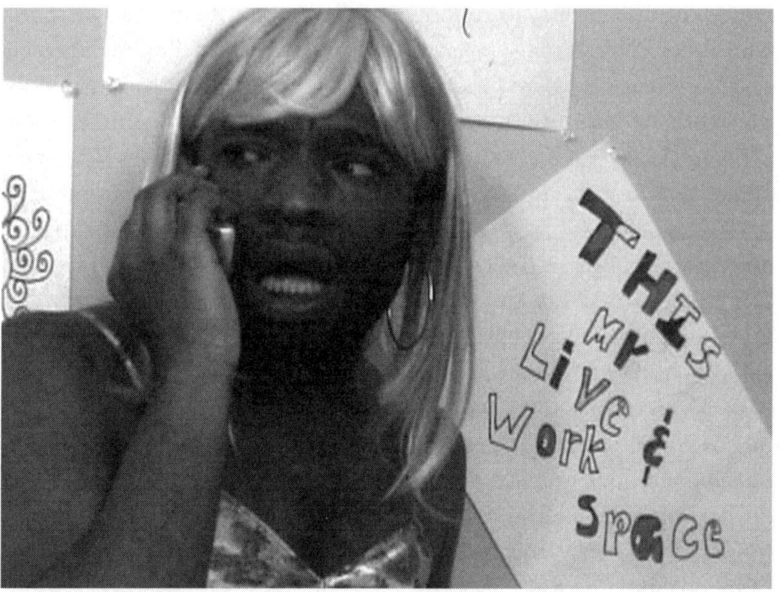

Figure 34 Kalup Linzy, *Conversations Wit De Churen IV: Play Wit De Churen* (2005) video, 15:49 min, colour, sound. © Kalup Linzy/Electronic Arts Intermix, NY

that is legible about identity – particularly the representational codes and visual markers of a repressive hetero-patriarchal society. In this regard, Linzy's art possesses a slippery quality that is only deceptively simplistic, but contains headier and more politically urgent meanings.

At the end of his review of the artist's Studio Museum debut, Holland Cotter stated the following regarding the political dimension of Linzy's work: 'I don't mean to spoil the fun by adding that he laces his work with shrewd home truths about race, class, sex, love, family, and stereotyping. He does, but you can ignore all that if you want.'[4] In a sense, Cotter is correct, and the critic pinpoints a quality in the artist's conceptual approach that relieves its viewers from necessarily engaging with the work's political dimension. Indeed, Linzy's humour and wit so palpably resonates on the surfaces of his videos and performances that one can easily look past its engagements with difficult subjects like racial marginalization and queer shame. In other ways, Cotter's review alludes to something that is perhaps more troubling, which is the rather dismissive way African-American art is treated in the art world. As minorities, black artists are told to get over their childish interests in racial sermonizing and to get down to the business of making good art. The political concerns of race and sexuality have always been dismissed as degenerative traits and therefore used as justification to brush aside the work of minority artists – characterizing it as deficient and less evolved. Linzy's success derives in part from his facility as an entertainer: he can make us laugh, but does he necessarily make us think?

This problematic way of interpreting African-American art surfaced quite prominently in the critical response to the 2011 exhibition *Now Dig This! Art and Black Los Angeles 1960–1980*. Organized by Columbia University Professor Kellie Jones, *Now Dig This!* debuted at Los Angeles' Hammer Museum before travelling to MoMA PS1 in Queens, NY. The exhibition focused on the history of African-American art in Los Angeles during a period of great political change. Responding to the conditions of racial segregation and violence, many black artists during this period chose a path of solidarity and collective resistance, forging a politically engaged aesthetic designed to resist the structures of inequality. The forging of this aesthetic has always been polarizing, not least because it necessitated the formation and policing of standards that placed limits on creativity. Forms of African-American art that resisted engagement with the black liberation struggle, or gestured defiantly towards expressive freedom, were marginalized, silenced, or ignored. Along those lines, as has been discussed in earlier chapters, the politically urgent concerns of women and queer communities were dismissed as oppositional and superfluous to the urgency of black male resistance. Both during and in response to the Black Art Movement's efforts to forge a unique and authentic expression, many artists and intellectuals have endeavoured to debunk the notion that there *is* a black aesthetic that is distinct from other creative expressions. In the 1973 essay 'Is There a Black Aesthetics?' Allan Shields suggests that an authentic and autonomous black aesthetic is largely mythical:

> A minor aspect of a major upheaval has been the suggested possibility of a distinguishable concept called 'black' aesthetics. At first flush it appears obvious that there are defensible senses in which a black aesthetics can be distinguished from other, general aesthetic theory. Is there not African art? Has not jazz itself come from the Negro culture of Africa? Can anyone seriously doubt the superior perspective of the black writer on his own social condition? Has not the blues singer developed from the Negro culture and have not some kinds of adolescent romance music been transformed

from the emotions of the Negro culture? Whoever has been moved by a black chorus and soloists singing spirituals knows the power of these subtle, strong voices fervently pleading their lot with deity. Their peculiar styles of singing, shouting, and speaking these songs give impressive testimony to the thesis of a distinctive, black feeling-tone range. The *prima facie* evidence is unmistakable: 'black' feeling and emotion, distinctive and recognizable in its palpable presence, has infused white culture and there is a black aesthetics of it.

> ... There is a limited sense in which black aesthetics can be meaningfully used as a concept, this sense is trivial and inconsequential and that there is no serious, supportable meaning of a theory of black aesthetics as distinguished from general aesthetic theory.[5]

In this now dated quotation, Shields echoes a viewpoint that has gone on to personify the Black Arts Movement's particular brand of racial essentialism. bell hooks echoes this sentiment in her writing about the pressures exerted by a movement that required painters, writers, and musicians to imaginatively evoke black nationhood and to re-create bonds with a mythical African past.[6] hooks elaborates: 'During this time, the Black Arts Movement was declared to be the "cultural arm of the black revolution." Art was to serve black people in the struggle for liberation. It was to call for and inspire resistance.'[7]

In the decades after the Black Arts Movement, intellectuals and cultural commentators advocated for leaving racial essentialism behind. Race should instead be viewed as a social and cultural construction – a byproduct of a particularly racial form of power and subordination.[8] English scholar and cultural theorist Paul Gilroy is widely known for his criticism of racial essentialism, particularly his impatience for what he has termed the 'essential black subject'. For Gilroy the tyranny of this concept has been an enduring, limiting constraint placed upon black people: 'The idea of blacks as a "national" or proto-national group with its own hermetically enclosed culture plays a key role in this mystification and, though seldom overtly named, the misplaced idea of a "national interest" gets invoked here as a means to silence dissent and censor political debate'.[9] Considering this legacy of critical thought, there is reason for understanding why there would be a less than enthusiastic response to black art forms advancing politically oppositional agendas. When *Now Dig This!* premiered at the MoMA, *New York Times* art critic Ken Johnson wrote a review that became somewhat of a *cause célèbre* in the art world – inspiring some of the most notable figures in the arts to publicly condemn the critic's (and by extension, *The New York Times*') unfortunate position on African-American art.

In his review, Johnson suggested that it was the politically aggressive nature of black art (as exemplified in the work on display in *Now Dig This!*) that explains why so few black artists have been embraced by the predominantly white high-end art world.[10] Johnson embraces an increasingly common viewpoint in the visual arts: a position that uncritically places creative inventiveness squarely on the shoulders of white male artists, while dismissively characterizing black art as a formally derivative, yet regressively political artistic genre. In his assessment of African-American assemblage artists, Johnson said the following:

> Herein lies the paradox. Black artists did not invent assemblage. In its modern form it was developed by white artists like Picasso, Kurt Schwitters, Marcel Duchamp, David Smith, and Robert Rauschenberg. For these artists assemblage was an expression of freedom from conservative aesthetics and parochial social mores. It did not come out of anything like the centuries-long black American experience of being viewed and treated as essentially inferior to white people. It was the art of people who already were about as free as anyone could be.[11]

The response to Johnson's review was swift and vehement, inspiring a group of artists and art world leaders to create a petition protesting against the influential newspaper and its writer. The ensuing debate argued the merits of Johnson's review, contemplating what appears to be its racial partiality, while focusing greater attention on the simplistic falsity of its assessments. Most commentators were less interested in gauging whether or not Johnson was intolerant (in fact, most believe he is not), but they were infuriated by the critic's ignorance about art history that took the form of uncritically expressed racial biases. Indeed it was problematic for a great many people in the art world that Johnson's views seemed so glaringly beneath the standards of veracity, rigour, and intellectual excellence expected of *The New York Times*.

According to writer Kyle Chayka, 'the embarrassing *Times* article creates a false distinction between artists working in an open playing field, freely interacting, adopting, and appropriating from each other. It ignores the difficulties black artists have faced and fails to adequately consider the inherent politics of art viewing.'[12] In her reportage on a Brooklyn Museum dialogue in response to the Ken Johnson debacle, writer Arianne Wack summarized the responses of panelists, Rich Blint, William Villalongo, Ademola Olugebefola, Mira Schor, and art historian Camara Holloway. In the spirited dialogue, Villalongo suggested that the problem resides in the notion of black art's marketability: 'the notion that a minority artist is commodifiable'. Blint elaborates, 'It's a disquieting idea; how do we reconcile ideas of "post-blackness," or the "disavowal of racial matter," with a market that capitalizes on the duality of art and activism, like critics filling a quota or affirmative action in art collecting?'[13]

At the close of Johnson's review, the critic makes a distinction between African-American art rooted in the struggle for black empowerment – which he derisively believes indulges 'social realist clichés, like the defiant fist' – 'and others for whom the black experience remains more a matter of conjecture'.[14] In the latter category, Johnson mentions African-American artists such as David Hammons, Robert Colescott, Jean-Michel Basquiat, Adrian Piper, Fred Wilson, Glenn Ligon, Kara Walker, and Jayson Musson, a.k.a. Hennessy Youngman – creative producers he characterizes as 'Duchampian tricksers' (in reference to the late French conceptual artist). Citing Hammons as the most successful exemplar of a black artist who transcends the politics of solidarity, Johnson suggests that the celebrated African-American conceptualist 'toys in surprising ways with signifiers of black culture, poetically unsettling entrenched representations of blackness on both sides of the racial divide'.[15] And working in this mode, Johnson believes there is a more elevated group of black artists who complicate how we think about prejudice and racial stereotyping.[16] Nevertheless, he rather forcefully asserts that the art of black solidarity gets less traction, because – as he proclaims – the post-modern art world is put off by overt assertions of *any* type of solidarity.[17] Of course, as Johnson admits in the closing of his review, the covert solidarity of liberal white folks is an enduring problem – though, rather predictably, he fails to implicate his own biases and complicity within that important admission.[18]

Interestingly, Johnson mentions Jayson Musson, a.k.a. Hennessy Youngman, a relatively young and emerging African-American artist, as an example of a cultural producer whose creative output transcends the politics of black solidarity. In 2010, Musson created the character

Hennessy Youngman, a persona that rapidly gained an online cult following. Through a series of comical videos posted on the social media site YouTube entitled ART THOUGHTZ, Musson's Hennessy Youngman alter ego comments on various aspects of the art world, with video titles like: *Grad School*, *The Studio Visit*, *Relational Aesthetics*, *Louise Bourgeois*, *Institutional Critique*, *On Beauty*, *Post-Structuralism*, and *How To Be A Successful Black Artist*. In the satirical shorts, Youngman speaks with an exaggerated hip-hop vernacular and dresses comically as a kind of street thug, with an elevated art world sensibility. In many respects, the videos function as a sight gag based upon the unlikely pairing of (what appears to be) an uneducated black man, who speaks intelligently and insightfully about the theoretical obsessions and value systems of the arts. Soon after debuting on the internet, ART THOUGHTZ became an online sensation – and as a result, Musson quickly found his way to art world superstardom. There are interesting parallels between Musson and Linzy: both have created personas who engage in elaborately staged performances and both have successfully tapped into the power of the internet as a means to distribute their work. However, in the case of each artist, the issue of satire emerges quite prominently in their critical approach.

Musson, Linzy and Post-Black Satire

I have written before about African-American satire as a polemical tool employed by certain black artists and intellectuals. However, there is a distinction to be made between satire and humour: a delineation that demarks different approaches to critiquing culture.[19] Scholar Darryl Dickson-Carr has written the most comprehensive volume dedicated to unravelling the genre. Entitled *African-American Satire* (2001), Dickson-Carr explored the use of satire in the history of black literature – a device that (in its wielding of racial caricatures) has often been misinterpreted as an embrace of harmful stereotypes. Satire's purpose, as Dickson-Carr suggests, is to push beyond mere entertainment: Its primary purpose is to act as an invaluable mode of social and political critique. Yet some critics may deem this same mode a threat when the 'wrong' parties are satirized, which happens fairly often. Without a doubt, satire tends to be 'politically incorrect.' . . . It is iconoclastic and frequently offensive on personal and political levels.[20]

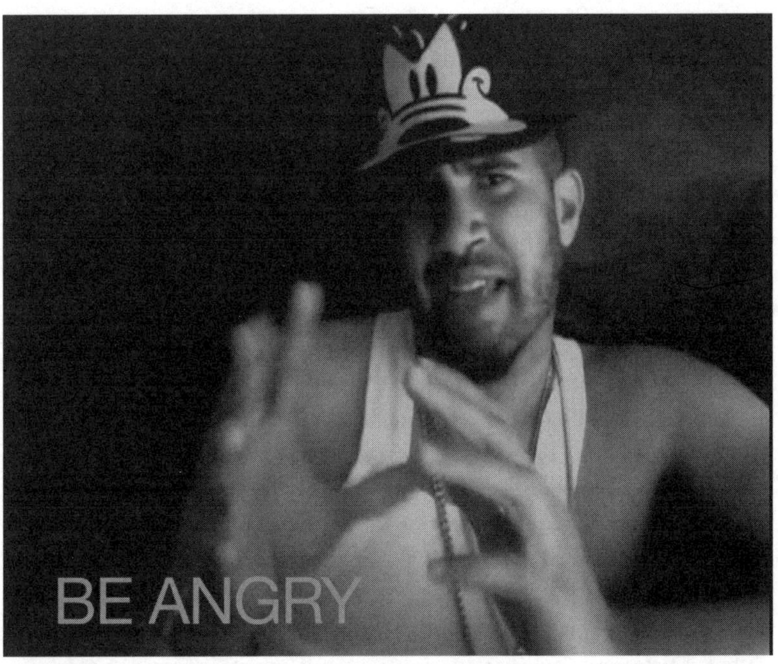

Figure 35 Jayson Musson, *Art Thoughtz* (Promotional image). © Salon 94 Gallery, NY

In his analysis, Dickson-Carr points out that the Black Arts Movement and its constructed black aesthetic were designed to create and promote racially uplifting representations of African-American life. There was a deep belief during the 1960s and 1970s that, through these images, the black community would be 'interpellated' and ultimately moved to political consciousness.[21] As Dickson-Carr points out, the movement's calls to cultural essentialism, promoted by some segments of the black arts and black aesthetic movements, were so dogmatic and dictatorial that they have become passé in the post-Civil Rights era. Differences among African-Americans, particularly along the lines of class, gender, and sexual orientation were unable to be ignored, 'nor can one set of experiences common to many African-Americans be accurately attributed to all'.[22] The scholar reminds us that the original intent of African-American literary satire was to lampoon the mechanisms of slavery and racism and to expose the sheer absurdity of these institutions. However, black forms of satire emerged over time that turned its critical lens upon the foibles and peccadilloes of African-American life, as well as on the hatreds and abuses of white America. For this reason, satire has not proven to be a popular genre among African-Americans.

Needless to say, blacks in the USA have always been subject to demeaning representations of themselves, caricatures and stereotypes that have relegated them to subhuman status. There are numerous examples of this throughout the nineteenth and twentieth centuries, though in the context of satirical representation, we might consider the famous prints of Currier & Ives, the New York-based firm that is considered by many to be one the best known and successful businesses of its kind in the USA. Founded by Nathaniel Currier (1813–1888) and James Merritt (1824–1895), the firm, that called itself 'Printmakers to the American People', is widely known for its print images of American life; historical events, portraits, pastoral scenes, Civil War battles, and patriotic events. Among the firm's idyllic and peaceful visual of American rural life, were images that advanced their bigoted worldview. In the 1880s and 1890s, Currier & Ives created a series called *Darktown Comics* that consisted of racist images of African-Americans that presented them satirically as 'buffoons and fools'.[23] One of the more notoriously offensive series is *The Darktown Fire Brigade – Saved!* (1884): a collection of images depicting the folly of buffoonish rural blacks as they unsuccessfully attempt to put out a fire. Imaged as inept and happy-go-lucky coons, Currier & Ives's 'darkies' represent the bitterness and fears of Northerners suspicious of life in the aftermath of abolition. The images of *Darktown Comics* exemplified the types of representation that proliferated at the time: images that satirically sent-up blacks who were now free and in the position of self-governance – such images depicted blacks as attempting to mimic the assumed competence of whites, but failing miserably in the process.

In response to this legacy, Dickson-Carr points out that during slavery, as well as in its aftermath, African-Americans were forced to create various complexly coded languages and expressions that enabled them to communicate covertly – but also allowed for the indirect expression of their frustrations.[24] He further explains that 'bitingly satiric humour was as much a part of these codes as any other rhetorical element, written into language of indirection that often satisfied those who held power even as it stymied them'.[25] Dickson-Carr saliently notes that the iconoclasm of African-American satire skewers the systematically oppressive mechanisms that have produced black victimization. However, satire also simultaneously ridicules the historical and present day injuries that African-Americans have inflicted upon themselves.[26] While Dickson-Carr's investigation focuses on satire in the literary works of writers Rudolph Fisher, Ishmael Reed, Ralph Ellison, Langston Hughes, John Oliver Killens, Cecil Brown, and George S. Schuyler, among others, the scholar's explication of the genre's sensibilities can be illuminating when considering the work of contemporary visual artists. The conceptual and aesthetic dictates of post-black have long been misunderstood and fall within existing debates around what might be described as the *proper* role of African-American cultural production, in response to the enduring presence of racial inequity.

Perhaps Musson, and Linzy, as post-black satirists, represent Ken Johnson's archetype of the 'Duchampian trickster' (to borrow the language of the *New York Times* critic) who parodies African-American culture for the amusement of the white cultural elite. Their ability and willingness to make the dominant culture laugh and to be safely amused by the folly of black folks is the crux of their success. Perceived as disarmed of their black rage, these artists tend to be viewed as more evolved: less threatening and above the oppositional politics of black solidarity. However, in Musson's case, the artist's gallery shows tend to be more conservative, tame, and muted when compared with the output of his irreverent alter ego Hennessy Youngman. In his first major exhibition *Halcyon Days* (2012), held at New York's Salon 94 Gallery, the artist presented a series of abstract paintings made from Coogi sweaters, the expensive and brightly coloured garments made famous by comedian Bill Cosby and rapper The Notorious B.I.G. The irony and cleverness of Musson's exhibition resided in his unwillingness to coon-it-up, so to speak, and in his resistance to creating racially inflammatory and stereotypical works in the guise of his alter ego. In contrast, he presented a cohesive series of traditional-looking paintings that only vaguely allude to what are rather esoteric signifiers of aspirational blackness. To a greater degree, Musson's Coogi paintings satirized both a history of modernist abstraction (a beloved and exclusive genre dominated by the mythically heroic gestures of

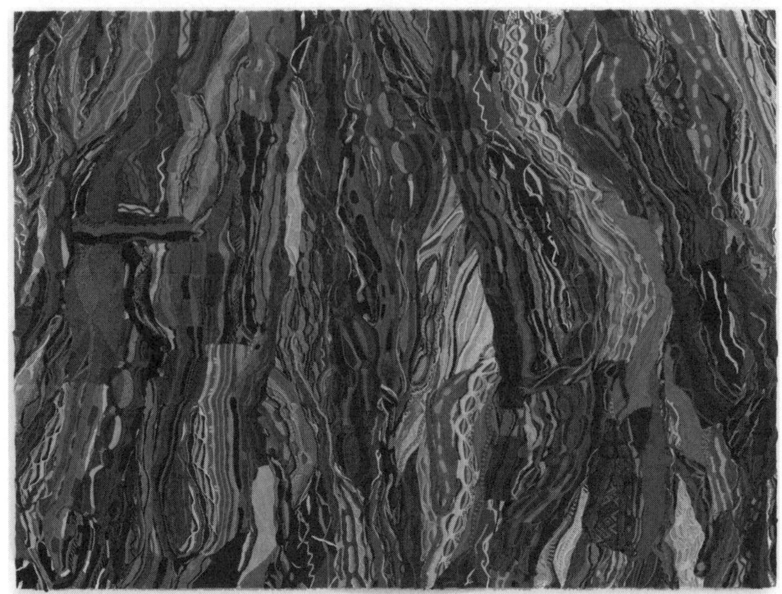

Figure 36 Jayson Musson, *Living Better Now* (2012). Mercerized cotton stretched on linen, 96 × 72 × 2 inches (244 × 183 × 5 cm). © Salon 94 Gallery, NY

white males) – as well as the representational demands placed upon African-American artists that they create whimsical, stereotypical, and racially problematic images of the black body. Having gained notoriety for his Hennessy Youngman persona, Musson's interest in modernist abstraction was perplexing for many critics because it defied the comedic self-deprecation that originally caught their attention. In an interview, Musson was asked to speak about the presence of blackness is his abstract works:

> Blackness is manifest in the works of artists of African decent. I don't believe Blackness to be a unified concept or to be located in a signature aesthetic identity. Yes, there are historical precedents that may dictate how past and present generations of Black artists make work and what they choose to make work about, but I see Blackness as an expansive field, which will be located in any and all investigations of Black artists no matter how far those investigations take them away from assumed notions of Black art. So yes, Blackness can be located in abstraction if a Black artist chooses to take up the task of producing abstract paintings.[27]

Clearly Musson is aware of the expectations placed upon black artists; in fact one of his ART THOUGHTZ videos was satirically dedicated to the topic. In *How to Be a Successful Black Artist* (2010), Hennessy Youngman pontificates sarcastically about the strategies and manoeuvres needed to become what he sardonically refers to as a 'successful nigga artist'. In one segment, he advocates for something he calls the 'jazz' principle: the idea that white people want to consume the 'exotic other' – suggesting that the 'nigger artist' needs to keep white folks entertained by always being different. And in a satirical jab at artist Kehinde Wiley, Youngman offers a strategy termed the 'dogs playing poker principle', a creative manipulation that consists of images depicting 'niggas doing white shit!' like sitting on a horse dressed as Napoleon.[28]

Musson's notion that blacks must 'keep white people entertained' is a concept that defines many of his artistic choices – particularly the repudiation of comic minstrelsy in his more serious gallery exhibitions. In many of the artist's videos a palpable bitterness lies just beneath the surface of their satirical wit – as well as the sense that Musson is well aware that his dopey Hennessy Youngman persona would achieve acclaim by employing the same 'dogs playing poker principle' that he so playfully skewers in his video. Youngman is the very personification of a 'nigga doing white shit': a sight gag that makes fun of the white-dominated art world's fetishistic thirst for racial stereotypes while also critiquing the black artist's complicity in his or her uncritical manufacture of problematic racial representations.

The tenor of Musson's biting humour recalls a scene in Spike Lee's satirical film *Bamboozled* (2000). Lee's opus tells the tale of Harvard-educated TV executive Pierre Delacroix, who works for a fictional network called CNS (Continental Network System). Disgruntled by institutionalized racism and structural barriers that prevent him from producing dignified and uplifting programming for African-American viewers, Delacroix (as a means to get fired) decides to create the most offensive televised programme possible: a modern-day minstrel show. Much to his dismay, the minstrel show becomes a huge success, plunging Delacroix into a dizzying state of guilt and despair that ultimately has disastrous consequences.

In one key scene, Delacroix (played by actor Damon Wayans) visits his standup comedian father Junebug (Paul Mooney) after one of his gigs. Despite his embarrassment over the coon-like minstrelsy of his father's stage performances, Delacroix reluctantly seeks out Junebug's advice about his professional predicament – to which he drunkenly recommends that his son simply: 'always keep 'em laughing!' and that 'Every nigger is an entertainer!'[29] This particular scene in many ways exemplifies the film's overall intent, which is to satirically parody the stifling and suffocating position of the black cultural producer who is caught between intra-cultural obligation (in this instance, the expectation of racial fidelity) and a rapacious, exploitative industry that demands that he/she produce comically stereotypical, demeaning, and self-deprecatory representations of black people (all for a chance at mainstream success).

The complexity of this impossible predicament tends to haunt the conceptual choices of African-American artists and informs the myriad ways these cultural producers effectively *play* with the quandary of complicity versus resistance: choices that obviously have great professional repercussions. In June 2014, Musson had his second solo exhibition at Salon 94 Gallery in New York. Entitled *Exhibit of Abstract Art*, the exhibition, much like its predecessor, mocked the pomposity of Euro-American modernism, through an inspired and witty appropriation of Ernie Bushmiller's *Nancy* comic strip (1933–1982). Bushmiller's comics made a habit of lampooning high modernist painting, distilling the self-proclaimed grandness of its expressive gestures into comically simplistic and reductive shapes. Musson paid tribute to the late cartoonist's aesthetic by recreating his jokey renditions of abstract paintings – albeit in grand scale. And interspersed throughout the gallery were large-scale fibreglass sculptures meant to monumentalize kitsch: toy-like ice cream cones, asymmetrical lamps, and a reductively rendered pink man, with a massive hole through his torso.[30] Interestingly, the subtlety, formal sophistication, and historical awareness of his exhibition were not received well by critics, or the art world in general – arguably because the satirical wit was completely absent. What Musson presented was a type of humour designed to mock the history and lofty aesthetic values of a white-dominated art world, but his comedic brand of racial self-flagellation was nowhere to be found. In sum, *Exhibit of Abstract Art* made good fun of modernism, while avoiding the comical exploitation and stereotyping of blackness expected of young African-American artists.

The critical response to *Exhibit of Abstract Art* seemed to articulate a rejection of Musson's desire to parody modernism, characterizing his

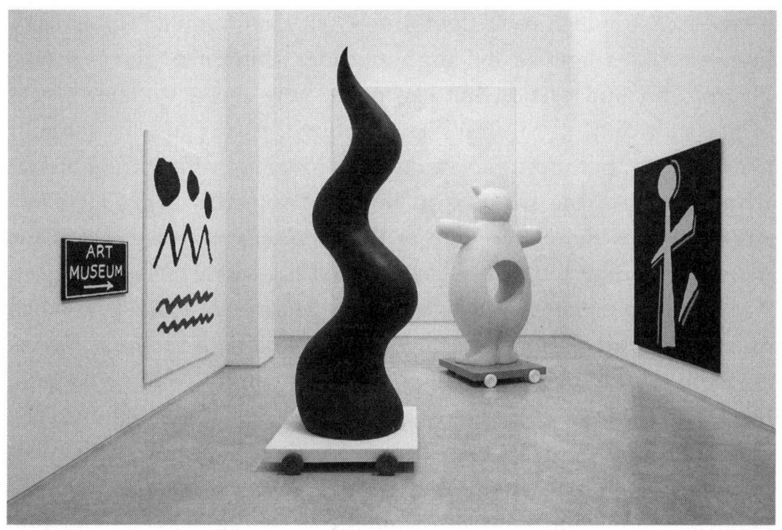

Figure 37 Jayson Musson, (Installation View) *Exhibit of Abstract Art* (2014). Salon 94 Gallery Bowery. © Salon 94 Gallery, NY

creative gestures as a failed attempt at satire devoid of humour. The controversial *New York Times* critic Ken Johnson had the following to say:

> Jayson Musson rose to fame in the hip-hop guise of his online video alter ego, Hennessy Youngman, who discourses hilariously and with rich profanity on the pretensions of contemporary art. In his non-video work, he also plays in the gap between high and low cultures but in a less biting, obliquely conceptual, Pop Art style.
>
> . . . Mr. Musson shares with Bushmiller a certain scepticism about Modern art. They both react to its snob appeal and elitist obscurantism. Paradoxically, Mr. Musson and his art belong to precisely the kind of high-society art world that Bushmiller made fun of. Underlying the cheerful, visually attractive surfaces of this show's works is a deeper ambivalence, a divided, insider-outsider state of mind that is expressed much more pointedly in Mr. Musson's videos. Which makes me wonder: If Hennessy Youngman made paintings and sculptures, what would they be like?[31]

Johnson's critique of Musson's humour expresses nostalgia for Hennessy Youngman's satirical *approach* to ridiculing art world pretensions – which took the form of self-deprecation. Youngman's humour makes light of the angry outsider's bitterness: the low class Negro who understands, but can never fully access the elite spaces of the art world. In Musson's gallery shows, it isn't just the humour that is absent, but most importantly, the longing of the racial outsider who peers into the window in hopes of someday being included. Arguably, it is the comic folly of the outsider's yearning that is the most entertaining and that, which Musson has wisely chosen to reject. According to writer Tiernan Morgan, 'Musson is at his best when his critiques are on point, his anger augmented with humour. *Exhibit of Abstract Art* works very well as a general parody of the art world, but it fails to delve deeper into its prejudices and contradictions. The artist's ART THOUGHTZ videos were successful, not just because they were extremely funny, but because they exposed deep rooted hypocrisies and contradictions within the art world.'[32] In contradiction to these sentiments, I would argue that in *Exhibit of Abstract Art*, anger is absolutely augmented with humour and his artworks are no less engaged with the process of exposing the art world's hypocrisies and contradictions. I posit that what is omitted from Musson's caustic wit (in the context of his gallery exhibitions) is the lowbrow racial minstrelsy that gives comic access to the unspeakable.

In the spirit of good satire, Linzy and Musson create a public forum from which to publicly ridicule the foibles of poor black people, while simultaneously (and cleverly, I might add) directing a judgmental glare at those with the impulse to do so. The adroitness of Linzy's satire comes out of a tradition of black comedy and musical performance with deep roots in African-American cultural traditions. In fact, I believe it necessary to consider this history when pondering the effectiveness of his production. Linzy is extremely aware of the racially disarming appeal of African-American musical performance and he exploits its jovial folksiness as a means to explore more heady themes. With that in mind, I'm interested in the relation between the survival of individuals who are both queerly and racially identified (to borrow the words of José Esteban Muñoz) and the notion that these subjects must *leave 'em laughing*! if they are to endure the annihilating and predatory nature of an intolerant society. The important connection between entertainment and survivorship is, in my estimation, key to forging a deeper understanding of Linzy's often-misunderstood video soap operas and stage performances.

Linzy and Musical Comedy

The interrelation between African-American survivorship and comedic musical performance traditions also provides context for understanding the deeper complexity of Linzy's visual and narrative choices. When queried about his interest in comedy and drama, he had the following to say:

> I think that I was always interested in both comedy and drama. I was very into *Def Comedy Jam* and stuff like that when I was in high school, and so, if you take something like *All My Churen*, it's a combination of the two – it follows the structure of a sitcom and a soap opera at the same time. But it all grew out of those aspirations of being a performer and an actor and filmmaker. I had all these dreams.[33]

Comedy and drama in Linzy's oeuvre intersect nicely with his interest in music – a relation that has a profound and lasting legacy in American entertainment history. In the last decade, there has been a renewed scholarly interest in black musical performance, particularly in Hollywood: an industry with a propensity for representing African-Americans with and through musical performance.[34]

Scholar Arthur Knight dedicated a book-length manuscript to focusing on what he designated as the 'most enduringly accepted, and even *loved* black cinematic figure, the musical performer'.[35] In Linzy's case, we might benefit from examining this archetype in relation to how the artist utilizes appropriation and politically wields what is often regarded as a non-threatening mode of African-American performance. As Knight illuminates, black performativity, and specifically Negro folk music, extends all the way back to slavery, but in Hollywood there was particular interest in African-American musical forms, which often took the shape of inserted musical numbers into films that were actually non-musicals.[36] However, in the late 1920s through 1950s, the form of the predominantly black-cast musical emerged, a phenomenon that forecasted the rise of the all black-cast cinematic dramas and crime stories of the 1960s and 1970s.[37] Oddly enough, the popularity of Linzy's musical comedy is both perplexing and entirely foreseeable, conjuring a query that Knight poses in his writing: 'Why were – and are – African-Americans so emphatically linked with music and musical performance in the American cinematic imagination?'[38] How is it that black musical performance has endured as the most significant expression of African-American *minority* culture? The importance of music to Afro-America is a subject that has been written about rather extensively, perhaps most notably by W.E.B. Du Bois. In his influential treatise, *The Souls of Black Folk*, the scholar proclaims that music is the Negro's greatest gift to American culture:

> By fateful chance, the Negro folk song – the rhythmic cry of the slave – stands to-day not simply as the sole American music, but as the most beautiful expression of human experience born this side the seas. It has been neglected, it has been, and is, half despised, and above all it has been persistently mistaken and misunderstood; but notwithstanding, it still remains as the singular spiritual heritage of the nation and the greatest gift of the Negro people.[39]

In his close reading of Du Bois' writings, Knight focuses attention on the late scholar's use of the word 'gift' to describe a cultural form that black folks brought to America. Knight effectively underscores how, for Du Bois, music embodied the most crucial and significant contribution that was *black folks' to give*: a gift borne of great sorrow, violence, and the physical toiling of black labour. The forms of black music: the spirituals and work songs provided 'soft, stirring melody in an ill-harmonized and unmelodious land'.[40] According to Knight, Du Bois' use of 'gift' is meant to denote a kind of property, an African-American possession that they *shared* and *mingled* with the dominant culture, even as it functioned as a vital tool of survivorship and intra-cultural communication.[41] However, 'gift' also suggests a quality that is essential to African-American people: an essence that black folks have that can only be *shared*, but never truly possessed by white culture.[42] As I move forward in my analysis of Linzy's iconography, it should be understood that Du Bois considered black musical performance as an African-American 'gift' that, while often read as demeaning and self-deprecating in the artist's comical performances, is a strategy that can also be understood as a shrewd and ingenious means to *leave 'em laughing*. Linzy employs a survival mechanism that mobilizes levity to transgress often impenetrable racial boundaries. As we will see, his approach often consists of performatively embodying stereotypes and caricatures that evoke painful and embarrassing memories of America's racially problematic past.

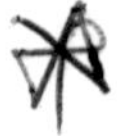

From November 2008 to January 2009, Kalup Linzy participated in *Prospect. 1 New Orleans*, a mega-exhibition organized by contemporary art curator Dan Cameron. Conceptualized in the tradition of long-standing biennials like the Venice Biennale and Istanbul Biennial, *Prospect. 1* showcased over 80 leading visual artists in an effort to culturally revitalize New Orleans in the aftermath of Hurricane Katrina. As his official entry to the exhibition, Linzy presented a video work entitled *Keys to Our Heart* (2008), a black-and-white piece in three vignettes, shot in the style of a classic 1940s Hollywood movie.[43] In this farcical period piece, the artist plays Lily, an ageing, bitter, and cynical older black woman who meddles deviously in the love affairs of others. Funded by the granting agency Creative Capital, *Keys to Our Heart* is more polished than many of the artist's earlier works – however, in keeping with his usual aesthetic, the dialogue is often profane and trite, and at times he inserts contemporary slang for its comic and anachronistic affect. The narrative follows a dramatic love triangle between John Jay (Joshua Seidner), Dinah (Alison Folland) and Lily (Linzy), characters whose paths cross tempestuously in a series of heated dialogues. The white John Jay struggles to maintain his troubled relationship with African-American Dinah in the midst of the meddling and misanthropic Lily, who harbours desires of her own.

In full drag as the embittered Lily, Linzy is more convincingly enmeshed in his character's melodramatic and mature womanliness. This is a shift from his usual drag, which could not be accurately described as an imitation of femininity, per se. The artist characterizes Lily as a Southern matriarch of sorts: the town's gossipy *grande dame*, who wreaks havoc with people's lives through a mix of rumour, bullying, and calculated subterfuge. Based on the cinematic performances of actors Joan Crawford and Bette Davis, her appearance is one of defiant sophistication: haughty and with an oppressive meticulousness that makes her that much more imposing and terrifying. Linzy renders Lily with a kind of deranged intensity. Her eyes bulge and her head always cocks slightly upwards with a cynical and slightly menacing forcefulness. The elaborate costuming allows Linzy to more fully embody his character, and as a result, his performance is arguably one of his best. Imaged as a woman with an oppressive and imposing sophistication, her dress arguably comprises the most crucial dimension of Lily's characterization. In one particular scene, we see Linzy's villain replete in a tightly coiffed French twist hairstyle, elaborate decorative

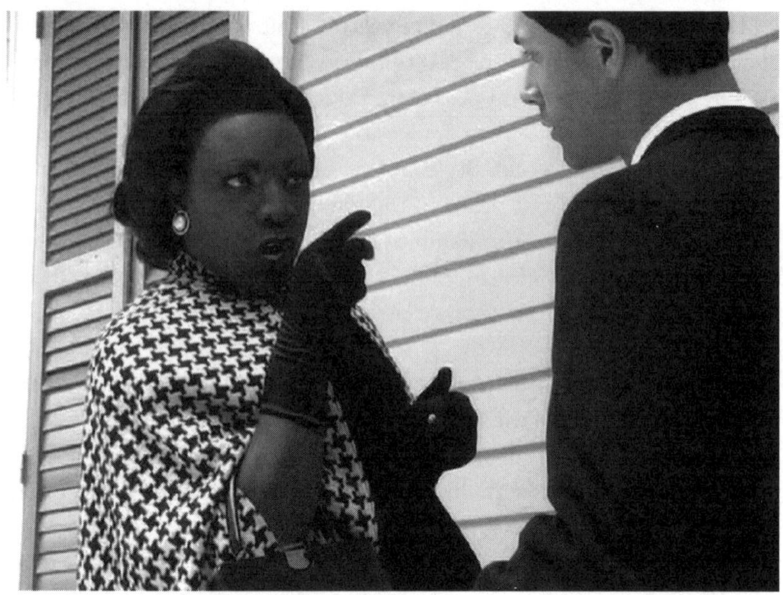

Figure 38 Kalup Linzy, *Keys to Our Heart* (2008). Video, 24:06 min, b&w, sound, English. © Kalup Linzy/Electronic Arts Intermix, NY

earrings, and dramatic makeup. Draped in a theatrical houndstooth cape, a pearl necklace, silk gloves and a black dress – Lily is all attitude: arms flailing, fingers pointing, and head rolling in a melodramatic and theatrical display. In one arm she holds a small leather purse, while the other daintily grasps a cigarette. A powerful mix of contradictions, Lily is both masculine and feminine; a kind of devious anti-hero that wields her power with a skillful grace.

Keys to Our Heart is a play on the social problem films of the 1940s–1960s, exploring the interracial relationship between John Jay and Dinah, two doomed lovers navigating the perils of Southern racism. Structurally, the film contains many of the traits that have made Linzy's work so successful: dubbed over voices, whimsical musical numbers, and the odd and surrealist grafting of stereotypically black voices onto white bodies. Through a clever process of modulating the pitch and tone of the audio, Linzy is able to record all of the character's lines using his own voice. This intentionally absurd and imperfect quality accounts for much of the video's humour, particularly, when the awkwardly slow cadence of his character's speech produces a disturbing comic affect. In a sense, the aural dimension of these films communicates a kind of horror... The bodies and sounds are always slightly disconnected, giving the character's interactions a strange quality of ventriloquism.

Linzy's inventiveness recalls the introduction of synchronized sound in films of the 1920s that enabled the integration of moving images with a range of acoustic elements, including music. According to Arthur Knight, the synchronized sound film aided Hollywood's existing fascination with the physicality of black performance, by joining 'coloured sight, to coloured sound'.[44] One of the consequences of this evolution was assigning a set of racially specific codes and ethnic markers to the bodies of black people. Linzy is aware of the ideological knottiness that informs the entertainment world's appropriation of African-American performers – though his work exhibits a particular consciousness around the cinematically-constructed racial coding that reduce us all to a series of legible types. The notion of joining 'coloured sight, to coloured sound' is always perverted in his work, disjointing and distorting the equilibrium between sight and sound, so that identity has fluidity and is never fixed. That fluidity is often communicated in the mobility granted a specifically Southern brand of black vernacular speech – a soulfulness and signifier of racial authenticity that Linzy generously spreads across all of his characters. If we think of black musical performance as an African-American 'gift' (in keeping with the writings of Du Bois), as a type of property, then in Linzy's case, there is no fundamentalist hold over it, no claimed ownership steeped in the problematic logic of racial essentialism. In the artist's creative universe, the visual and aural markers of blackness are always transferable.

In *Keys to Our Heart*, the racial fluidity is light-heartedly communicated through the two main white characters, John Jay and Sally Sue. In a particularly confrontational scene, the strait-laced John Jay looks like a stiff Southern gentleman in his black suit as he glares at Lily with a perplexed blankness while she proclaims:

> When dealing with a woman like Dinah and myself, you can't give us all the things we really desire. We need to be challenged. Don't treat us like queens. Treat us like shit and we'll love you! We're wounded John Jay... Save the romantic shit for girls like Sally Sue![45]

Belying his refined and seemingly educated exterior, John Jay's voice has a precise, albeit dopey drawl to it that sounds distinctly, if not stereotypically black: an audible feature that, in its racially heightened (if not somewhat offensive) affect, recalls the comic absurdity of blackface. We see this quality again in Sally Sue: a character whose shrill voice intentionally resonates with troubling racial caricaturing. These deliberately inserted sound elements play satirically with the racial coding that always subtends cinematic characterization – elements used not only to denote race, but also class, notions of sophistication, and social value. The milquetoast Sally Sue looks like a pampered Southern belle. She appears svelte in her feminine dresses, yet her digitally-altered shrieking voice takes on a crudely racialized and stereotypical tonality. Her faux African-American dialect recalls the coon song genre that was popular until the 1920s, however what Linzy ridicules is the stilted etiquette (and veneer of white civility) of the Old South. While giving advice to the beleaguered John Jay (in his pursuit of Dinah), Sally Sue advises: 'Bitches can be turned around John Jay. . . . give it some time, why don't you talk to her again!'[46] The dubbing of a contemporary and distinctly black brand of profanity, over the genteel and stereotypically white looking Sally Sue, has a melodramatic irony that is as unsettling as it is hilarious. To add more ironic texture, Linzy includes music by the singer Lil Johnson, an African-American performer in the 1920s and 1930s who recorded lewd blues and Hokum songs that had an intentionally cheeky brand of sexual suggestiveness. As comedic farce, Johnson's Hokum songs spoofed African-American life in the tradition of blackface minstrelsy, where racial and sexual stereotypes were embodied and lampooned with an exaggerated ludicrousness. Within *Keys to Our Heart* we hear the 1937 song 'If It Don't Fit (Don't Force It)' by Lil Johnson and Barrel House Annie. The lyrics are a mix of lewdness and sexually suggestive metaphor:

> If it don't fit don't force it,
> Cause you'll make your momma mad.
> If it don't fit don't force it,
> Cause you'll only get in bad.
>
> Changed the lock cause you stayed out till four,
> Your key didn't fit, you tried to break down the door!
> If it don't fit don't force it,
> Cause you'll make your momma mad.

Now it may stretch, it may not tear at all,
But you'll never pack that big mule up in my stall!
If it don't fit don't force it,
Cause you'll make your momma mad.[47]

In one scene, Lily sings to Dinah, playfully performing Lil Johnson's 1936 'Get 'Em from the Peanut Man (Hot Nuts)' with comic swagger:

Selling nuts! Hot nuts!
Anybody here wanna buy my nuts?
Selling nuts, hot nuts
I've got nuts for sale
Selling one for five, two for ten
If you buy 'em once, you'll buy 'em again
Selling nuts, hot nuts,
You buy 'em from the peanut man!

Nuts! Hot nuts!
Anybody here wanna buy my nuts?
Selling nuts, hot nuts
I've got nuts for sale
They tell me your nuts is mighty fine
But I bet your nuts isn't hard as mine
Selling nuts, hot nuts,
You buy 'em from the peanut man![48]

The choice of tune is fitting, considering Lily's illicit, yet hidden desires that will ultimately be narratively revealed in dramatic fashion. Lil Johnson's particular brand of dirty blues dealt with socially taboo subjects through clever forms of innuendo and racially coded *double entendres*. Linzy's canny use of dirty blues in his video-based works alludes to the layering of meaning, not simply in music's suggestiveness, but also within the moving image itself. Things are never really what they seem and the images, like the music, conceal a more in-depth and intellectual engagement with the complexities of identity. Linzy's awareness of these historical tropes gives context for understanding some of his conceptual and narrative choices, particularly the rather lengthy history of ridiculing the black Southern underclass – which the artist attempts to subvert in *Keys to Our Heart*. In many respects, Linzy takes and reworks the traditions of the dirty blues, Hokum, and the coon song – musical forms with deep roots in American culture – and reworks them by injecting biting satire that transcends their origins in a lengthy history of anti-black racism and allows them to be mobilized across the boundaries of identity.

Queering the Churen: Kalup's Bodies/Warhol's Bodies

Critical interpretations of Kalup Linzy's production often refer to the artist's comic use of drag in his videos and stage performances, yet there is reticence around discussing his queerness in any direct way. In fact, like the response to Musson's work, critics tend to openly articulate their ambivalence for overt political statements or activist-oriented declarations about identity that may arise in certain pieces. What we often see are critical assessments that allude to the presence of identity politics as a series of juvenile sentiments that dumb down artistic production. Art critic Steven Stern's reading of Linzy's conceptual approach cites the artist's interventions into discussions of identity, yet creates a framework through which to look beyond their obvious centrality:

> All of Linzy's work displays an obvious affection for his pop-cultural models his sensibility resonates with the outmoded and sentimental. There is certainly degree of camp here, and plenty of canny play with stereotypes of race and gender, but to speak of the artist's work simply in terms of satire and subversion might be to miss the point. Throwing a monkey wrench into any notion of identity politics, he foregrounds instead the odd, twisty process of identification itself.[49]

In Stern's analysis, to read Linzy's references to queerness for their obvious attempts at *satire* and *subversion* is to 'miss the point'. While I agree that there are many dimensions to Linzy's production that bear critical unpacking, it is rather odd that the queerness of this artist's work (and how it intersects with race and class) is not intellectually attended to, in favour of fixating on more esoteric musings about form and humour. The very obvious presence of a black man in what could be described as an unconvincing form of drag is an elephant in the room that must be explored.

However, there is precedent in art historical discourse for overlooking queer iconography and aesthetics (and queer desire for that matter) in the production of many notable artists, particularly the late Andy Warhol. Recent efforts at theorizing Andy Warhol have attempted to re-contextualize him within gay discourse, or to examine him through the perspective of psychoanalysis, critical race theory, and even feminism. Books such as *Pop Out*,[50] or even *The Andy Warhol Diaries*,[51] refreshingly highlight Warhol's gayness or 'swishiness' (that was so deeply ingrained in his cultural production) as a critical strategy for understanding his life and work. In the 1990s, revisionist scholarship began to emerge that focused on recovering Warhol's queerness, unpacking its iconographic presence in his more notable works. However, engaging his queerness necessitated a re-examination of Warhol's films – particularly his cinematic exploits with collaborator Paul Morrissey. In his book *The Cinematic Body*, American cultural critic Steven Shaviro cites a 1967 interview between Gretchen Berg and Warhol in which the artist stated: 'all of my films are artificial but then everything is sort of artificial. I don't know where the artificial stops and the real starts.'[52] The connection between artificiality and queerness (as a representational mode) is a theme I intend to explore in greater detail – because in both Warhol and Linzy's works, the construction of an absurdly artificial world gives popular representation a strangeness and a semiotic vulnerability that dramatically alters our perception of these forms.

There are many striking similarities between Warhol's films and the video works of Kalup Linzy, but I want to explore this relationship in the service of exploring each artist's self-conscious wielding of queerness, not simply as a means to make gay subjectivities present – but rather to *queer* representation: to push our reading of bodies into a more nebulous and less ideologically over-determined terrain. According to Shaviro, Warhol's films engage critically with the capitalist production of simulacra, which he characterizes as resulting in a regime of unlimited and totalizing artificiality:[53] 'Capitalist commodity production culminates in a regime of unlimited artificiality, first expressed by mechanical reproduction and by the cinema, but brought to its highest pitch through the ubiquity of electronic media (TV, video, computers).'[54] Shaviro makes reference to Jean Baudrillard's notion of the *hyperreal*, 'a condition in which the "contradiction between the real and the imaginary is effaced. The unreal is no longer that of the dream or of fantasy, of a beyond or a within, it is that of *a hallucinatory resemblance of the real with itself.*'[55] It is already widely understood that Warhol was fascinated by the artificiality of celebrity and capitalist consumer culture, but there has been little writing on how his homosexuality informed this obsession.

That said, there is a similar trend forming in the critical response to Linzy's video works that I intend to explore. To accomplish this, however, there is a need to revisit some of the critical themes that have emerged in revisionist assessments of Warhol's art. I'm intrigued by Shaviro's thinking regarding Warhol's fascination with artificiality. This fixation runs through his entire body of work, from the celebrity portraits to his screen tests and satirical films. The relation between artificiality and Baudrillard's *hyperreal* (the collapsing of the real and the imaginary) in Warhol can certainly apply to a formal reading of Linzy's video works, which are similarly obsessed with the artifice of capitalist consumer culture. The relationship between Warhol and Linzy was explored in the 2012 exhibition *Regarding Warhol: Sixty Artists, Fifty Years*, held at The Metropolitan Museum of Art. In a reassessment of the late artist's interest in the imagery of everyday life and the commonplace banality of popular representation, *Regarding Warhol* looked at a range of artists who were influenced by Warhol. The show presented works by artists including Hans Haacke, Sigmar Polke, Robert Gober, and Jeff Koons, alongside the much a younger generation of artists, to which Linzy belongs. Interestingly, one section of the exhibition, entitled 'Queer Studies: Camouflage and Shifting Identities', made a point of unpacking Warhol's impact and importance 'as an artist who broke new ground in representing issues of sexuality and gender in the post-war period'.[56] However, in relation to Linzy, I am also intrigued by Shaviro's notion of capitalist representation as a *regime of unlimited artificiality* that is most potently expressed by mechanical forms, like the cinema, video, and computers. Warhol's embrace of the camera (and especially the moving image) exemplifies Shaviro's claims. This understanding also applies quite strikingly to Linzy, whose appropriation and successful wielding of digital technologies has been the key to his success.

Warhol's career as a filmmaker is actually more extensive then one might believe. In fact, he was extremely prolific as a producer of moving images. Between 1963 and 1968, he produced over 60 films and was known for shooting short film portraits (called 'screen tests') of visitors to his studio The Factory. Most recognized as a successful painter, Warhol actually embraced a range of media forms including photography, film, and music. He was known to socialize with everyone from major celebrities to drag queens and bohemian street people. The populist dimension of his career and working method serves to illuminate many of his creative and intellectual leanings, and this facet of his personality has emerged as one of the central factors in queer re-readings of his expansive body of work. In interviews and in his diaristic entries, Warhol often spoke publicly about class and race, in relation to his ever-increasing social status: sentiments that are now often linked to his sexual radicalism. Throughout his career, Warhol lived openly as a gay man, which was in contrast to the repressiveness of the times. In fact, he did this long before the gay liberation movement began to pick up steam. In his film works, queerness became a more overtly discussed topic that expressed itself satirically and in terms of humorous depictions of queer shame and repressed sexual desires.

The notion of queer shame is germane to any critical unpacking of Warhol and Linzy's filmic efforts, as evidenced in their farcical fascination with drag and transvestitism. Though Warhol's aesthetic was, at least in part, informed by the relationship between his white working class roots and ambivalence towards his sexuality, which only began to surface in his film work. Linzy has often spoken about his own humble beginnings among the black working poor in the rural South – and as is evidenced in his irreverent videos, the underbelly of African-American life is often juxtaposed with the abject presence of the sexually marginal. All of this is imaged with a humorous edge, though the notion of queer shame is potentially a useful lens through which to understand his unique vision. In critical interpretations of Warhol's queerness, the relation between shame and his apparent shyness (a quality that he often spoke about) emerges as a crucial dimension to the artist's highly constructed professional persona:

> There are different ways for individual people to take over space – to command space. Very shy people don't even want to take up the space that their body actually takes up, whereas very outgoing people want to take up as much space as they can . . .
>
> I've always had a conflict because I'm shy and yet I like to take up a lot of personal space. Mom always said, 'Don't be pushy, but let everybody know

> you're around.' I wanted to command more space than I was commanding, but then I knew I was too shy to know what to do with the attention if I did manage to get it. That's why I love television. That's why I feel that television is the media I'd most like to shine in.[57]

According to Eve Kosofsky Sedgwick, in this brief quotation, there are hints that Warhol was conscious about his identity and his social position. However, the scholar suggests that Warhol's neuroses around economic and sexual marginality were potentially the catalyst for artworks that – in their satirical and playful dimensions – simultaneously ridiculed and valorized the visual tropes and warped value systems promoted in popular television programming. For Sedgwick, Warhol's shame/shyness matrix was the catalyst for creative work based on a highly constructed and politicized personal presence – and a new form of critical and performative efficacy. Among its many themes, Sedgwick suggests that Warhol's constructed identity (embodied in his shyness) explored what it may mean to be a white (queer) in a queer-hating world... and what it may mean to be a white (queer) in a white-supremacist one.[58] In her analysis of Warhol's life and work, Sedgwick characterizes this bashfulness as a particularly 'Queer' shyness that was infused with a shame for his physical presence as well as for his whiteness. She cites a quote by Warhol describing his inability or unwillingness to look at maids, many of whom were of colour:

> Some people just aren't embarrassed by the idea of somebody else cleaning up after them... It's so awkward when you come face to face with a maid. I've never been able to pull it off. Some people I know are very comfortable looking at maids... but I can't handle it. When I go to a hotel, I find myself trying to stay there all day so the maid can't come in. I make a point of it. Because I just don't know where to put my eyes... where to look, what to be doing while they're cleaning. It's actually a lot of work avoiding the maid, when I think about it.[59]

Sedgwick views this passage as a manifestation of Warhol's shame that specifically relates to his white male privilege. She describes his embarrassment as a kind of 'queer' whininess with racist overtones. However, this shyness or embarrassment could more aptly be related to his working class upbringings. Perhaps, his guilt is related to a social

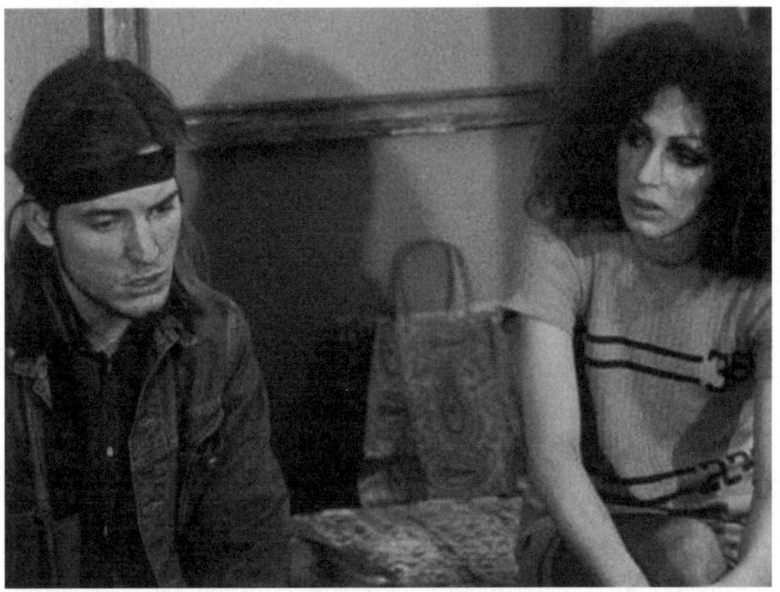

Figure 39 Andy Warhol and Paul Morrissey, *Trash* (1970). Film, colour, screen shot by author

consciousness about the working poor, and those on the social and economic margins.

Sedgwick describes Warhol's cultivated 'childlikeness' or what she calls his 'faggy air' as a component of his 'more-than-casual' racism. One can deduce from Warhol's uncomfortable preoccupation with the plight of the poor in his cinematic works that he was thinking politically about the underbelly of capitalist excess in which he was participating. Warhol was keenly aware of his underprivileged roots. This realization informed his gaze, specifically his satirical engagement with the carnivalesque nature of high society and celebrity – and the marginal (and often queer) figures that existed along their periphery. We see this evidenced in several of his films, particularly the narrative B-movies *Lonesome Cowboys* (1968), *Flesh* (1968), *Trash* (1970), and *Heat* (1972). Each of these films starred actor Joe Dallesandro. In the latter three, the actor played male leads who were street hustlers, prostitutes, or drug addicts.

Thematically, many of these campy and satirical films depicted the trials and tribulations of the outsider who exists on the margins of wealth and power and who constantly navigates predatory behaviour, violence, exploitation, and the perils of street life. Directed by Paul Morrissey and produced by Warhol, *Trash* explores the underbelly of contemporary urban life, as viewed through the lens of Joe (Joe Dallesandro), a drugged out, though remarkably handsome vagrant. The film chronicles Joe's experiences as he wanders the New York streets in search of his next fix. With each new experience in his quest for drugs, Joe encounters abuse at the hands of those who wish to exploit him sexually. Unable to physically perform, he drifts from one frustrating scenario to the next. *Trash*, as J.J. Murphy illuminates, 'attempts to comment on the relaxed mores brought about by 1960s hippie culture, a development that the conservative Morrissey absolutely detested'.[60] In Murphy's account, Dallesandro's drug addicted Joe was meant to symbolize the consequences and fallout of the 1960s culture of sex and drugs – 'the degradation that Morrissey saw as resulting from failed experiments with personal freedom'.[61] Apparently, the irony of this intention, as Murphy points out, is that in the film's commercial success, the political message was lost and *Trash* was instead viewed as a chic comedy that celebrated excess, rather than critiquing it.[62]

Warhol's films were known for their intentionally poor production: bad lighting, shaky and out-of-focus camerawork, microphones visibly hanging above the actor's heads, and no discernable editing technique. The awkwardness of the production is all part of the fun, but it also enabled a greater focus on the actor's physical presence and behaviour. The intensity of the camera's gaze in Warhol's films has been likened to the voyeuristic aesthetics of pornography: the cinematic cheapness, the blunt sexual straightforwardness, and the intentionally bad dialogue. Each scenario in *Trash* plays like a pornographic film, where the protagonist unwittingly finds himself in situations that quickly lead to the suggestion of a sexual encounter that is ultimately unfulfilled. However, Warhol's movies utilize and exploit the titillation of the pornographic structure as a means to build tension. But in the end, there is no actual sex. This visual frankness – which reads as an emptied-out, porn-like quality – appears to be devoid of content, beyond the simple desire to gaze upon the stupidity and awkwardness of bodies. The effect of Warhol's bitingly satirical, pseudo-pornographic approach is that he tends to highlight what Shaviro calls the seductive stupidity of the body.[63] In other words, as the scholar suggests, the films are 'marked with *literalism* with which they evacuate all other significance and content' in order to capture the physical awkwardness and folly of their human subjects.[64]

In many respects, the most compelling and confrontational subjects of Warhol's films were his transvestites and drag queens. The artist's fascination with the real and the artificial found its perverse union in these incendiary characterizations. The very intentional artificiality of drag fails so spectacularly in its effort to achieve authenticity, that it conveys a certain truth. That truth is believed to be the *modus operandi* of Warhol's films: to mobilize the truly *bad* acting of amateur performers to cut through the lie of cinematic artifice. No actor better exemplified this characteristic than Holly Woodlawn (Born Haroldo Santiago Franceschi Rodriguez Danhakl), the Puerto Rican-born transgender actress and Warhol superstar. Woodlawn received acclaim for her role in *Trash*, where she plays Holly, the drug addicted, trash-collecting roommate of Joe (Dallesandro).

In some of the film's most humorous moments, Woodlawn's transvestite heroine badgers her roommate for sex and drugs, while Joe nods off in a drug-induced stupor. The acting in these scenes is intentionally bad and embodies the desired truthfulness that Warhol wanted to achieve. In fact that ultimate truthfulness was in the failure of the transvestite to 'naturalize the artifice' of successfully passing as a woman.[65] The drag queen relates to the notion of 'passing' through the embodiment of both sexes, yet they don't 'originate their own image', according to Shaviro...on the contrary, 'they both subvert and reinforce traditional stereotypes of gender'.[66] Drag contains both the normative and the perverse, while still remaining subversive – although what is most meaningful in regard to Warhol's filmic production is that they perform the cinematic ideal of femininity. And it is in their ultimate failure to achieve realness that exposes the deep ideological dysfunction at the heart of hetero-patriarchal femininity. The drag queen embodies the duality of Warhol's obsessions: the grandiose excessiveness of Hollywood celebrity and glamorous hyper-femininity, combined with bad performance and the spectacle of the marginal and the sexually abject. In her symbolic aspects, Holly Woodlawn is a surrogate for these characteristics, but a more complete and fully realized one – what Thomas Waugh calls, 'the gay subject par excellence.'[67]

Warhol's interest in pornography plays an important role in the Woodlawn scenes. Warhol regarded the oft-discussed 'pornographic gaze' and its objectifying nature as an enticing tool to engage the audience. He stated, 'People are alienated by one another, and Porn gets you excited about people.'[68] In *Trash*, the camera always gazes upon Holly with a curious fascination and a mix of voyeuristic curiosity, titillation and boredom.

Warhol's greatness as a painter, a taste-maker, as well as his genre-defining sense of cool, are all believed to exist because of his political vacuity and personal blankness: his ability to evacuate his persona and his artwork of any activist or socially redeeming agenda. A great deal of critical effort has gone into theorizing this supposedly post-modern quality of self-consciously rising above all meaning and all sense of social obligation. Of course, the truth is a bit more complex. Overt expressions of queer solidarity, not unlike expressions of racial fidelity, are not looked upon favourably in the art world – where exploitive images of racial and sexual difference are permissible (even desired) while identity politics and resistance to inequity is punished and shamed (or condescendingly brushed aside). Warhol understood that to be a great artist is to, at least on the surface, feign disinterest in the plight of the underclass, even while his images defiantly represent that very constituency. That is perhaps why the imaging of Warhol's street denizens, queer hustlers, and transvestites always took a satirical tone . . . it was imbued with a comic whimsy that never seemed to take itself seriously enough to communicate a coherent message.

Collaborating with, portraying, and publicly socializing with racial minorities, transvestites and street hustlers at a time when the country was at its height of repressiveness (pre-Civil Rights, pre-Stonewall) was an extremely political gesture, and one that could potentially tarnish Warhol's more conservative and respectable painting practice. Yet still, the post-modern reading of the artist's 'superficiality and blankness' prevail over what Shaviro calls a 'hermeneutics of suspicion' about the supposed political dimension of the artist's practice: an attempt to '*decipher* the work, interpreting symptoms, searching for signs of repression, uncovering latent meanings'.[69] For Shaviro, Warhol has gone to great length to empty out his work, to eliminate depth and to reveal the ubiquity of the commodity form – to present nothing but surfaces.[70] However, I am sceptical of analyses suggesting, as Shaviro does, that Warhol's art and films have no content at all – that they are completely and totally porous.

When considering the larger impact of Warhol's oeuvre on recent generations of artists such as Linzy, it is imperative to move beyond apolitical readings. Furthermore, it is not simply in the formal and structural logics of his films, or even in their satirical wit, where comparisons can be drawn. I argue that Warhol's work is deeply embedded with meaning and with a representational politics of the body that was at the vanguard of sexual radicalism. In his historical account of Warhol's queer activism, Mark Rosenthal reminds us that: 'by the early 1970s, cross-dressing, gender-bending, and androgyny had become part of the mainstream culture with "sexual radicals"'.[71] These individuals, Warhol included, 'helped make ubiquitous the camp aesthetics of "artifice" and "decadence"'.[72] What I find most salient about Warhol's impact on younger artists is the way in which he rather forcefully created a uniquely queer desiring gaze that, according to J.J. Murphy, explored the intersection between documentary and fiction.[73] For Murphy, Warhol's bizarre brand of realism has enormous relevance today, especially when considering the emergence of reality television. Warhol's insistence on the parody and satirical send-up of Hollywood, bears great significance to Kalup Linzy's iconographic and narrative proclivities. In a dialogue with Alex Allenchey, Linzy was asked to consider his use of parody and satire in comparison to Andy Warhol's similar strategy:

> Allenchey: Your 2006 video *Conversations wit de Churen V: As da Art World Might Turn*, which lampoons both the serial, daytime soap-opera and the art world, is on display in the Met show alongside Warhol's *Lonesome Cowboys*, itself a parody of the Western movie genre. How important is satire for you as a tool in your art, and what do you use it to accomplish?
>
> Linzy: I love satire, and I love what I satirize. Yes, satire can be used as political propaganda to demoralize and dehumanize, but that's not what I'm doing. I am role-playing, satirizing, and paying tribute at the same time to the genre of the soap opera. I also want to keep people coming back to my work. Those who enjoy it and follow it know there is always another episode around the corner.[74]

A striking link appears between Linzy and Warhol when considering their fixation with celebrity, kitsch, and the vulgarity of popular culture. Although, I want to foreground their political engagement and means of exerting pressure against the repressive social mores of their respective generations. The imperative of survival in a deeply homophobic and deeply racist society hovers ominously over everything they produce. An ethos of survival emanates from Linzy's work, one that is both black and queer. This attitude is steeped in the traditions of African-American musical performance, but also in the abject representation of sexual outsiders and economically underprivileged racial minorities. What is most significant about this relation is not the *queering* as a form of sexual radicalism, but rather their effort to queer representation and ultimately the stifling and repressive logic of normativity in its many manifestations. The bad acting, the transvestitism, the banality, and the pornographic aesthetics, have the function of perverting all that is legible – particularly the demeaning effects of social, economic, sexual, and racial divisions and hierarchies.

Linzy's *Keys to Our Heart* – in its spoof of old Hollywood films like *What Ever Happened to Baby Jane* (1962) starring Bette Davis and Joan Crawford – embodies several of the characteristics of Warhol's filmic melodramas, most notably the bad acting and awkward production values. Linzy has often spoken about his youth and the importance of TV dramas and daytime soap operas to his family. Having been raised among the working poor in rural Florida, TV was the primary outlet for entertainment and the hub of social activity in his small town. Warhol was similarly intrigued by soap operas; in fact, he directed a film entitled *Soap Opera* in 1964 – but Linzy's tribute to the genre strays into more politically fraught terrain. While Warhol's creation consists primarily of 'narrative episodes, interrupted by a series of product commercials' – Linzy's soaps feel more closely aligned with the genre in form and structure.[75] In their comedic element and racially subversive casting, the artist's video works comment on the mainstream soap opera's hyper-constructed fantasy of white American wealth, opulence, and excess. Largely devoid of black bodies, the sanitized world of the soap opera is, in many ways, the antithesis of Linzy's Southern black working class roots. In an interview, Linzy spoke about the importance of television in his early life:

> My obsession with the soap opera was in full blossom by the time I entered junior high school. When I wasn't interested in cartoons or escaping into

> the woods with my cousins in my hometown Stuckey, Florida, I would sit with my grandmother and watch the stories. By the time I got to high school, I had been bitten by the acting bug – I was always artistically inclined as a child, but the soap opera is what nurtured my acting (or dare I say . . . dramatic aspirations).[76]

One of the central questions that arises in relation to Linzy's makeshift soaps is whether or not the gender bending constitutes a form of drag. Steven Shaviro rightly suggests that, in the case of Warhol, drag signified falsity and hyperbolic exaggeration – and spoke to the artificiality of all gender constructions.[77] In many ways, the old Hollywood glamour model of femininity was a kind of drag that was so completely overstated in its construction of ideal womanhood, that it completely deviated from reality. Shaviro reads Warhol's drag as a testament to the artist's fixation with the artifice and the superficiality of surfaces, though he doesn't speak about it in terms of identity politics, or in terms of the sexual radicalism of the period, that permeated the worlds of music, stage performance, and visual culture.

It is virtually impossible to adequately discuss Warhol's artistic production out of the context of homophobia and the anti-homosexual legal system of the 1950s and 1960s. It was within this milieu that Warhol operated – yet; we might also consider that Linzy's sexually and racially radical work emerged in the wake of the rise of America's first African-American president (Barack Obama) and an ever-more aggressive (and successful) LGBT rights movement. Linzy's artistic strategy embraces the utopian vision of the globalization era – an anti-essentialist ethos that is critical of fundamentalist ties to pernicious markers of identity (race, gender, sexuality, class, and nationhood). In that regard, Linzy's gender-bending approach may not be drag, at least not in its more stereotypical understanding. Aside from *Keys to Our Heart*, Linzy never appears to be very interested in accurately imitating femininity, in that his maleness is never fully submerged within a performative ruse. In contrast, his characters are always rooted in what Richard Dyer calls an 'idea of (male) masculinity'.[78] There is no naturalizing of femininity or an assertion of any kind of 'biological androgyny or real in-betweenism'.[79] Locating drag (specifically in reference to the 'queen' who wears women's clothing) as one of the predominant features of gay male ghetto culture's expression of camp,

Dyer makes an important distinction between camp behaviour and a camp attitude:

> The latter [camp attitude] implies an ironic stance towards official or mainstream images or representations. Camp in this sense is profoundly denaturalizing. Far from expressing a sense of what is natural, it constantly draws attention to the artifices attendant on the construction of images of what is natural. Camp, drag, and macho self-consciously play the signs of gender, and it is in the play and exaggeration that an alternative sexuality is implied – a sexuality, that is, that recognizes itself as in a problematic relationship to the conventional conflation of sexuality and gender.[80]

In its phantasmagoric excessiveness, Linzy's drag seems to accurately personify the tenets of camp, although, it seems that his gender bending contains a desire to queer popular representation – to denaturalize it by destabilizing what is racially coherent, as well as recognizably and stereotypically masculine and feminine. The crossing over and remixing of identities, combined with racial fluidity, is arguably more about creating a world defined by a quality of whimsical strangeness, than by a desire to make a coherent political statement about gay rights. With that in mind, I am intrigued by how Linzy combines queer drag, feminist sentiment, and racial commentary in his video work. *Keys to Our Heart* does this quite successfully, as evidenced in a hilarious scene between Lily and Dinah, where the latter complains about her struggles with her embattled lover John Jay:

> Dinah: 'He wanted to make love . . . I was not trying to make love! Just because he bought me two outfits, did not mean he was gonna get him some. I don't care how *good* the lovin' is . . . He was too much for me last night.'
>
> Lily: 'I know that's right . . . *Hold back the pussy girl!*'[81]

Lily's manipulative and toxic feminism has a force that is so convincingly overwrought that it seems to deviate from stereotypical articulations of queer drag. Yet it also tends to reconcile the opposition between *camp behaviour* and a *camp attitude* that Dyer speaks of. In *Keys to Our Heart* we see a bit of both identifications, though the film may more accurately inspire allusions to black comedy traditions in which African-American men dress as women as a form of farcical entertainment. In the past 20 years, a divisive debate has begun to stir about the mainstream popularity of this comedic form, that contemplates it social function, and broader impacts on black self-esteem. Stephane Dunn contemplates mainstream black comedic drag as a culturally safe means to take on the often-problematic conditions of African-American life:

> For black male entertainers, comedy has been a sort of sacred space for taking the profane to its most explicit level and freely exploring the peculiarities of navigating race and gender both in the larger society and within the black community. Thus it is not surprising that comedy operates as the safe popular space for black masculinity masquerading in black maternal feminine excess; it has proven extremely durable in the black imagination and popular entertainment generally. Imagining and culturally inhabiting the racial other has provided those empowered to use it to work out all kinds of cultural and psychic crises.
>
> What has not been as thoroughly investigated thus far is how becoming Big Mama in drag, for black men, is more than a matter of mindless entertainment, simple comedic fun and moneymaking. It enables black men to become feminine in a sense or to imagine occupying an otherness that is taboo and at least temporarily transgress or operate outside the social restraints imposed upon black masculinity.[82]

Making reference to popular comedy films like the Martin Lawrence vehicle *Big Momma's House* (2000) and the movies of Tyler Perry, in which the actor plays Mabel 'Madea' Simmons, a towering elderly matriarch with a sharp tongue – Dunn suggests that black men in drag enable the frank consideration of problematic issues in the African-American community. However, these representations are also disarming in their comedic lightheartedness, removing the intimidating menace that stereotypically looms over the public lives of black men in the USA. In *Keys to Our Heart*, Linzy doesn't simply exploit the subversive quality of drag in the spirit of Warhol; he also creates a similarly pornographic aesthetic that lampoons the form's iconic mix of titillation and boredom.[83] It is rather apparent that these films aim to be ridiculous, but also to leverage that quality as a means of social critique.

Like Warhol, Linzy rejects intellectualism and overt expressions of political activism. However, their respective satirical approaches enable a form of cultural critique so rooted in the comically absurd that it seems to provide refuge from the stoicism of identity politics. In a similar vein, Tyler Perry's Madea makes it somehow OK to speak openly about intolerance and to make politically confrontational declarations about intra-cultural responsibility, racism, and the self-defeating tendencies of black folk. In a sense, Madea advances a political point of view, while simultaneously defusing it with comedic outrageousness. It is a quality that we see in the moving images of both Warhol and Linzy: a calculated form of semiotic slipperiness that mixes the incendiary with the ridiculous.

Melody Set Me Free, Free At Last

Rejecting meaning, while pushing the boundaries of good taste (around the social mores of sexuality, race, and class) is all part of the joke. These qualities converge in Linzy's *Melody Set Me Free* (2007–2012), an episodic soap opera about the melodramatic goings-on surrounding an *American Idol*-style talent show. In *Melody* we see the return of KK Queen as she struggles to balance her business, the demands of family, various torrid relationships, and the threat of personal and professional rivals. Linzy plays KK Queen in drag once again, as well as the role of beleaguered daughter Patience. Filmed in a succession of dramatic episodes, Linzy produced a feature edit at over an hour and thirty minutes (of seasons 2 and 3), which pushed the artist's comic form into new terrain. Focusing on KK Queen's fledging and threatened record company, the feature edit feels more complete and follows a tangled narrative of double-crossing and deceit. The increased length brought additional texture and elevated the artist's creative gestures beyond the status of being a simple sight gag.

What stands out most prominently in the longer version is Linzy's wielding of blackness: a feature that, like most of his works, he spreads across both white and black performers. The racial malleability has a blunt comic force in the shorter videos, but it loses some of its humorous appeal in the feature and starts to feel more overtly critical. In a sense, *Melody* makes us aware of the construction and mobilization of stereotypes in the representational field – yet Linzy's use of stereotype also feels quite demeaning. In the main, Linzy

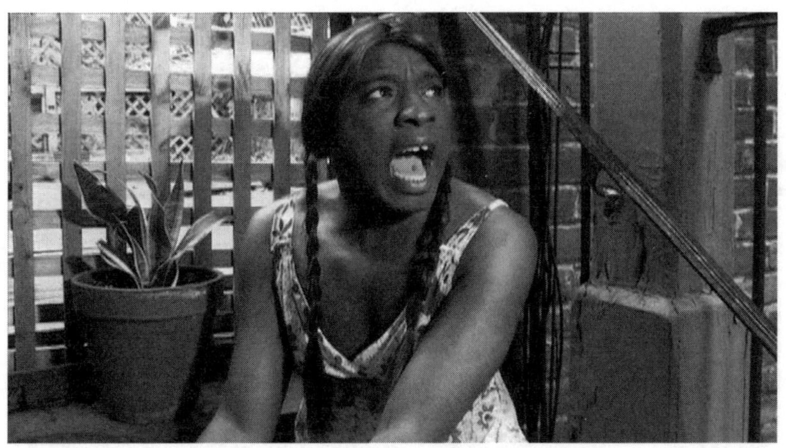

Figure 40 Kalup Linzy, *Melody Set Me Free* (2007). Video, 15:16 min, colour, sound [Production Still #1]. © Kalup Linzy/Electronic Arts Intermix, NY

sends-up the folly of the Southern black poor who, in his fictional narratives, balance the pressures of the elite and high-powered worlds of art and entertainment.

It is the visual and audible clash of contradictory elements that provides much of the humour – but in the end, this humour is enacted primarily at the expense of African-Americans. In *Melody*, the characters embody a range of troubling racial stereotypes: hustlers, greedy power-hungry bitches, shallow R&B singers and misogynistic rappers, whiny malcontents, or vicious sex-crazed alcoholics. Linzy's videos present heterosexual black men as lascivious dopes whose voices are modulated, giving them an unintelligent sounding drawl with which to spew their sexist banter. Interspersed throughout the piece are humorous performances that spoof African-American popular music genres like R&B and especially rap. The effect of white performers in racial minstrelsy and black men either in drag (or in positions of ridicule) begins to take its toll as the film progresses.

What is conveyed is a mix of queer and racial shame, masquerading as comedy, because we see queerness played for cheap laughs – and a kind dopey ineffectual blackness that, in its amusing ineptness, is something to giggle at and be playfully embodied by white performers. Hovering over this work is the question of why Linzy has decided

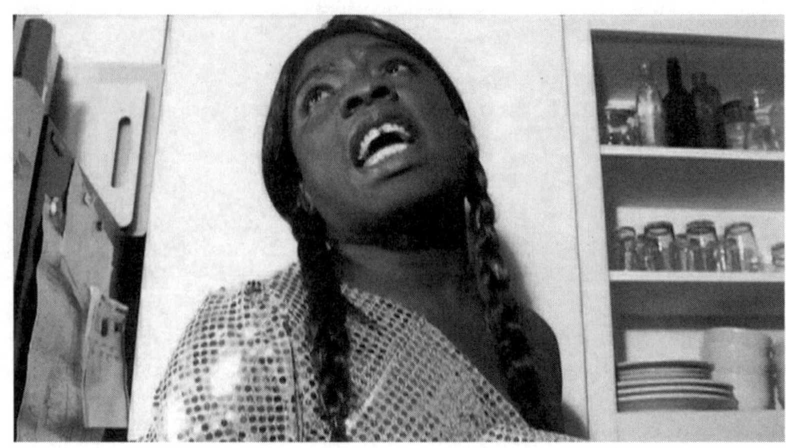

Figure 41 Kalup Linzy, *Melody Set Me Free* (2007). Video, 15:16 min, colour, sound [Production Still #2]. © Kalup Linzy/Electronic Arts Intermix, NY

to mock that which, for many in the black community, would be the most embarrassing depictions of black people. However, in the context of post-blackness, this creative approach epitomizes its defiant politics. In its post-ness, Linzy's art rejects racial fidelity and the long-standing demand placed upon African-American artists that they must only produce positive, affirming, and dignified images of black people. In fact, Linzy's work thrusts him rather forcefully beyond the limits of racial obligation, which can be as confining as the forces of racism and homophobia.

In *Melody*, like so many of his video pieces, Linzy explores the communal bonds and survivorship of African-American women, and the telephone is always the glue that keeps them connected. For scholar Tavia Nyong'o, it is the telephone wire that holds Linzy's social universe together. 'Often an intergenerational link between mothers and children, the telephone is also a promiscuous device: a device of promiscuity.'[84] The contentious and often fraught bonds of family are always complexly and intelligently interwoven into Linzy's stories, but he most effectively presents strong black women in the mode of those who populated his Southern rural upbringing. It is in this regard that Linzy's art is a tribute of sorts. Although his depictions are mocking, they grant a kind of grand presence to the lives of black women who exist almost completely in the shadows: the factory workers and the domestics – those for whom the *television* and the *telephone* are the most powerful means for them to 'connect, attach, and identify'.[85] As technologies, the TV and telephone were eerily present in both Warhol's celebrity fandom as well as in his diaristic accounts.

When discussing the artist's posthumously published text *The Andy Warhol Diaries* (1989), his former secretary Pat Hackettt recounts having daily phone conversations with Warhol about the gossipy events of the previous day. These humorous anecdotes were recorded and formed the basis for the 807-page book.[86] In fact, the most amusing dimension of the diaries are Warhol's recollections of gossip-laden phone calls between friends, in which cruel observations were gleefully shared. The tempestuous phone interactions between Linzy's heroines playfully recall Warhol's diary entries, which in their lengthy unfolding, narratively play out like the intrigue of a soap opera. Linzy's injection of blackness into the soap opera genre creates a strange affect where the racial other (the Southern black female viewer) can populate what are almost exclusively melodramatic narratives about mythic and sentimentalized American whiteness.[87] While blackness seems promiscuously spread across white performers, there is another more sinister ventriloquism at work, one where the deceitful acts of the gratuitously wealthy are reanimated by the spirits and desires of black female fandom.

In almost every dimension, Linzy's videos unearth the messiness of black culture, airing dirty laundry through narratives that are simultaneously vulgar and sexually explicit – yet they are even more troublesome in their vulgarizing of the Civil Rights movement's assimilationist and racially recuperative ambitions. However, in their defiance of this legacy, Linzy's comic stories are narratives of survival and transcendence – they are satirical meditations on the plight of those who are both queerly and racially identified, yet they are also tributes to the resilience of African-American women. If we find the artist's images somewhat hard to swallow, it is because Linzy understands that our dignity as people is bound up in the form and expression of its representation. The mandate to create ennobled and recuperative images of blackness (that is demanded of African-American artists) is a restricting and racially confining framework that has never had a place for black queer subjectivities. In that sense, his production gestures towards something new, a post-black futurity, and a fantasy space for the dreams and longing of those on the margins of racial and sexual normativity. Pondering the complexity of Linzy's art recalls the famous and enduringly relevant passage from W.E.B. Du Bois' essay, 'Our Spiritual Strivings':

> The Negro is a sort of seventh son, born with a veil, and gifted with second-sight in this American world, – a world which yields him no self-consciousness, but only lets him see himself through the revelation of the other world. It is a peculiar sensation, this double-consciousness, this sense of always looking at one's self through the eyes of others, of measuring one's soul by the tape of a world that looks on in amused contempt and pity. One feels his two-ness, – an American, a Negro; two souls, two thoughts, two un-reconciled strivings; two warring ideals in one dark body, whose dogged strength alone keeps it from being torn asunder.[88]

These words have never been more pertinent than in our post-black era: a time when African-Americans are still struggling to achieve Du Bois' dreams of equality. But what has always been perverse about that dream is the troubling dance of refusal and acquiescence around acknowledging the lives and struggles of black queer subjectivities: a constituency waiting impatiently for reciprocity, equality, and dignity both from within and beyond the African-American community. There is something generative in Linzy's imaginative universe that oscillates between a dignified 'queer world-making'[89] and a refusal to look at one's self (to borrow the words of Du Bois) through the lens of another's amused contempt and pity. In the end, what we see is the creation of a black queer utopia that, in its enigmatic and satirical wielding of stereotype, fruitfully reimagines the ideological and representational logics of blackness beyond the limits of fetishism and fantasy.

In its overt and unapologetic queerness, Linzy's art – as misunderstood as it may be – is at the vanguard of the most radical traditions of African-American performativity. And in its resplendent and phantasmagoric excess is the imagining of an alternative universe where aberrant sexualities and the racially abject can rise above the ideological markers of dysfunction and despondence – that, in their stereotypical logics, confine black and queer subjects to a vexed social position defined by a condition of irrecoverable marginalia. Emerging from their rejection of this impossible condition, Linzy's creations (in their profane and bawdy naughtiness) demonstrate that within his world anything is possible – but more profoundly arises the revelation that in the logic of his post-black queerness, *we are all Kalup's churen.*

Notes

Introduction

1. K. Anthony Appiah, 'Identity, Authenticity, Survival: Multicultural Societies and Social Reproduction', in *Multiculturalism: Examining the Politics of Recognition*, ed. Amy Gutmann (Princeton: Princeton University Press, 1994), pp. 162–163.
2. Robert Farris Thompson, 'Afro Modernism', *Artforum International* (1991), p. 91. Also see: Nana Adusei-Poku, 'Iwishiwas-Post-Black Aesthetics, Post-Black or Post-Colonial?' in *Heimatkunde*, http://heimatkunde.boell.de/2012/12/18/iwishiwas-post-black-aesthetics-post-black-or-post-colonia. Viewed, 1 September 2014.
3. Thelma Golden, 'Post . . . ,' in *Freestyle* (New York: The Studio Museum in Harlem, 2001), p. 14.
4. Amelia Jones, 'Multiculturalism, Intersectionality, and "Post-Identity"', in *Seeing Differently: A History and Theory of Identification and the Visual Arts* (London: Routledge Press, 2012). Also see: Amelia Jones, 'The "Post-Black" Bomb', in *Tema Celeste 90* (March-April 2002), pp. 52–55.
5. Golden, p. 14.
6. Ibid., p. 14.
7. Thelma Golden, 'My Brother', in *Black Male: Representations of Masculinity in Contemporary American Art* (New York: Whitney Museum of American Art, 1994), p. 20.
8. Kobena Mercer and Isaac Julien, 'True Confessions', in *Black Male: Representations of Masculinity in Contemporary American Art* (New York: Whitney Museum of American Art, 1994), p. 196.
9. Mercer and Julien, p. 196.
10. Ibid., p. 196.

11. Ibid., p. 197.
12. Ibid., p. 198.
13. Angela Y. Davis, 'Black Nationalism: The Sixties and the Nineties', in *Black Popular Culture*, ed. Gina Dent and Michele Wallace (New York: Dia Centre for the Arts, 1992), p. 322.
14. To read more on black feminist critiques of the Civil Rights and Black Power movements, see: Gloria T. Hull's *But Some of Us Are Brave: All the Women Are White, All the Blacks Are Men: Black Women's Studies* (New York: The Feminist Press at CUNY, 1993); Michele Wallace's *Black Macho and the Myth of the Superwoman* (New York: Verso Classics, 1999); Lynn Olson's *Freedom's Daughters: The Unsung Heroines of the Civil Rights Movement from 1830 to 1970* (New York: Scribner, 2002); Elaine Brown's memoir *A Taste of Power: A Black Woman's Story* (New York: Anchor Books, 1993); bell hooks' *Ain't I a Woman: Black Women and Feminism* (New York: South End Press, 1999); Angela Y. Davis' *Angela Davis: An Autobiography* (International Publishers, 1989) and Bettye Collier-Thomas and V.P. Franklin's *Sisters in the Struggle: African-American Women in the Civil Rights-Black Power Movement* (New York: NYU Press, 2001).
15. bell hooks, 'An Aesthetic of Blackness: Strange and Oppositional', in *Lenox Avenue: A Journal of Interarts Inquiry*, Vol. 1 (1995) pp. 66–67.
16. Ibid., p. 68.
17. E. Patrick Johnson and Mae G. Hendersen, 'Introduction: Queering Black Studies/"Quaring" Queer Studies', in *Black Queer Studies: A Critical Anthology* (Durham: Duke University Press, 2005), p. 3.
18. Ibid., p. 3.
19. Ibid., p. 3.
20. Ibid., p. 4.
21. Ibid., p. 4.
22. Shawn Michelle Smith, 'The Art of Scientific Propaganda', in *Photography on the Colour Line* (Durham: Duke University Press, 2004), p. 43.
23. Ibid., p. 43. Also see: W.E.B. Du Bois, 'Criteria of Negro Art' (1926), in *W.E.B. Du Bois: Writings*, ed. Nathan Higgins (New York: Library of America, 1986), p. 999.
24. Also of note: Ytasha L. Womack, *Post Black: How a New Generation is Redefining African American Identity* (Chicago: Chicago Review Press, 2010).
25. Touré, 'Dedication', in *Who's Afraid of Post-Blackness?: What It Means To Be Black Now* (New York: Free Press, Simon & Schuster, Inc., 2011), p. v.
26. Touré, 'Forty Million Ways To Be Black', in *Who's Afraid of Post-Blackness?: What It Means To Be Black Now* (New York: Free Press, Simon & Schuster, Inc., 2011), p. 5.

27. Ibid., p. 7.
28. John Blake, 'Running Afoul of the Soul Patrol', in *The Chicago Tribune*, http://articles.chicagotribune.com/1992-04-06/news/9201310779_1_soul-patrol-black-african-american-students, 6 April 1992.
29. To read more about the relationship between post-blackness and notions of black authenticity, see the following: Derek Conrad Murray, 'Post post-black: some politically incorrect thoughts on the reception and contemplation of African-American Art', in *Art Journal*, Winter 2007, vol. 66, no. 4, pp. 112–4; Derek Conrad Murray and Soraya Murray, 'On Art and Contamination: Performing Authenticity in Global Art Practices', *Nka: Journal of Contemporary African Art 22/23* (Spring/Summer 2008): 88–93; Thelma Golden, 'Post . . . ', in *Freestyle*, Studio Museum in Harlem, 2001, pp. 14–15; Paul C. Taylor 'Post-Black, Old Black', in *African American Review*, Vol. 41 (Winter 2007), pp. 625–640; Richard Schur, 'Post-soul Aesthetics in Contemporary African American Art'. *African American Review*, Vol. 41 (Winter 2007), pp. 641–654; Darnell Moore, 'Post-racial Rhetorics and the Depoliticization of Blackness', in *Darkmatter: In the Ruins of Imperial Culture* 9.2, Centre for Cultural Studies Research, University of East London, 2013; Bertram D. Ashe, Crystal Anderson, Mark Anthony Neal, Evie Shockley, Alexander Weheliye. 'These – Are – The "Breaks": A Roundtable Discussion on Teaching the Post-Soul Aesthetic', in *African American Review*, Vol. 41, No. 4, Post-Soul Aesthetic (Winter, 2007), pp. 787–803.
30. Michael Eric Dyson, 'Tour(é)ing Blackness', in *Who's Afraid of Post-Blackness?: What It Means To Be Black Now* (New York: Free Press, Simon & Schuster, Inc., 2011), pp. xii–xiii.
31. Ibid., p. xv.
32. Touré, p. 8.
33. Randall Kennedy, *Sellout: The Politics of Racial Betrayal* (New York: Vintage Books, 2009). See also: Randall Kennedy, *Nigger: The Strange Career of a Troublesome Word* (New York: Vintage Books, 2003).
34. Ibid., p. 186.
35. Randall Kennedy, 'The Fallacy of Touré's Post-Blackness Theory', in *The Root*, http://www.theroot.com/articles/culture/2011/08/whos_afraid_of_postblackness_tours_postblackness_theory.html, 11 August 2011. Viewed, 5 September 2014, p. 1.
36. Ibid., p. 2.
37. Ibid., p. 3.
38. Cornel West, 'On Black Nationalism', in *The Cornel West Reader* (New York: Civitas Books, 1999), p. 522.
39. Ibid., p. 523.
40. Ibid., p. 522.

41. Ibid., p. 522.
42. Judith Butler, 'Gender is Burning: Questions of Appropriation and Subversion', in *Bodies That Matter: On the Discursive Limits of 'Sex'* (London: Routledge, 1993), p. 121.
43. Isaac Julien, 'Black is, Black Ain't: Notes on De-Essentializing Black Identities', in *Black Popular Culture*, ed. Gina Dent and Michele Wallace (Seattle: Bay Press, 1992), p. 258.
44. Ibid., p. 258.
45. E. Patrick Johnson, 'Manifest Faggotry: Queering Masculinity in African-American Culture', in *Appropriating Blackness: Performance and the Politics of Authenticity* (Durham: Duke University Press, 2003), p. 48.
46. Ibid., p. 48.
47. Ibid., p. 51.
48. Roderick A. Ferguson, 'Something Else to Be: *Sula*, *The Moynihan Report*, and the Negations of Black Lesbian Feminism', in *Aberrations in Black: Toward a Queer of Color Critique* (Minneapolis: University of Minnesota Press, 2004), p. 113.
49. Ibid., p. 115.
50. Johnson, p. 51. Also see: Marlon Riggs, 'Black Macho Revisited: Reflections of a SNAP!! Queen', in *Brother to Brother: New Writings by Black Gay Men*, ed. Essex Hemphill (Boston: Alyson Press, 1991), pp. 253–257.
51. Johnson, 'Manifest Faggotry,' p. 51.
52. Ibid., p. 51.
53. Ibid., p. 53. To read Cleaver's passage in its entirety, see: Eldridge Cleaver, *Soul on Ice* (New York: Laurel, 1968), p. 30. For more on the Cleaver/Baldwin rift, see: Lee Edelman, 'The Part for the W(h)ole: Baldwin, Homophobia, and the Fantasmatics of "Race"', in *Homographesis: Essays in Gay Literary and Cultural Theory* (New York: Routledge Press, 1994).
54. Ibid., p. 53.
55. Ibid., p. 53.
56. Touré, 'How to Build More Baracks,' in *Who's Afraid of Post-Blackness?: What It Means To Be Black Now* (New York: Free Press, Simon & Schuster, Inc., 2011), p. 178.
57. Ibid., pp. 180–181.
58. Barack Obama, *The Audacity of Hope: Thoughts on Reclaiming the American Dream* (New York: Crown Press, 2006), p. 231.
59. Tavia Nyong'o, 'Introduction: Antebellum Genealogies of the Hybrid Future', in *The Amalgamation Waltz: Race, Performance, and the Ruses of Memory* (Minneapolis: University of Minnesota Press, 2009), p. 1.
60. Stanley Crouch, 'What Obama Isn't: Black Like Me', in *Daily News*, http://www.nydailynews.com/archives/opinions/obama-isn-black-

race-article-1.585922, 2 November 2006, p. 1. Viewed, 7 September 2014.

61. Nyong'o, p. 2.
62. Crouch, p. 1.
63. E. Patrick Johnson, 'Blackness and Authenticity: What's Performance Got to Do with It?', in *Appropriating Blackness: Performance and the Politics of Authenticity* (Durham: Duke University Press, 2003), p. 6.
64. Henry Louis Gates, Jr., 'Who Designed the March on Washington', in *The African Americans: many Rivers to Cross*, w/ Henry Louis Gates, Jr., www.pbs.org, http://www.pbs.org/wnet/african-americans-many-rivers-to-cross/history/100-amazing-facts/who-designed-the-march-on-washington/. Viewed, 7 September 2014, p. 1.
65. Peter Dreier, 'Obama Awards Bayard Rustin the Presidential Medal of Freedom', in bill.moyers.com, http://billmoyers.com/2013/08/10/obama-awards-bayard-rustin-the-presidential-medal-of-freedom/, 10 August 2013. Viewed, 8 September 2014, p. 1.
66. Ibid., p. 1.
67. Ibid., p. 1.
68. For additional writings on the life and thoughts of Bayard Rustin, see: John D'Emilio, *Lost Prophet: The Life and Times of Bayard Rustin* (Chicago: University of Chicago Press, 2004); Devon W. Carbado, *Time on Two Crosses: The Collected Writings of Bayard Rustin* (New York: Cleis Press, 2003); Michael G. Long, *I Must Resist: Bayard Rustin's Life in Letters* (San Francisco: City Lights Publishers, 2012); Jervis Anderson, *Bayard Rustin: Troubles I've Seen: A Biography* (New York: HarperCollins, 1997).
69. Gates, Jr., p. 1. Also see: George Chauncey, Jr., and Lisa Kennedy, 'Time on Two Crosses: An Interview with Bayard Rustin', in *Village Voice*, 30 June 1987, pp. 27–28; Redvers Jeanmarie, 'An Interview with Bayard Rustin', *Other Countries: Black Gay Voices*, 1 (1988), pp. 3–16; John D'Emilio, 'Reading the Silences in a Gay Life: The Case of Bayard Rustin', in *The Seductions of Biography* (London: Routledge, 1996) pp. 59–68.
70. Touré, 'Keep It Real Is a Prison', in *Who's Afraid of Post-Blackness?: What It Means to Be Black Now* (New York: Free Press, Simon & Schuster, Inc., 2011), p. 42.
71. Rashid Johnson in conversation with Touré: Touré, 'Keep It Real Is a Prison', in *Who's Afraid of Post-Blackness?: What It Means to Be Black Now* (New York: Free Press, Simon & Schuster, Inc., 2011), p. 42.
72. Glenn Ligon in conversation with Touré: Touré, 'Keep It Real Is a Prison', in *Who's Afraid of Post-Blackness?: What It Means to Be Black Now* (New York: Free Press, Simon & Schuster, Inc., 2011), p. 25.

73. Thelma Golden, 'To Be Real', in *Black Romantic* (New York: The Studio Museum in Harlem, 2002), p. 14.
74. Ibid., p. 14.
75. Ibid., p. 14.
76. Paul Gilroy, *The Black Atlantic: Modernity and Double Consciousness* (Cambridge: Harvard University Press, 1995). See also: Brent Hayes Edwards, *The Practice of Diaspora: Literature, Translation, and the Rise of Black Internationalism* (Cambridge: Harvard University Press, 2003).
77. In this quotation, Ligon makes reference to the exhibition *Mirage: Enigmas of Race, Difference and Desire*, held at the Institute of Contemporary Arts (inIVA), London, 12 May–16 July 1995. See: David A. Bailey, and Kobena Mercer, *Mirage: Enigmas of Race, Difference and Desire* (London: ICA/inIVA, 1995).
78. Glenn Ligon. Huey Copeland, 'Post/Black/Atlantic: A Conversation with Thelma Golden and Glenn Ligon,' in *Afro-Modern: Journeys in the Black Atlantic*, eds. Tanya Barson, Peter Gorschlüter (Liverpool: Tate; 2009), p. 1.
79. Ibid., http://www.liv.ac.uk/media/livacuk/csis-2/blackatlantic/research/Copeland_text_defined.pdf, Viewed, September 8, 2014.
80. Cornel West, 'Christian Love and Heterosexism,' in *The Cornel West Reader* (New York: Civitas Books, 1999), p. 402.
81. Ibid., p. 403.
82. Ibid., p. 403.
83. Ibid., p. 403.
84. Ibid., p. 404.
85. Ibid., p. 405.
86. Marlon T. Riggs, 'Unleash the Queen,' in *Black Popular Culture*, ed. Gina Dent and Michele Wallace (Seattle: Bay Press, 1992), p. 103.
87. Ibid., pp. 102–103.
88. Ibid., p. 104.

1 Looking for Ligon: Towards an Aesthetic Theory of Blackness

1. Ralph Ellison, *Invisible Man* (New York: Vintage International, 1995), p. 3.
2. Susanna Newbury, 'Glenn Ligon's America', in *Nka: Journal of Contemporary African Art*, Number 31, Fall 2012, pp. 36–45.
3. Okwui Enwezor, 'Text, Subtext, and Intertext: Painting Language and Signifying in the Work of Glenn Ligon', in Rothkopf, *Glenn Ligon: AMERICA* (New York: Whitney Museum of American Art, 2011), p. 60.

4. Ibid., p. 51.
5. Ibid., p. 51.
6. Robert Hughes, 'The Whitney Biennial: A Fiesta of Whining', in *Time Magazine*, Monday, 22 March 1993.
7. For critical writing on Mapplethorpe's *The Black Book* and the problem of racial fetishism, see: Kobena Mercer, 'Reading Racial Fetishism: The Photographs of Robert Mapplethorpe', in *Welcome to the Jungle: New Positions in Black Cultural Studies* (London: Routledge, 1994), pp. 171–220; David Marriott, 'Murderous Appetites: Photography and Fantasy', in *On Black Men* (New York: Columbia University Press, 2000), pp. 23–42.
8. Thelma Golden, 'What's White . . . ?' in *1993 Whitney Biennial* (New York: Whitney Museum of American Art, 1993), p. 30.
9. For writing on the intersection of racial identity, contemporary art and ethnography, see: Hal Foster, 'The Artist as Ethnographer', in *The Return of the Real* (Cambridge: The MIT Press, 1996), pp. 171–204. Also see: Derek Conrad Murray and Soraya Murray, 'Uneasy Bedfellows: Canonical Art Theory and the Politics of Identity', in *Art Journal*, Vol. 65, no. 1, Spring 2006, pp. 22–39; Amelia Jones, 'Multiculturalism, Intersectionality, and "Post-Identity"', in *Seeing Differently: A History and Theory of Identification and the Visual Arts* (London: Routledge, 2012), pp. 117–169.
10. Enwezor, *AMERICA*, p. 52.
11. Ibid., p. 52.
12. Julia Kristeva, *Powers of Horror: An Essay on Abjection* (New York: Columbia University Press, 1982).
13. Yve-Alain Bois and Rosalind E. Krauss, 'The Use Value of "Formless', in *Formless: A User's Guide* (New York: Zone Books, 1997), pp. 13–42.
14. Kristeva, *Powers of Horror*, p. 69.
15. For writings on Kristeva's abjection and the visual arts, see: Hal Foster, 'Obscene, Abject, Traumatic', in *October*, #78 (Fall 1996); Hal Foster, 'Whatever Happened to Postmodernism?', in *The Return of the Real: The Avant-Garde at the End of the Century* (Cambridge: The MIT Press, 1996); Hal Foster, 'The Politics of the Signifier', in *October* #66 (Fall 1993); Derek Conrad Murray and Soraya Murray, 'Uneasy Bedfellows: Canonical Art Theory and the Politics of Identity', in *Art Journal*, Vol. 65, no. 1, Spring 2006, pp. 22–39.
16. Bois and Krauss, p. 15.
17. Ibid., p. 18.
18. The art critic Clement Greenberg, in his influential essay 'Modernist Painting', argued that works of art should endeavour to achieve a formal

autonomy and uniqueness that depends upon the specificity of the chosen medium. According to Greenberg, the progressive modernist is called upon to eliminate all inessential elements. In his modernist value system, each art searches for 'purity' and absolute autonomy not only from other advanced art forms – but also from popular or mass culture. See: Clement Greenberg, 'Avant-Garde and Kitsch', in *Partisan Review* 6 (Fall 1939), pp. 34–49; Clement Greenberg, 'Modernist Painting', in *The Collected Essays and Criticism, Volume 4: Modernism with a Vengeance, 1957–1969* (Chicago: University of Chicago Press, 1995), pp. 85–93.

19. Enwezor, *AMERICA*, p. 52.
20. Ibid., p. 52.
21. Ibid., p. 54.
22. Cornel West, 'On Black Nationalism', in *The Cornel West Reader* (New York: Civitas Books, 1999), p. 522.
23. Thelma Golden, 'My Brother', in *Black Male: Representations of Masculinity in Contemporary American Art* (New York: Whitney Museum of American Art, 1994), p. 34.
24. For critical writing on the subject of African-American satire, see: Darryl Dickson-Carr, 'Introduction', in *African-American Satire* (Columbia: University of Missouri Press, 2001); Derek C. Maus and James J. Donahue, *Post-Soul Satire: Black Identity After Civil Rights* (Jackson: University of Mississippi Press, 2014); Derek Conrad Murray, 'Post-Black Art and the Resurrection of African-American Satire', in *Post-Soul Satire: Black Identity After Civil Rights* (Jackson: University of Mississippi Press, 2014).
25. Thelma Golden, 'My Brother', p. 34.
26. Darby English, 'Beyond Black Representational Space', in *How to See A Work of Art In Total Darkness* (Cambridge: MIT Press, 2007), p. 33.
27. Ibid., p. 33.
28. For an in depth discussion of Clement Greenberg's formalism relative to the politics of identity, see: Ann Eden Gibson's *Abstract Expressionism: Other Politics* (New Haven: Yale University Press, 1997); Lisa Bloom, 'Ghosts of Ethnicity: Rethinking Art Discourses of the 1940s and 1980s', in *With Other Eyes: Looking at Race and Gender in Visual Culture*, ed. Lisa Bloom (Minneapolis: University of Minnesota Press, 1999); Clement Greenberg, 'Self-hatred and Jewish Chauvinism: Some Reflections on "Positive Jewishness"', *Commentary* (November 1950). Reprinted in *Clement Greenberg, The Collected Essay and Criticism: Affirmations and Refusals, 1950–1956* (Chicago: The University of Chicago Press, 1993); Florence Rubenfeld, 'Highbrow and Jewishness: Twin Poles of Identity', in *Clement Greenberg: A Life* (Minneapolis: University of Minnesota Press,

1997) and Louis Kaplan, 'Reframing Self-Criticism: Clement Greenberg's "Modernist Painting" in Light of Jewish Identity', in *Jewish Identity in Modern Art History*, ed. Catherine M. Soussloff (Berkeley: University of California Press, 1999), pp. 180–199.

29. Homi Bhabha, '"The Other Question" Stereotype, discrimination and the Discourse of Colonialism', in *The Location of Culture* (London: Routledge Press, 1994), p. 94.
30. Ibid., p. 114.
31. Stuart Hall, 'The Spectacle of the Other', in *Representation: Cultural Representation and Signifying Practices*, ed. Stuart Hall (London: Sage Publications, 1997), p. 258.
32. Henry Louis Gates, Jr., 'Preface', in *Black Male: Representations of Masculinity in Contemporary American Art* (New York: Whitney Museum of American Art, 1994), p. 13.
33. Holland Cotter, 'Black and White, but Never Simple,' in *The New York Times*, http://www.nytimes.com/2007/10/12/arts/design/12walk.html?ref=karawalker&_r=3&, 12 October 2007; Lucy McKeon, 'The Controversies of Kara Walker', in *Hyperallergic.com*, http://hyperallergic.com/67125/the-controversies-of-kara-walker/, 19 March 2013.
34. Michael D. Harris, 'The Language of Appropriation: Fantasies and Fallacies', in *Coloured Pictures: Race & Visual Representation* (Chapel Hill: The University of North Carolina Press, 2003), p. 215.
35. Ibid., p. 202.
36. In this passage, I am making reference to Polish/British (given nationality in 1886) novelist Joseph Conrad's 1899 novella *Heart of Darkness*. In the novella, Conrad metaphorically characterizes the continent of Africa as a dystopia that is devoid of logic and reason (in the darkness), even though he is simultaneously critical of the colonial project. See: Joseph Conrad, *Heart of Darkness* (New York: W.W. Norton & Company, Inc., 1971). Conrad's novella has been influential on the work of revisionist scholars endeavoring to contest ideologically problematic representations of Africa. See art historian Olu Oguibe's canonical essay, 'In the Heart of Darkness', in *The Culture Game* (Minneapolis: University of Minnesota Press, 2004).
37. bell hooks, 'An Aesthetic of Blackness – Strange and Oppositional', in *Lenox Avenue: A Journal of Interarts*, Vol. 1 (1995), p. 66.
38. Ibid., p. 67.
39. Ibid., p. 67.
40. Ibid., p. 68.
41. Ibid., p. 68.
42. Ibid., p. 69.
43. Ibid., p. 69.

44. Huey Copeland in conversation with Glenn Ligon and Thelma Golden, 'Post/Black/Atlantic: A Conversation with Thelma Golden and Glenn Ligon', in *Afro Modern: Journeys in the Black Atlantic*, Barson T, Gorschlüter P, eds (Liverpool: Tate, 2010), pp. 76–81.
45. Ibid., p. 4.
46. Ibid., p. 5.
47. Lauren DeLand, 'Black Skin, Black Masks: The Citational Self in the Work of Glenn Ligon', in *Criticism*, Vol. 54, No. 4, Fall 2012, p. 507.
48. Ibid., p. 509.
49. Ibid., p. 509.
50. Greg Tate, 'Nigs R Us, or How Blackfolk Became Fetish Objects', in *Everything But the Burden: What White People are Taking From Black Culture* (New York: Broadway Books, 2003), p. 4.
51. Ibid., p. 4.
52. Karl Marx, 'The Commodity', in *Capital: Volume 1: A Critique of Political Economy* (New York: Penguin Classics, 1992), pp. 125–156.
53. Alessandra Raengo, 'Optic Black: Blackness as Phantasmagoria,' in Akil Houston, ed., *Beyond Blackface: Africana Images in the US Media* (Kendall Hunt Publishing, 3rd edition, 2010), p. 159.
54. Ibid. Raengo cites W. T. Lhamon as the originator of the term 'optic black'. See W. T. Lhamon, 'Optic Black: Naturalizing the Refusal to Fit', in Harry J. Elam, Jr., and Kennell Jackson, eds., *Black Cultural Traffic: Crossroads in Global Performance and Culture* (Ann Arbor: University of Minnesota Press, 2005), pp. 111–140.
55. Bill Brown, 'Reification, Reanimation, and the American Uncanny', in *Critical Inquiry* 32 (Winter 2006), p. 185.
56. For an in-depth critical analysis of black performance history, see: Arthur Knight, *Disintegrating the Musical: Black Performance and American Musical Film* (Durham: Duke University Press, 2002).
57. Raengo, 'Optic Black', p. 160.
58. Ibid., p. 160.
59. Brown, p. 183.
60. Raengo, p. 160.
61. Harry J. Elam, Jr., 'Change Clothes and Go: A Postscript to Postblackness', in *Black Cultural Traffic: Crossroads in Global Performance and Popular Culture*, ed. Harry J. Elam Jr. and Jackson Kennell (Ann Arbor: The University of Michigan Press, 2005), p. 386.
62. Ibid., p. 386.
63. Kerry James Marshall, 'Notes on Career and Work', in *Kerry James Marshall* (New York: Harry N. Abrams, Inc., Publishers, 2000), p. 117.
64. Ibid., p. 118.

65. Ibid., p. 117.
66. Ibid., p. 117.
67. Ibid., p. 117.
68. Enwezor, *AMERICA*, p. 54.
69. Ibid., p. 60.
70. Thelma Golden, 'A Conversation between Glenn Ligon and Thelma Golden', in Rothkopf, *Glenn Ligon: AMERICA*, p. 244.
71. Scott Rothkopf, 'Glenn Ligon: AMERICA', in *Glenn Ligon: AMERICA* (New York: Whitney Museum of American Art, 2011), p. 40.
72. Ibid., p. 40.
73. Carter Ratcliff, 'Introduction', in *Andy Warhol* (New York: Abbeville Press, 1983), p. 8.
74. Ibid., p. 8.
75. Ibid., p. 28.
76. Ibid., p. 29.
77. Ibid., p. 29.
78. DeLand, 'Black Skin, Black Masks,' p. 510.
79. Ibid., p. 510.
80. Ibid., p. 510.
81. Ibid., p. 515.

2 Kehinde Wiley's Black Utopia: Racial Fetishism and the Queering of Masculinity

1. Richard Dyer, 'Seen to be believed: some problems in the representation of gay people as typical', in *The Matter of Images: Essays on Representation* (London: Routledge, 1993), p. 19.
2. Slavoj Žižek, *The Perverts Guide to Ideology*, Dir. Sophie Fiennes, Perf. Slavoj Žižek (Zeitgeist Films, 2012).
3. Christopher Beam, 'Outsource to China,' in *NY Magazine*, http://nymag.com/arts/art/rules/kehinde-wiley-2012–4/, 22 April 2012. Viewed, 24 July 2014, p. 2.
4. Ibid., p. 2.
5. Ibid., p. 2.
6. Ibid., p. 2.
7. Ibid., p. 2.
8. Kobena Mercer, 'Busy in the Ruins of Wretched Phantasia', in *Mirage: Enigmas of Race, Difference and Desire* (London: Institute of Contemporary Arts, ICA/inIVA, 1995), p. 20.
9. Ibid., p. 20.
10. Kerry James Marshall, 'Notes on Career and Work', in *Kerry James Marshall* (New York: Harry N. Abrams, Inc., Publishers, 2000), p. 119.

11. Kehinde Wiley and Peter Halley, 'A Conversation with Kehinde Wiley and Peter Halley', in *Kehinde Wiley* (New York: Rizzoli, 2011), p. 162.
12. Terry Sultan, 'This Is the Way We Live', in *Kerry James Marshall* (New York: Harry N. Abrams, Inc., Publishers, 2000), p. 16.
13. Wiley, 'A Conversation with Kehinde Wiley,' p. 162.
14. Cornel West, 'The New Cultural Politics of Difference', in *The Cultural Studies Reader*, Second Edition, ed. Simon During (London: Routledge, 1993), p. 262.
15. Ibid., p. 262.
16. Ibid., p. 263.
17. Wiley, p. 162.
18. Beam, 'Outsource to China,' p. 1.
19. Ibid., p. 1.
20. Ibid., p. 1.
21. Ibid., p. 1.
22. Clement Greenberg, 'Modernist Painting', in *Clement Greenberg: The Collected Essays and Criticism, Modernism with a Vengeance, 1957–1969, Vol. 4* (Chicago: The University of Chicago Press, 1993), p. 93.
23. Ibid., p. 86.
24. Ibid., p. 86.
25. Kobena Mercer, *Welcome to the Jungle: New Positions in Black Cultural Studies* (London: Routledge, 1994), p. 137.
26. bell hooks, 'Feminism Inside: Toward a Black Body Politic', in *Black Male: Representations of Masculinity in Contemporary American Art* (New York: Whitney Museum of American Art, 1994), p. 136.
27. Ibid., p. 138.
28. Ibid., p. 138.
29. Thelma Golden, 'My Brother', in *Black Male: Representations of Masculinity in Contemporary American Art* (New York: Whitney Museum of American Art, 1994), p. 33.
30. Ibid., p. 33.
31. Ibid., p. 33.
32. hooks, 'Feminism Inside,' p. 140.
33. Michele Wallace and Gina Dent, *Black Popular Culture*, ed. Gina Dent (Seattle: Bay Press, 1992).
34. For additional writings on queer sexual politics, see: Judith Halberstam, *In a Queer Time & Place: Transgender Bodies, Subcultural Lives* (New York: New York University Press, 2005); Judith Halberstam, *The Queer Art of Failure* (Durham: Duke University Press, 2011); Sara Ahmed, *Queer Phenomenology: Orientations, Objects, Others* (Durham: Duke University Press, 2006); Lauren Berlant and Lee Edelman, *Sex, or the Unbearable*

(Durham: Duke University Press, 2014); Lee Edelman, *No Future: Queer Theory and the Death Drive* (Durham: Duke University Press, 2004).

35. E. Patrick Johnson, 'Introduction: Queering Black Studies/"Quaring" Queer Studies' in *Black Queer Studies: A Critical Anthology* (Durham: Duke University Press, 2005), p. 3.
36. Ibid., p. 3.
37. Ibid., p. 4.
38. Roderick A. Ferguson, 'Queer of Colour Critique, Historical Materialism and Canonical Sociology', in *Aberrations in Black: Toward a Queer of Colour Critique* (Minneapolis: University of Minnesota Press, 2004), p. 3.
39. Aliyyah I. Abdur-Rahman, 'Against the Closet: Racial Logic and the Bodily Basis/Biases of Sexual Identity', in *Against the Closet: Black Political Longing and the Erotics of Race* (Durham: Duke University Press, 2012), p. 3.
40. For critical writing that explores the relation between homosexuality, race, censorship and AIDS activism in contemporary art and popular visual representation, see: José Esteban Muñoz, *Cruising Utopia: The Then and There of Queer Futurity* (New York: New York University Press, 2009); José Esteban Muñoz, *Disidentifications: Queers of Colour and the Performance of Politics* (Minneapolis: University of Minnesota Press, 1999); Richard Meyer, *Outlaw Representation: Censorship and Homosexuality in Twentieth-Century American Art* (New York: Beacon Press, 2004); Catherine Lord and Richard Meyer, *Art and Queer Culture* (London: Phaidon Press, 2013); Christopher Reed, *Art and Homosexuality: A History of Ideas* (Oxford: Oxford University Press, 2011); Harmony Hammond, *Lesbian Art in America* (New York: Rizzoli Press, 2000); Amelia Jones, *Seeing Differently: A History and Theory of Identification and the Visual Arts* (London: Routledge Press, 2012); Douglas Crimp, *AIDS: Cultural Analysis/Cultural Activism* (Cambridge: The MIT Press, 1988).
41. Henry Louis Gates, 'The Black Man's Burden', in *Black Popular Culture*, ed. Gina Dent (Seattle: Bay Press, 1992), p. 79. *Looking For Langston*'s queer appropriation of the celebrated African-American poet generated controversy. See: Manthia Diawara, 'The Absent One: The Avant-Garde and the Black Imaginary in *Looking for Langston*', *Wide Angle* 13, no. 3/4 (July–October 1991): 96–109; Roy Grundmann, 'Black Nationhood and the Rest in the West: An Interview with Isaac Julien', *Cineaste* 21, 1/2 (1995): pp. 28–31.
42. Ibid., p. 79.
43. Ibid., p. 79.
44. Ibid., p. 80.

45. Stuart Hall, 'The Spectacle of the "Other"', in *Representation: Cultural Representation and Signifying Practices* (London: Sage Publications, 1997), p. 262.
46. Ibid., p. 262; also see: Kobena Mercer, 'Black Masculinity and the Sexual Politics of Race', in *Welcome to the Jungle: New Positions in Black Cultural Studies* (London: Routledge, 1994), pp. 138–138.
47. Kobena Mercer, 'Black Masculinity and the Sexual Politics of Race', in *Welcome to the Jungle: New Positions in Black Cultural Studies* (London: Routledge, 1994), p. 133.
48. Ibid., p. 133.
49. Ibid., p. 133.
50. Yomi Abiola, 'Jonte Demarcus Moaning,' in *Vogue* magazine, http://www.vogue.it/en/vogue-black/the-black-blog/2013/06/jonte-demarcus-moaning#ad-image281271 http://www.vogue.it/en/vogue-black/the-black-blog/2013/06/jonte-demarcus-moaning#ad-image 281271. 25 June 2013. Viewed, 24 July 2014.
51. Alex Hawgod, 'Michael David Quattlebaum, Jr.', in *Interview Magazine*, http://www.interviewmagazine.com/culture/michael-david-quattlebaum-jr/#_. Viewed, 24 July 2014.
52. Sewell Chan, 'Financial Crisis Was Avoidable, Inquiry Finds', in *The New York Times*, http://www.nytimes.com/2011/01/26/business/economy/26inquiry.html?_r=0, 25 January 2011. Viewed, 29 July 2014.
53. Derek Conrad Murray, 'Kehinde Wiley: Splendid Bodies', in *Nka: Journal of Contemporary African Art*, #21 (Fall 2007), p. 92.
54. Beam, 'Outsource to China,' p. 2.
55. Wiley and Halley, p. 164.
56. Phillip Brian Harper, 'Walk-On Parts and Speaking Subjects: Screen Representations of Black Gay Men', in *Black Male: Representations of Masculinity in Contemporary American Art* (New York: Whitney Museum of American Art, 1994), p. 141.
57. Harper, p. 141.
58. Jack Fritscher, 'White Art, Black Men: Racism is Essentially Sex', in *Mapplethorpe: Assault with a Deadly Camera* (New York: Hastings House, 1994), p. 207.
59. Ibid., p. 207.
60. For critical responses to William Friedkin's *Cruising*, see: Vito Russo, *The Celluloid Closet: Homosexuality in the Movies* (New York: Harper & Row Publishers, 1985); Thomas Waugh, *The Fruit Machine: Twenty Years of Writing on Queer Cinema* (Durham: Duke University Press, 2000); Ellis Hanson, *Out Takes: Essays on Queer Theory and Film* (Durham: Duke University Press, 1999); David Greven, *Psycho Sexual: Male Desire in*

Hitchcock, De Palma, Scorsese, and Friedkin (Austin: University of Texas Press, 2013).

61. David Greven, *Psycho Sexual: Male Desire in Hitchcock, De Palma, Scorsese, and Friedkin* (Austin: University of Texas Press, 2013), p. 18.
62. Ibid., p. 18.
63. Fritscher, 'White Art, Black Men,' p. 207.
64. Ibid., p. 251.
65. Ibid., p. 251.
66. Ibid., p. 279.
67. Ibid., p. 284.
68. Mercer, *Welcome to the Jungle*, p. 142.
69. Ibid., p. 132.
70. Ibdi., p. 132.
71. Ibid., p. 132.
72. Ibid., p. 132.
73. Kehinde Wiley, 'Forty Million Ways to Be Black', in *Who's Afraid of Post-Blackness?: What It Means to Be Black Now* (New York: Free Press, 2011), p. 8.
74. Kobena Mercer, 'Reading Racial Fetishism: The Photographs of Robert Mapplethorpe', in *Welcome to the Jungle: New Positions in Black Cultural Studies* (London: Routledge, 1994), p. 173. See also Mercer's revised critical position on Mapplethorpe's *The Black Book* series: Kobena Mercer, 'Skin Head Sex Thing: Racial Difference and the Homoerotic Imaginary', in *The Masculinity Studies Reader*, edited by Rachel Adams and David Savran (Wiley-Blackwell Press, 2002), pp. 188–200.
75. Ibid., p. 173.
76. Ibid., p. 174.
77. Ibid., p. 176.

3 Loving Aberrance: Mickalene Thomas and the Queering of Black Female Desire

1. Daphne Brooks, 'Introduction', in *Bodies in Dissent: Spectacular Performances of Race and Freedom, 1850–1919* (Durham: Duke University Press, 2006), p. 7.
2. bell hooks, 'Facing Difference: The Black Female Body', in *Art on My Mind: Visual Politics* (New York: The New Press, 1995), p. 96.
3. Griselda Pollock, 'About Canons and Culture Wars', in *Differencing the Canon: Feminism and the Writing of Art's Histories* (London: Routledge Press, 1999), p. 4.
4. Ibid., p. 5.

5. To read more about Linda Nochlin's uniquely revisionist approach to art historical scholarship, see: Linda Nochlin, *Women, Art and Power and Other Essays* (New York: Icon Editions, 1989); Linda Nochlin, *Representing Women* (New York: Thames & Hudson, 1999); Linda Nochlin, *The Politics of Vision: Essays on Nineteenth-Century Art and Society* (Westview Press, 1991) and Linda Nochlin, *The Body in Pieces: The Fragment as a Metaphor of Modernity* (New York: Thames & Hudson, 2001).
6. Edward Said, *Orientalism* (New York: Vintage Book, 1979).
7. Griselda Pollock, 'Feminist Mythologies and Missing Mothers', in *Differencing the Canon: Feminism and the Writing of Art's Histories* (London: Routledge Press, 1999), p. 135.
8. Ibid., p. 135.
9. Nicole Fleetwood, 'Excess Flesh: Black Women Performing Hypervisibility', in *Troubling Vision: Performance, Visuality, and Blackness* (Chicago: University of Chicago Press, 2011), p. 105.
10. Donald Kuspit, 'Seminal Entropy: The Paradox of Modern Art', in *The End of Art* (Cambridge: Cambridge University Press, 2004), p. 71.
11. Ibid., pp. 71–73.
12. Derek Conrad Murray and Soraya Murray, 'Uneasy Bedfellows: Canonical Art Theory and the Politics of Identity', in *Art Journal*, Vol. 65, no. 1 (Spring 2006), p. 36.
13. Murray and Murray, p. 37. Also see: Rosalind Krauss et al., 'The Politics of the Signifier,' in *October* 66 (Fall 1993), p. 3.
14. Hal Foster, 'Obscene, Abject, Traumatic', in *Cindy Sherman: October Files* (Cambridge: The MIT Press, 2006), p. 186.
15. Ibid., p. 187.
16. Fleetwood, 'Excess Flesh,' p. 105.
17. Deborah Willis, 'Introduction', in *Posing Beauty: African-American Images 1980s to the Present* (New York: W.W. Norton & Company, 2009), p. xiii.
18. Ibid., p. xiv.
19. Albert Boime, *The Art of Exclusion: Representing Blacks in the Nineteenth Century* (Washington: Smithsonian Institution Press, 1990).
20. Ibid., pp. 91–92.
21. Ibid., p. 98.
22. Ibid., p. 20.
23. Denise Murrell, 'The Anterior as Muse: Recent Paintings by Mickalene Thomas', in *Mickalene Thomas: Origin of the Universe* (Santa Monica: Santa Monica Museum of Art, 2012), p. 21.
24. Griselda Pollock, 'A Tale of Three Women: Seeing in the Dark, Seeing Double, at Least, with Manet', in *Differencing the Canon: Feminism and the Writing of Art's Histories* (London: Routledge Press, 1999), p. 279.

25. Judith Wilson, 'Getting Down to Get Over: Romare Bearden's Use of Pornography and the Problem of the Black Female Body in Afro-U.S. Art', in *Black Popular Culture* (Seattle: Bay Press, 1992), p. 112.
26. Ibid., p. 114.
27. Ibid., p. 113.
28. Ibid., p. 113.
29. Ibid., p. 113.
30. Ibid., p. 118.
31. Mickalene Thomas and Lisa Melandri, 'Points of Origin: An Interview with Mickalene Thomas', in *Mickalene Thomas: Origin of the Universe* (Santa Monica: Santa Monica Museum of Art, 2012), pp. 37–38.
32. Amelia Jones, 'Feminism, Incorporated: Reading "Postfeminism" in an Anti-Feminist Age', in *Afterimage*, v. 20, no. 5 (Rochester, NY, December 1992), p. 315.
33. George Baker, 'Photography's Expanded Field', in *October* 114, (Fall 2005), p. 121.
34. Laura Mulvey, 'A Phantasmagoria of the Female Body', in *Cindy Sherman* (Paris: Editions Jeu de Palme, 2006), p. 287.
35. Jones, 'Feminism, Incorporated,' p. 315.
36. Mulvey, 'A Phantasmagoria of the Female Body,' p. 288.
37. Jones, 'Feminism, Incorporated,' p. 315.
38. The connection between photography and colonialism, as well as the link between the exoticization of women and people of colour in relation to imperial expansion has been well explored. See: Malek Alloula, *The Colonial Harem* (Minneapolis: University of Minnesota Press, 1986); Eric Breitbart, *A World On Display: Photographs from the St. Louis World's Fair, 1904* (Albuquerque: University of New Mexico Press, 1997); Shawn Michelle Smith, *Photography on the Colour Line: W.E.B. Du Bois, Race, and Visual Culture* (Durham & London: Duke University Press, 2004).
39. Kellie Jones, '(Un)Seen & Overheard: Pictures by Lorna Simpson', in *Lorna Simpson* (London: Phaidon Press, 2002), p. 28.
40. Ibid., p. 28.
41. Carrie Mae *Weems' Kitchen Table Series* (1990) was inspired by Laura Mulvey's canonical essay 'Visual Pleasure and Narrative Cinema' (originally published in 1975), which explores, from a feminist perspective, the representation of women in the history of cinema. See: Laura Mulvey, 'Visual Pleasure and Narrative Cinema', in *Visual and Other Pleasures* (New York: Palgrave Macmillan, 2009), pp. 14–30.
42. Evelynn Hammonds, 'Toward a Genealogy of Black Female Sexuality: The Problematic of Science', in *Feminist Genealogies, Colonial Legacies, Democratic Futures*, ed. M. Jacqui Alexander and Chandra Talpade Mohanty (New York: Routledge Press, 1997), p. 171.

43. Ibid., p. 171.
44. Patricia Hill Collins, 'The Sexual Politics of Womanhood', in *Black Feminist Thought* (London: Routledge Press, 2000), p. 134.
45. Ibid., p. 134.
46. Ibid., p. 135.
47. Ibid., p. 135.
48. Ibid., p. 135.
49. Ibid., p. 135.
50. Ibid., p. 135.
51. Laura Mulvey, 'Visual Pleasure and Narrative Cinema', in *Visual and Other Pleasures* (New York: Palgrave Macmillan, 2009), pp. 19–25.
52. bell hooks, 'The Politics of Radical Black Subjectivity', in *Yearning: Race, Gender, and Cultural Politics* (Boston: South End Press, 1990), p. 16.
53. Ibid., p. 16.
54. Ibid., p. 17.
55. bell hooks, 'Representations: Feminism and Black Masculinity', in *Yearning: Race, Gender, and Cultural Politics* (Boston: South End Press, 1990), p. 66.
56. hooks, p. 66.
57. Slavoj Žižek, 'Tolerance as an Ideological Category', in *Critical Inquiry* Vol. 34, No. 4 (Summer 2008), p. 660.
58. Ibid., p. 660.
59. Mulvey, 'Visual Pleasure and Narrative Cinema,' p. 285.
60. Ibid., p. 286.
61. Ibid., p. 286.
62. Ibid., p. 286.
63. hooks, 'Black Subjectivity', p. 21.
64. Griselda Pollock, *Differencing the Canon: Feminism and the Writing of Art's Histories* (London: Routledge Press, 1999).
65. Black female contributions to art history have been a consistent presence within the field, but they have also been relegated to a marginal position, with notable exceptions being the scholarship of Deborah Willis who in 2000 was awarded the coveted MacArthur Fellowship and more recently the celebrated scholarly and curatorial efforts of Columbia University Professor Kellie Jones, specifically her celebrated exhibition and book *Now Dig This!: Art and Black Los Angeles* (New York: Prestel, 2011).
66. Some notable black female contributions to art history include: Samella Lewis, *African-American Art and Artists* (Berkeley: University of California Press, 2003); Lowery Stokes Sims, et al, *Betye Saar: Extending the Frozen Moment* (Berkeley: University of California Press, 2005); Kellie Jones, *Now Dig This!: Art and Black Los Angeles* (New York: Prestel, 2011);

Cherise Smith, *Enacting Others: Politics of Identity in Eleanore Antin, Nikki S. Lee, Adrian Piper, and Anna Deavere Smith* (Durham: Duke University Press, 2011); Michele Wallace, 'Why Are There No Great Black Artists? The Problem of Visuality in African-American Culture,' in *Michele Wallace: Dark Designs & Visual Culture* (Durham: Duke University Press, 2004), pp. 184–194; bell hooks, *Art on My Mind* (New York: The New Press, 1994); Valerie Cassell Oliver, *Double Consciousness: Black Conceptual Art Since 1970* (Houston: Museum of Contemporary Art Houston, 2005); Gwendolyn DuBois Shaw, *Seeing the Unspeakable: The Art of Kara Walker* (Durham: Duke University Press, 2004); Sharon F. Patton, *African-American Art* (Oxford: Oxford University Press, 1998); Kymberly N. Pinder, *Race-ing Art History: Critical Readings in Race and Art History* (London: Routledge Press, 2002); Jacqueline Francis, *Making Race: Modernism and 'Radical Art' in America* (Seattle: University of Washington Press, 2012); Deborah Willis, *Black: A Celebration of a Culture* (New York: Hylas Publishing, 2003); Judith Wilson et al., *Bob Thompson* (Berkeley: University of California Press, 1998); Bridget Cooks, *Exhibiting Blackness: African-Americans and the American Art Museum* (Amherst: University of Massachusetts Press, 2011).

67. Angela Carter, 'Black Venus', in *Black Venus and Other Stories* (London: Picador, 1985), p. 9. Also see: Griselda Pollock, 'A Tale of Three Women: Seeing in the Dark, Seeing Double, at Least, with Manet', in *Differencing the Canon: Feminism and the Writing of Art's Histories* (London: Routledge Press, 1999), p. 270.
68. Pollock, 'A Tale of Three Women', p. 299.
69. Richard J. Powell, 'Re/Birth of a Nation', in *Rhapsodies in Black: Art of the Harlem Renaissance* (Hayward Gallery, the Institute of International Visual Arts and the University of California Press, 1997), p. 25.
70. Aliyyah I. Abdur-Rahman, 'Against the Closet: Racial Logic and the Bodily Basis/Biases of Sexual Identity', in *Against the Closet: Black Political Longing and the Erotics of Race* (Durham: Duke University Press, 2012), p. 2.
71. Ibid., p. 3.
72. Jennifer C. Nash, 'Introduction: Reading Race, Reading Pornography', in *The Black Body in Ecstasy: Reading Race, Reading Pornography* (Durham: Duke University Press, 2014), p. 2.
73. Ibid., p. 3. See also: Ariane Cruz, 'Pornography: A Black Feminist Woman Scholar's Reconciliation', in *The Feminist Porn Book: The Politics of Producing Pleasure*, ed. Tristan Taormino, Celine Parreñas Shimizu, Constance Penley, Mireille Miller-Young (New York: The Feminist Press, 2013), pp. 215–227; Jillian Hernandez, 'Carnal Teachings: Raunch Aesthetics as Queer Feminist Pedagogies in Yo! Majesty's Hip Hop

Practice', *Women and Performance: A Journal of Feminist Theory 24* (1), 2014; 'Nicki Minaj and Pretty Taking All Fades: Performing the Erotics of Feminist Solidarity', *The Feminist Wire*, co-authored with Anya M. Wallace, 6 March 2014; Mireille Miller-Young, *A Taste for Brown Sugar: Black Women in Pornography* (Durham: Duke University Press, 2014); Mireille Miller-Young, 'Interventions: The Deviant and Defiant Art of Black Women Porn Directors', in *The Feminist Porn Book: The Politics of Producing Pleasure*, ed. Tristan Taormino, Celine Parreñas Shimizu, Constance Penley, Mireille Miller-Young (New York: The Feminist Press, 2013), pp. 105–120.

74. Ibid., p. 3.
75. Mickalene Thomas and Lisa Melandri, 'Points of Origin: An Interview with Mickalene Thomas', in *Mickalene Thomas: Origins of the Universe*, ed. Lisa Melandri (Santa Monica: Santa Monica Museum of Art, 2012), pp. 39–40.
76. Antke Engel, 'The Elegantly Strong Triad: Defamiliarizing the Family in Works by LaToya Ruby Frazier and Henrik Olesen,' in *E-Flux Journal*, http://www.e-flux.com/journal/the-elegantly-strong-triad-defamiliarizing-the-family-in-works-by-latoya-ruby-frazier-and-henrik-olesen/, #52, February, 2014. Viewed, 10 August 2014.

4 We're All Kalup's Churen

1. José Esteban Muñoz, 'Famous and Dandy Like B. 'n' Andy: Race, Pop, and Basquiat', in *Pop Out: Queer Warhol* (Durham: Duke University Press, 1996), p. 145.
2. Holland Cotter, 'Art in Review; Kalup Linzy', in *The New York Times*, March 25, 2005, http://query.nytimes.com/gst/fullpage.html?res=9506E1D6173FF936A15750C0A9639C8B63. Viewed, 17 August 2014, p. 1.
3. Benjamin H.D. Buchloh, 'Andy Warhol's One-Dimensional Art: 1956–1966', in Michelson, Annette, *Andy Warhol* (Cambridge: The MIT Press, 2001), p. 28.
4. Cotter, 'Art in Review,' p. 1.
5. Allan Shields, 'Is There a Black Aesthetics?', in *Leonardo*, vol. 6, No. 4 (Autumn, 1973), p. 319.
6. bell hooks, 'An Aesthetics of Blackness – Strange and Oppositional', in *Lenox Avenue: A Journal of Interarts Inquiry*, vol. 1 (1995), p. 67.
7. Ibid., p. 67.
8. Paul Gilroy, 'The Dialectics of Diaspora Identification', in *Theories of Race and Racism: A Reader*, ed. Les Black and John Solomos (London: Routledge Press, 2000), p. 492.

9. Ibid., p. 492.
10. Ken Johnson, 'Forged from the Fires of the 1960s: 'Now Dig This! Art & Black Los Angeles', at MoMA PS1,' in *The New York Times*, October 25, 2012, http://www.nytimes.com/2012/10/26/arts/design/now-dig-this-art-black-los-angeles-at-moma-ps1.html?pagewanted=all&_r=0. Viewed, 18 August 2014.
11. Ibid., p. 1.
12. Kyle Chayka, 'Critical Problems: New York Times, Race, and Gender', in *Hyperallergic.com*, http://hyperallergic.com/61027/critical-problems-the-new-york-times-race-and-gender/, 27 November 2012. Viewed, 18 August 2014.
13. Arianne Wack, 'Are We Post-Black Art?', in *Hyperallergic.com*, http://hyperallergic.com/65694/are-we-post-black-art/, 22 February 2013. Viewed, 18 August 2014.
14. Johnson, 'Forged From the Fires of the 1960s,' p. 1.
15. Ibid., p. 1.
16. Ibid., p. 1.
17. Ibid., p. 1.
18. Ibid., p. 1.
19. For additional writing on the relationship between African-American satire and Post-Black Art, see the following essay: Derek Conrad Murray, 'Post-Black Art and the Resurrection of African-American Satire', in *Post-Soul Satire: Black Identity After Civil Rights* (Jackson: University Press of Mississippi, 2014), pp. 3–21.
20. Darryl Dickson-Carr, 'Introduction', in *African-American Satire: The Sacredly Profane Novel* (Columbia: University of Missouri Press, 2001), p. 5.
21. Darryl Dickson-Carr, 'Black Satire in the Post-Civil Rights Era', in *African-American Satire: The Sacredly Profane Novel* (Columbia: University of Missouri Press, 2001), p. 167.
22. Ibid., p. 167.
23. John Dorsey, 'Currier & Ives' America Could Be a Dark Place', in the *Baltimore Sun*, 26 June 1997, http://articles.baltimoresun.com/1997-06-26/features/1997177066_1_currier-ives-ives-print-unintentionally-funny. Viewed, 19 August 2014.
24. Darryl Dickson-Carr, 'Introduction', in *African-American Satire: The Sacredly Profane Novel* (Columbia: University of Missouri Press, 2001), p. 3.
25. Ibid., 'Introduction', p. 3.
26. Darryl Dickson-Carr, 'Toward A Theory of African American Satire', in *African-American Satire: The Sacredly Profane Novel* (Columbia: University of Missouri Press, 2001), p. 17.

27. Jayson Musson, 'Jayson Musson: "Halcyon Days," a conversation with Adrienne Edwards', in *Performa Magazine*, http://performamagazine.tumblr.com/post/28436292376/jayson-musson-halcyon-days. Viewed, 19 August 2014.
28. Hennessy Youngman, 'ART THOUGHTZ: How To Be A Successful Black Artist', YouTube Video, 8:42, posted by Hennessy Youngman, 7 October 2010, https://www.youtube.com/watch?v=3L_NnX8oj-g.
29. Arthur Knight, 'Coda: Bamboozled?', in *Disintegrating the Musical: Black Performance and American Musical Film* (Durham: Duke University Press, 2002), p. 244.
30. Tiernan Morgan, 'Jayson Musson's Joke Without a Punchline', in *Hyperallergic.com*, 15 May 2014, http://hyperallergic.com/126452/jayson-musson-exhibit-of-abstract-art/. Viewed, 20 August 2014, p. 1.
31. Ken Johnson, 'Jayson Musson: "Exhibit of Abstract Art"', in *The New York Times*, 12 June 2014, http://www.nytimes.com/2014/06/13/arts/design/jayson-musson-exhibit-of-abstract-art.html?_r=0. Viewed, 20 August 2014.
32. Morgan, 'Jayson Musson's Joke Without a Punchline,' p. 1.
33. Kalup Linzy and Chan Marshall, 'Kalup Linzy', in *Interview Magazine*, http://www.interviewmagazine.com/art/kalup-linzy/. Viewed, 17 August 2014.
34. Arthur Knight, 'Coda: Bamboozled?', in *Disintegrating the Musical: Black Performance and American Musical Film* (Durham: Duke University Press, 2002), p. 244. Arthur Knight, 'Introduction: Disintegrating the Musical?', in *Disintegrating the Musical: Black Performance and American Musical Film* (Durham: Duke University Press, 2002), p. 2. For additional writing on race, performance and the black body, see: Alexander G. Weheliye, *Habeas Viscus: Racializing Assemblages, Biopolitics, and Black Feminist Theories of the Human* (Durham: Duke University Press, 2014); Michelle Ann Stephens, *Skin Acts: Race, Psychoanalysis, and the Black Male Performer* (Durham: Duke University Press, 2014).
35. Ibid., p. 3.
36. Ibid., p. 2.
37. Ibid., p. 2.
38. Ibid., p. 3.
39. W.E.B. Du Bois, 'Of the Sorrow of Songs', in *The Souls of Black Folk* (New York: Bantam Books, 1980), p. 178.
40. W.E.B. Du Bois, *The Souls of Black Folk in Writings*, ed. Nathan Huggins (1903; reprint, New York: New American Library, 1986), p. 545.
41. Knight, 'Coda: Bamboozled?' p. 5.
42. Ibid., p. 5.

43. Chan Marshall, 'Kalup Linzy', in *Interview Magazine*, http://www.interviewmagazine.com/art/kalup-linzy/. Viewed, 21 August 2014.
44. Knight, 'Coda: Bamboozled?' p. 7. For additional writing on the synchronization of sound and race, see: Alice Maurice, 'Cinema at Its Source: Synchronizing Race and Sound in the Early Talkies', *Camera Obscura* 17, no. 1 (2002), pp. 1–71.
45. Kalup Linzy, 'Keys to Our Heart', YouTube Video, 4:00 posted by Kalup Linzy, 5 August 2008, https://www.youtube.com/watch?v=SEuGJ7OCX0c&list=UUzpneftB0RVauO8JLr94iSw.
46. Ibid.
47. Lil Johnson & Barrel House Annie, 'If It Don't Fit (Don't Force It),' in lyricsplayground.com, http://lyricsplayground.com/alpha/songs/i/ifitdontfit.shtml. Viewed, 23 August 2014.
48. Lil Johnson, 'Get 'Em From the Peanut Man (Hot Nuts)', in lyricsmode.com, http://www.lyricsmode.com/lyrics/l/lil_johnson/get_em_from_the_peanut_man_hot_nuts.html. Viewed, 23 August 2014.
49. Steven Stern, 'Kalup Linzy', in *Frieze Magazine*, Issue 122, April 2009, http://www.frieze.com/issue/article/kalup_linzy/. Viewed, 23 August 2014.
50. Jennifer Doyle, Jonathan Flatley and José Esteban Muñoz, eds., *Pop Out* (Durham and London: Duke University Press, 1996).
51. Andy Warhol, *The Andy Warhol Diaries*, ed. Pat Hackett (New York: Time Warner Books, 1989). For more on the relation between Andy Warhol and queerness, see: Roy Grundmann, *Andy Warhol's Blow Job* (Penn: Temple University Press, 2003); Matthew Tinkcom, *Working Like a Homosexual: Camp, Capital, Cinema* (Durham: Duke University Press, 2002); Kathryn Bond Stockton, *Beautiful Bottom, Beautiful Shame: Where 'Black' Meets 'Queer'* (Durham, NC: Duke University Press, 2006).
52. Steven Shaviro, 'Warhol's Bodies', in *The Cinematic Body* (Minneapolis: University of Minnesota Press, 1993), p. 201. Also see: Gretchen Berg, 'Nothing to Lose: An Interview with Andy Warhol', in *Andy Warhol: Film Factory*, ed. Michael O'Prey (London: British Film Institute, 1989).
53. Ibid., p. 201.
54. Ibid., p. 201.
55. Shaviro, p. 201. Also see: Jean Baudrillard, *Simulations*, trans. Paul Foss, Paul Patton and Phillip Beitchman (New York: Semiotext(e), 1983).
56. This citation comes from press materials for the exhibition *Regarding Warhol: Sixty Artists, Fifty Years* (September 18–31 December 2012), held at The Metropolitan Museum of Art, http://www.metmuseum.org/about-the-museum/press-room/exhibitions/2012/regarding-warhol. Viewed, 24 August 2014.

57. Andy Warhol, *The Philosophy of Andy Warhol* (New York: Harcourt Brace Jovanovich, 1975), pp. 146–147. See also: Eve Kosofsky Sedgwick, 'Queer Performativity: Warhol's Shyness/Warhol's Whiteness', in *Pop Out: Queer Warhol* (Durham: Duke University Press, 1996), pp. 134–135.
58. Eve Kosofsky Sedgwick, Ibid., p. 135.
59. Ibid., p. 141.
60. J.J. Murphy, 'Paul Morrissey Films: Confidential Stories', in *The Black Hole of the Camera: The Films of Andy Warhol* (Berkeley: University of California Press, 2012), p. 235.
61. Ibid., p. 235.
62. Ibid., p. 235.
63. Shaviro, 'Warhol's Bodies,' p. 201.
64. Ibid., p. 210.
65. Ibid., p. 227.
66. Ibid., p. 227.
67. Thomas Waugh, 'Cockteaser', in *Pop Out*, ed. Jennifer Doyle, Jonathan Flatley and José Estaban Muñoz (Durham and London: Duke University Press, 1996), p. 53.
68. Jennifer Doyle, 'Tricks of the Trade: Pop Art/Pop Sex', in *Pop Out*, ed. Jennifer Doyle, Jonathan Flatley and Jose Esteban Munoz (Durham and London: Duke University Press, 1996), p. 197.
69. Shaviro, 'Warhol's Bodies,' p. 205.
70. Ibid., p. 205.
71. Mark Rosenthal, 'Identities: Gay, Camouflaged, and Hybrid', in *Regarding Warhol: Sixty Artists, Fifty Years* (New York: The Metropolitan Museum of Art, 2012), p. 88.
72. Ibid., p. 88.
73. Murphy, pp. 252–253.
74. Alex Allenchey, 'Meet the Artist: Kalup Linzy,' in *Artspace.com*, 10 October 2012, http://www.artspace.com/magazine/interviews_features/kalup_linzy_interview. Viewed, 22 August 2014.
75. Murphy, 'The Early Films of Andy Warhol', in *The Black Hole of the Camera: The Films of Andy Warhol* (Berkeley: University of California Press, 2012), p. 46.
76. Kalup Linzy, 'My Epic Love Affair with the Soap Opera', in *The Huffington Post*, 23/04/2012, http://www.huffingtonpost.com/kalup-linzy/my-epic-love-affair-with-soaps_b_1444619.html. Viewed, 26 August 2014.
77. Shaviro, 'Warhol's Bodies,' p. 227.
78. Richard Dyer, 'Seen to be Believed: Some Problems in the Representation of Gay People as Typical', in *The Matter of Images: Essays on Representation* (London: Routledge, 1993), p. 38.

79. Ibid., p. 38.
80. Ibid., pp. 38–40.
81. Kalup Linzy, 'Keys to Our Heart', Video, 5:42, posted by *Art21.org*, 21 December 2012, http://www.art21.org/newyorkcloseup/films/kalup-linzy-likes-it-a-little-bit-off/.
82. Stephane Dunn, 'Black Masculinity in Big Mama Disguise', in *Interpreting Tyler Perry: Perspectives on Race, Class, Gender, and Sexuality* (Routledge Transformations in Race and Media), ed. Jamel Sante Cruze Bell and Ronald L. Jackson II (London: Routledge, 2014), pp. 61–62.
83. Shaviro, 'Warhol's Bodies,' p. 237.
84. Tavia Nyong'o, 'Brown Punk: Kalup Linzy's Musical Anticipations', in *The Drama Review*, Vol. 54, No. 3 (Fall 2010), p. 76.
85. Ibid., p. 76.
86. Andy Warhol and Pat Hackett, *The Andy Warhol Diaries* (New York: Grand Central Publishing, 1989).
87. Nyong'o, 'Brown Punk,' p. 78.
88. W.E.B. Du Bois, 'Our Spiritual Strivings', in *The Souls of Black Folk* (New York: Bantam Books, 1980), pp. 2–3.
89. Nyong'o, 'Brown Punk,' p. 82.

Bibliography

Abdur-Rahman, Aliyyah I., *Against the Closet: Black Political Longing and the Erotics of Race* (Durham: Duke University Press, 2012).

Abiola, Yomi, 'Jonte Demarcus Moaning', in *Vogue Magazine*, http://www.vogue.it/en/vogue-black/the-black-blog/2013/06/jonte-demarcus-moaning#ad-image281271 http://www.vogue.it/en/vogue-black/the-black-blog/2013/06/jonte-demarcus-moaning#ad-image281271. 25 June 2013. Viewed, 24 July 2014.

Allenchey, Alex, 'Meet the Artist: Kalup Linzy', in *Artspace.com*, 10 October 2012, http://www.artspace.com/magazine/interviews_features/kalup_linzy_interview. Viewed, 22 August 2014.

Alloula, Malek, *The Colonial Harem* (Minneapolis: University of Minnesota Press, 1986)

Anderson, Jervis, *Bayard Rustin: Troubles I've Seen: A Biography* (New York: Harper Collins, 1997).

Appiah, K. Anthony, 'Identity, Authenticity, Survival: Multicultural Societies and Social Reproduction', in *Multiculturalism: Examining the Politics of Recognition,* ed. Amy Gutmann (Princeton: Princeton University Press, 1994), pp. 149–163.

Bailey, David A., and Kobena Mercer, *Mirage: Enigmas of Race, Difference and Desire* (London: ICA/inIVA, 1995).

Baker, George, 'Photography's Expanded Field', in *October* 114 (Fall 2005), 120–140.

Barson, Tanya and Peter Gorschlüter (eds), *Afro-Modern: Journeys in the Black Atlantic* (Liverpool: Tate, 2009).

Baudrillard, Jean, *Simulations*, trans. Paul Foss, Paul Patton and Phillip Beitchman (New York: Semiotext(e), 1983).

Beam, Christopher, 'Outsource to China', in *NY Magazine*, http://nymag.com/arts/art/rules/kehinde-wiley-2012–4/, 22 April 2012. Viewed, 24 July 2014.

Berg, Gretchen, 'Nothing to Lose: An Interview with Andy Warhol', in *Andy Warhol: Film Factory*, ed. Michael O'Prey (London: British Film Institute, 1989).

Berlant, Lauren, and Lee Edelman, *Sex, or the Unbearable* (Durham: Duke University Press, 2014).

Bhabha, Homi, *The Location of Culture* (London: Routledge Press, 1994).

Blake, John, 'Running Afoul of the Soul Patrol', in *The Chicago Tribune*, http://articles.chicagotribune.com/1992-04-06/news/9201310779_1_soul-patrol-black-african-american-students, 6 April 1992.

Bloom, Lisa, *With Other Eyes: Looking at Race and Gender in Visual Culture* (Minneapolis: University of Minnesota Press, 1999).

Boime, Albert, *The Art of Exclusion: Representing Blacks in the Nineteenth Century* (Washington: Smithsonian Institution Press, 1990).

Bois, Yve-Alain, and Rosalind E. Krauss, *Formless: A User's Guide* (New York: Zone Books, 1997).

Breitbart, Eric, *A World On Display: Photographs from the St. Louis World's Fair, 1904* (Albuquerque: University of New Mexico Press, 1997).

Brooks, Daphne, *Bodies in Dissent: Spectacular Performances of Race and Freedom, 1850–1919* (Durham: Duke University Press, 2006).

Brown, Bill, 'Reification, Reanimation, and the American Uncanny', in *Critical Inquiry* 32 (Winter 2006), pp. 175–207.

Brown, Elaine, *A Taste of Power: A Black Woman's Story* (New York: Anchor Books, 1993).

Butler, Judith, *Bodies That Matter: On the Discursive Limits of 'Sex'* (London: Routledge, 1993).

Carbado, Devon W., *Time on Two Crosses: The Collected Writings of Bayard Rustin* (New York: Cleis Press, 2003).

Carter, Angela, *Black Venus and Other Stories* (London: Picador, 1985).

Chan, Sewell, 'Financial Crisis Was Avoidable, Inquiry Finds', in *The New York Times*, http://www.nytimes.com/2011/01/26/business/economy/26inquiry.html?_r=0, 25 January 2011. Viewed, 29 July 2014.

Chauncey, George, Jr., and Lisa Kennedy, 'Time on Two Crosses: An Interview with Bayard Rustin', in *Village Voice*, 30 June 1987, pp. 27–28.

Chayka, Kyle, 'Critical Problems: New York Times, Race, and Gender', in *Hyperallergic.com*, http://hyperallergic.com/61027/critical-problems-the-new-york-times-race-and-gender/, 27 November 2012. Viewed, 18 August 2014.

Cleaver, Eldridge, *Soul on Ice* (New York: Laurel, 1968).

Collier-Thomas, Bettye, and V.P. Franklin, *Sisters in the Struggle: African-American Women in the Civil Rights-Black Power Movement* (New York: NYU Press, 2001).

Collins, Patricia Hill, *Black Feminist Thought* (London: Routledge Press, 2000).

Conrad, Joseph, *Heart of Darkness* (New York: W.W. Norton & Company, Inc., 1971).

Cooks, Bridget, *Exhibiting Blackness: African-Americans and the American Art Museum* (Amherst: University of Massachusetts Press, 2011).

Cotter, Holland, 'Art in Review; Kalup Linzy', in *The New York Times*, March 25, 2005, http://query.nytimes.com/gst/fullpage.html?res=9506E1D6173FF936A15750C0A9639C8B63. Viewed, 17 August 2014, p. 1.

Cotter, Holland, 'Black and White, but Never Simple', in *The New York Times*, http://www.nytimes.com/2007/10/12/arts/design/12walk.html?ref=karawalker&_r=3&, 12 October 2007.

Crimp, Douglas, *AIDS: Cultural Analysis/Cultural Activism* (Cambridge: The MIT Press, 1988).

Crouch, Stanley, 'What Obama Isn't: Black Like Me', in *Daily News*, http://www.nydailynews.com/archives/opinions/obama-isn-black-race-article-1.585922, 2 November 2006.

Davis, Angela Y., *Angela Davis: An Autobiography* (International Publishers, 1989).

DeLand, Lauren, 'Black Skin, Black Masks: The Citational Self in the Work of Glenn Ligon', in *Criticism*, Vol. 54, No. 4, Fall 2012, pp. 507–537.

Dent, Gina, and Michele Wallace, *Black Popular Culture* ed. (New York: Dia Center for the Arts, 1992).

Dickson-Carr, Darryl, *African-American Satire* (Columbia: University of Missouri Press, 2001).

Dorsey, John, 'Currier & Ives' America Could Be a Dark Place', in the *Baltimore Sun*, 26 June 1997, http://articles.baltimoresun.com/1997-06-26/features/1997177066_1_currier-ives-ives-print-unintentionally-funny. Viewed, 19 August 2014.

Dreier, Peter, 'Obama Awards Bayard Rustin the Presidential Medal of Freedom', in *bill.moyers.com*, http://billmoyers.com/2013/08/10/

obama-awards-bayard-rustin-the-presidential-medal-of-freedom/, 10 August 2013. Viewed, 8 September 2014. p. 1.

Du Bois, W.E.B., *The Souls of Black Folk* (New York: Bantam Books, 1980).

———, *The Souls of Black Folk in Writings*, ed. Nathan Huggins (1903; reprint, New York: New American Library, 1986).

———, '*W.E.B. Du Bois: Writings*, ed. Nathan Higgins (New York: Library of America, 1986).

Dunn, Stephane, 'Black Masculinity in Big Mama Disguise', in James Santa Cruze Bell and Ronald L. Jackson II (eds), *Interpreting Tyler Perry: Perspectives on Race, Class, Gender, and Sexuality* (London: Routledge, 2014), pp. 57–68.

Dyer, Richard, *The Matter of Images: Essays on Representation* (London: Routledge, 1993).

Edelman, Lee, *Homographesis: Essays in Gay Literary and Cultural Theory* (New York: Routledge Press, 1994).

———, *No Future: Queer Theory and the Death Drive* (Durham: Duke University Press, 2004).

Edwards, Brent Hayes, *The Practice of Diaspora: Literature, Translation, and the Rise of Black Internationalism* (Cambridge: Harvard University Press, 2003).

Elam, Harry J., Jr., and Kennell Jackson (eds), *Black Cultural Traffic: Crossroads in Global Performance and Culture* (Ann Arbor: University of Minnesota Press, 2005).

Ellison, Ralph, *Invisible Man* (New York: Vintage International, 1995).

D'Emilio, John, 'Reading the Silences in a Gay Life: The Case of Bayard Rustin', in Mary Rhiel and David Suchoff (eds), *The Seductions of Biography* (London: Routledge, 1996) pp. 59–68.

———, *Lost Prophet: The Life and Times of Bayard Rustin* (Chicago: University of Chicago Press, 2004).

Engel, Antke, 'The Elegantly Strong Triad: Defamiliarizing the Family in Works by LaToya Ruby Frazier and Henrik Olesen', in *E-Flux Journal*, http://www.e-flux.com/journal/the-elegantly-strong-triad-defamiliarizing-the-family-in-works-by-latoya-ruby-frazier-and-henrik-olesen/, #52, February, 2014 (Viewed 08/10/2014).

English, Darby, *How to See a Work of Art in Total Darkness* (Cambridge: MIT Press, 2007).

Ferguson, Roderick A., *Aberrations in Black: Toward a Queer of Color Critique* (Minneapolis: University of Minnesota Press, 2004).

Fleetwood, Nicole, *Troubling Vision: Performance, Visuality, and Blackness* (Chicago: University of Chicago Press, 2011).

Foster, Hal, 'The Politics of the Signifier', in *October* #66 (Fall 1993), pp. 3–27.

———, 'Obscene, Abject, Traumatic', in *October*, #78 (Fall 1996), pp. 106–124.

———, *The Return of the Real* (Cambridge: The MIT Press, 1996).

———, *Cindy Sherman: October Files* (Cambridge: The MIT Press, 2006).

Francis, Jacqueline, *Making Race: Modernism and 'Radical Art' in America* (Seattle: University of Washington Press, 2012).

Fritscher, Jack, *Mapplethorpe: Assault with a Deadly Camera* (New York: Hastings House, 1994).

Gates, Henry Louis, Jr., 'Who Designed the March on Washington', in *The African Americans: Many Rivers to Cross*, w/ Henry Louis Gates, Jr., *www.pbs.org*, http://www.pbs.org/wnet/african-americans-many-rivers-to-cross/history/100-amazing-facts/who-designed-the-march-on-washington/. Viewed, 7 September 2014.

Gibson's, Ann Eden, *Abstract Expressionism: Other Politics* (New Haven: Yale University Press, 1997).

Gilroy, Paul, *The Black Atlantic: Modernity and Double Consciousness* (Cambridge: Harvard University Press, 1995).

———, 'The Dialectics of Diaspora Identification', in Les Black and John Solomos (eds), *Theories of Race and Racism: A Reader* (London: Routledge Press, 2000) pp. 490–502.

Golden, Thelma, *1993 Whitney Biennial* (New York: Whitney Museum of American Art, 1993).

———, *Black Male: Representations of Masculinity in Contemporary American Art* (New York: Whitney Museum of American Art, 1994).

———, *Freestyle* (New York: The Studio Museum in Harlem, 2001).

———, *Black Romantic* (New York: The Studio Museum in Harlem, 2002).

Greenberg, Clement, 'Avant-Garde and Kitsch', in *Partisan Review 6* (Fall 1939), pp. 34-49.

———, 'Self-hatred and Jewish Chauvinism: Some Reflections on "Positive Jewishness"', *Commentary* (November 1950).

———, *The Collected Essays and Criticism, Volume 4: Modernism with a Vengeance, 1957–1969* (Chicago: University of Chicago Press, 1995).

Greven, David, *Psycho Sexual: Male Desire in Hitchcock, De Palma, Scorsese, and Friedkin* (Austin: University of Texas Press, 2013).

Grundmann, Roy, *Andy Warhol's Blow Job* (Penn: Temple University Press, 2003).

Halberstam, Judith, *In a Queer Time and Place: Transgender Bodies, Subcultural Lives* (New York: New York University Press, 2005).

———, *The Queer Art of Failure* (Durham: Duke University Press, 2011).

Hall, Stuart (ed), *Representation: Cultural Representation and Signifying Practices* (London: Sage Publications, 1997).

Hammond, Harmony, *Lesbian Art in America* (New York: Rizzoli Press, 2000).

Hammonds, Evelynn, 'Toward a Genealogy of Black Female Sexuality: The Problematic of Science', in *Feminist Genealogies, Colonial Legacies, Democratic Futures,* ed. M. Jacqui Alexander and Chandra Talpade Mohanty (New York: Routledge Press, 1997).

Hanson, Ellis, *Out Takes: Essays on Queer Theory and Film* (Durham: Duke University Press, 1999).

Harris, Michael D., *Coloured Pictures: Race & Visual Representation* (Chapel Hill: The University of North Carolina Press, 2003).

Hawgod, Alex, 'Michael David Quattlebaum, Jr.', in *Interview Magazine*, http://www.interviewmagazine.com/culture/michael-david-quattlebaum-jr/#_. Viewed, 24 July 2014.

Hernandez, Jillian, 'Carnal Teachings: Raunch Aesthetics as Queer Feminist Pedagogies in Yo! Majesty's Hip Hop Practice', *Women and Performance: A Journal of Feminist Theory 24* (1), 2014, pp. 88–106.

hooks, bell, 'An Aesthetic of Blackness: Strange and Oppositional', in *Lenox Avenue: A Journal of Interarts Inquiry*, Vol. 1 (1995) pp. 65–72.

———, in *Art on My Mind: Visual Politics* (New York: The New Press, 1995).

———, *Yearning: Race, Gender, and Cultural Politics* (Boston: South End Press, 1990).

———, *Ain't I a Woman: Black Women and Feminism* (New York: South End Press, 1999).

Hughes, Robert, 'The Whitney Biennial: A Fiesta of Whining', in *Time Magazine*, Monday, 22 March 1993.

Hull, Gloria T., *But Some Of Us Are Brave: All the Women Are White, All the Blacks Are Men: Black Women's Studies* (New York: The Feminist Press at CUNY, 1993).

Johnson, E. Patrick, *Appropriating Blackness: Performance and the Politics of Authenticity* (Durham: Duke University Press, 2003).

——— and Mae G. Hendersen (eds), *Black Queer Studies: A Critical Anthology* (Durham: Duke University Press, 2005).

Johnson, Ken, 'Jayson Musson: "Exhibit of Abstract Art"' *in The New York Times*, 12 June 2014, http://www.nytimes.com/2014/06/13/arts/

design/jayson-musson-exhibit-of-abstract-art.html?_r=0. Viewed, 20 August 2014.

———, 'Forged from the Fires of the 1960s: 'Now Dig This! Art & Black Los Angeles', at MoMA PS1', in *The New York Times,* 25 October 2012, http://www.nytimes.com/2012/10/26/arts/design/now-dig-this-art-black-los-angeles-at-moma-ps1.html?pagewanted=all&_r=0. Viewed, 18 August 2014.

Jones, Amelia, 'Feminism, Incorporated: Reading "Postfeminism" in an Anti-Feminist Age', in *Afterimage*, v. 20, no. 5 (Rochester, NY, December 1992), pp. 10–15.

———, 'The "Post-Black" Bomb', in *Tema Celeste* 90 (March–April 2002) pp. 52–55.

———, *Seeing Differently: A History and Theory of Identification and the Visual Arts* (London: Routledge Press, 2012).

Jones, Kellie, *Lorna Simpson* (London: Phaidon Press, 2002).

———, *Now Dig This!: Art and Black Los Angeles* (New York: Prestel, 2011).

Kaplan, Louis, 'Reframing Self-Criticism: Clement Greenberg's "Modernist Painting" in Light of Jewish Identity', in *Jewish Identity in Modern Art History*, ed. Catherine M. Soussloff (Berkeley: University of California Press, 1999), pp. 180–199.

Kennedy, Randall, *Nigger: The Strange Career of a Troublesome Word* (New York: Vintage Books, 2003).

———, *Sellout: The Politics of Racial Betrayal* (New York: Vintage Books, 2009).

———, 'The Fallacy of Touré's Post-Blackness Theory', in *The Root*, http://www.theroot.com/articles/culture/2011/08/whos_afraid_of_post blackness_tours_postblackness_theory.html, 11 August 2011. Viewed, 5 September 2014.

Knight, Arthur, *Disintegrating the Musical: Black Performance and American Musical Film* (Durham: Duke University Press, 2002).

Krauss, Rosalind, et al., 'The Politics of the Signifier', in *October* 66 (Fall 1993), pp. 3–27.

Kristeva, Julia, *Powers of Horror: An Essay on Abjection* (New York: Columbia University Press, 1982).

Kuspit, Donald, *The End of Art* (Cambridge: Cambridge University Press, 2004).

Lewis, Samella, *African-American Art and Artists* (Berkeley: University of California Press, 2003).

Linzy, Kalup, 'Keys to Our Heart', Video, 5:42, posted by *Art21.org*, 21 December 2012, http://www.art21.org/newyorkcloseup/films/kalup-linzy-likes-it-a-little-bit-off/

——— and Chan Marshall, 'Kalup Linzy', in *Interview Magazine*, http://www.interviewmagazine.com/art/kalup-linzy/. Viewed, 17 August 2014.

———, 'My Epic Love Affair with the Soap Opera', in *The Huffington Post*, 04/23/2012, http://www.huffingtonpost.com/kalup-linzy/my-epic-love-affair-with-soaps_b_1444619.html. Viewed, 26 August 2014.

Long, Michael. G, *I Must Resist: Bayard Rustin's Life in Letters* (San Francisco: City Lights Publishers, 2012).

Lord, Catherine and Richard Meyer, *Art and Queer Culture* (London: Phaidon Press, 2013).

Marriott, David, *On Black Men* (New York: Columbia University Press, 2000).

Marshall, Kerry James, *Kerry James Marshall* (New York: Harry N. Abrams, Inc., Publishers, 2000).

Marx, Karl, *Capital: Volume 1: A Critique of Political Economy* (New York: Penguin Classics, 1992).

Maurice, Alice, 'Cinema at Its Source: Synchronizing Race and Sound in the Early Talkies', *Camera Obscura* 17, no. 1 (2002), pp. 31–71.

Maus, Derek C. and James J. Donahue (eds), *Post-Soul Satire: Black Identity After Civil Rights* (Jackson: University of Mississippi Press, 2014).

McKeon, Lucy, 'The Controversies of Kara Walker', in *Hyperallergic.com*, http://hyperallergic.com/67125/the-controversies-of-kara-walker/, 19 March 2013.

Melandri, Lisa, *Mickalene Thomas: Origin of the Universe* (Santa Monica: Santa Monica Museum of Art, 2012).

Mercer, Kobena, *Welcome to the Jungle: New Positions in Black Cultural Studies* (London: Routledge, 1994).

———, 'Busy in the Ruins of Wretched Phantasia', in *Mirage: Enigmas of Race, Difference and Desire*, ed. Ragnar Farr (London: Institute of Contemporary Arts, ICA/inIVA, 1995), pp. 15–53.

———, 'Skin Head Sex Thing: Racial Difference and the Homoerotic Imaginary', in *The Masculinity Studies Reader*, eds. Rachel Adams and David Savran (Wiley-Blackwell Press, 2002), 188–200.

Meyer, Richard, *Outlaw Representation: Censorship and Homosexuality in Twentieth-Century American Art* (New York: Beacon Press, 2004).

Michelson, Annette (ed.), *Andy Warhol* (Cambridge: The MIT Press, 2001).

Miller-Young, Mireille, *A Taste for Brown Sugar: Black Women in Pornography* (Durham: Duke University Press, 2014).

Moore, Darnell, 'Post-racial Rhetorics and the Depoliticization of Blackness', in *Darkmatter: In the Ruins of Imperial Culture* 9.2, Centre for Cultural Studies Research, University of East London, 2013.

Morgan, Tiernan, 'Jayson Musson's Joke without a Punchline', in *Hyperallergic.com*, 15 May 2014, http://hyperallergic.com/126452/jayson-musson-exhibit-of-abstract-art/. Viewed, 20 August 2014. p. 1.

Mulvey, Laura, 'A Phantasmagoria of the Female Body', in *Cindy Sherman* (Paris: Editions Jeu de Palme, 2006).

———, *Visual and Other Pleasures* (New York: Palgrave Macmillan, 2009).

Muñoz, José Esteban, *Disidentifications: Queers of Color and the Performance of Politics* (Minneapolis: University of Minnesota Press, 1999).

———, *Cruising Utopia: The Then and There of Queer Futurity* (New York: New York University Press, 2009).

——— et al. (eds), *Pop Out: Queer Warhol* (Durham: Duke University Press, 1996).

Murphy, J.J., *The Black Hole of the Camera: The Films of Andy Warhol* (Berkeley: University of California Press, 2012).

Murray, Derek Conrad, 'Kehinde Wiley: Splendid Bodies', in *Nka: Journal of Contemporary African Art*, #21 (Fall 2007), pp. 90–101.

———, 'Post post-black: some politically incorrect thoughts on the reception and contemplation of African-American Art', in *Art Journal*, Winter 2007, vol. 66, no. 4, pp. 112–114.

——— and Soraya Murray, 'Uneasy Bedfellows: Canonical Art Theory and the Politics of Identity', in *Art Journal,* Vol. 65, no. 1, Spring 2006, pp. 22–39.

——— and Soraya Murray, 'On Art and Contamination: Performing Authenticity in Global Art Practices', *Nka: Journal of Contemporary African Art 22/23* (Spring/Summer 2008), pp. 88–93.

Musson, Jayson, 'Jayson Musson: "Halcyon Days', a conversation with Adrienne Edwards", in *Performa Magazine*, http://performamagazine.tumblr.com/post/28436292376/jayson-musson-halcyon-days. Viewed, 19 August 2014.

Nash, Jennifer C., *The Black Body in Ecstasy: Reading Race, Reading Pornography* (Durham: Duke University Press, 2014).

Newbury, Susanna, 'Glenn Ligon's America', in *Nka: Journal of Contemporary African Art*, No. 31, Fall 2012, pp. 36–45.

Nochlin, Linda, *The Politics of Vision: Essays on Nineteenth-Century Art and Society* (Westview Press, 1991).

———, *Representing Women* (New York: Thames & Hudson, 1999).

———, *The Body in Pieces: The Fragment as a Metaphor of Modernity* (New York: Thames & Hudson, 2001).

Nyong'o, Tavia, *The Amalgamation Waltz: Race, Performance, and the Ruses of Memory* (Minneapolis: University of Minnesota Press, 2009).

———, 'Brown Punk: Kalup Linzy's Musical Anticipations', in *The Drama Review,* Vol. 54, No. 3 (Fall 2010), pp. 71–86.

Obama, Barack, *The Audacity of Hope: Thoughts on Reclaiming the American Dream* (New York: Crown Press, 2006).

Oguibe, Olu, *The Culture Game* (Minneapolis: University of Minnesota Press, 2004).

Oliver, Valerie Cassell, *Double Consciousness: Black Conceptual Art since 1970* (Houston: Museum of Contemporary Art Houston, 2005).

Olson's, Lynn, *Freedom's Daughters: The Unsung Heroines of the Civil Rights Movement from 1830 to 1970* (New York: Scribner, 2002).

Patton, Sharon F., *African-American Art* (Oxford: Oxford University Press, 1998).

Pinder, Kymberly N., *Race-ing Art History: Critical Readings in Race and Art History* (London: Routledge Press, 2002).

Pollock, Griselda, *Differencing the Canon: Feminism and the Writing of Art's Histories* (London: Routledge Press, 1999).

Powell, Richard J., 'Re/Birth of a Nation', in *Rhapsodies in Black: Art of the Harlem Renaissance* (Hayward Gallery, the Institute of International Visual Arts and the University of California Press, 1997), pp. 14–34.

Raengo, Alessandra, 'Optic Black: Blackness as Phantasmagoria in Akil Houston, ed. *Beyond Blackface: Africana Images in the US Media* (Kendall Hunt Publishing, 3rd edition, 2010).

Ratcliff, Carter, *Andy Warhol* (New York: Abbeville Press, 1983).

Redvers, Jeanmarie, 'An Interview with Bayard Rustin', *Other Countries: Black Gay Voices*, 1 (1988): pp. 3–16.

Reed, Christopher, *Art and Homosexuality: A History of Ideas* (Oxford: Oxford University Press, 2011).

Riggs, Marlon, 'Black Macho Revisited: Reflections of a SNAP!! Queen', in *Brother to Brother: New Writings by Black Gay Men*, ed. Essex Hemphill (Boston: Alyson Press, 1991) pp. 253–57.

Rosenthal, Mark, 'Identities: Gay, Camouflaged, and Hybrid', in *Regarding Warhol: Sixty Artists, Fifty Years* (New York: The Metropolitan Museum of Art, 2012).

Rothkopf, Scott (ed), *Glenn Ligon: AMERICA* (New York: Whitney Museum of American Art, 2011).

Rubenfeld, Florence, *Clement Greenberg: A Life* (Minneapolis: University of Minnesota Press, 1997).

Russo, Vito, *The Celluloid Closet: Homosexuality in the Movies* (New York: Harper & Row Publishers, 1985).

Said, Edward, *Orientalism* (New York: Vintage Book, 1979).

Schur, Richard, 'Post-soul Aesthetics in Contemporary African American Art.' *African American Review*, Vol. 41 (Winter 2007), pp. 641–654.

Shaviro, Steven, *The Cinematic Body* (Minneapolis: University of Minnesota Press, 1993).

Shaw, Gwendolyn DuBois, *Seeing the Unspeakable: The Art of Kara Walker* (Durham: Duke University Press, 2004).

Shields, Allan, 'Is There a Black Aesthetics?', in *Leonardo*, Vol. 6, No. 4 (Autumn, 1973), pp. 319–323.

Sims, Lowery Stokes, et al. (eds), *Betye Saar: Extending the Frozen Moment* (Berkeley: University of California Press, 2005).

Smith, Cherise, *Enacting Others: Politics of Identity in Eleanore Antin, Nikki S. Lee, Adrian Piper, and Anna Deavere Smith* (Durham: Duke University Press, 2011).

Smith, Shawn Michelle, *Photography on the Color Line: W.E.B. Du Bois, Race, and Visual Culture* (Durham: Duke University Press, 2004).

Stephens, Michelle Ann, *Skin Acts: Race, Psychoanalysis, and the Black Male Performer* (Durham: Duke University Press, 2014).

Stern, Steven, 'Kalup Linzy', in *Frieze Magazine*, Issue 122, April 2009, http://www.frieze.com/issue/article/kalup_linzy/. Viewed, 23 August 2014.

Stockton, Kathryn Bond, *Beautiful Bottom, Beautiful Shame: Where 'Black' Meets 'Queer'* (Durham, NC: Duke University Press, 2006).

Taormino, Tristan, et al. (eds), *The Feminist Porn Book: The Politics of Producing Pleasure* (New York: The Feminist Press, 2013).

Tate, Greg, *Everything But the Burden: What White People are Taking From Black Culture* (New York: Broadway Books, 2003).

Taylor, Paul C., 'Post-Black, Old Black', in *African American Review*, Vol. 41 (Winter 2007) pp. 625–640.

Thompson, Robert Farris, 'Afro Modernism', in *Artforum International* (Sept. 1991), pp. 91–94.

Tinkcom, Matthew, *Working Like a Homosexual: Camp, Capital, Cinema* (Durham: Duke University Press, 2002).

Touré, *Who's Afraid of Post-Blackness?: What It Means to Be Black Now* (New York: Free Press, Simon & Schuster, 2011).

Wack, Arianne, 'Are We Post-Black Art?', in *Hyperallergic.com,* http://hyperallergic.com/65694/are-we-post-black-art/, 22 February 2013. Viewed, 18 August 2014.

Wallace, Michele, *Black Macho and the Myth of the Superwoman* (New York: Verso Classics, 1999).

———, *Dark Designs & Visual Culture* (Durham: Duke University Press, 2004).

Warhol, Andy, *The Philosophy of Andy Warhol* (New York: Harcourt Brace Jovanovich, 1975).

———, *The Andy Warhol Diaries*, ed. Pat Hackett (New York: Time Warner Books, 1989).

Waugh, Thomas, *The Fruit Machine: Twenty Years of Writing on Queer Cinema* (Durham: Duke University Press, 2000).

Weheliye, Alexander G., *Habeas Viscus: Racializing Assemblages, Biopolitics, and Black Feminist Theories of the Human* (Durham: Duke University Press, 2014).

West, Cornel, 'The New Cultural Politics of Difference', in *The Cultural Studies Reader*, Second Edition, ed. Simon During (London: Routledge, 1993), pp. 256–267.

———, *The Cornel West Reader* (New York: Civitas Books, 1999).

Wiley, Kehinde, *Kehinde Wiley* (New York: Rizzoli, 2011).

Willis, Deborah, *Black: A Celebration of a Culture* (New York: Hylas Publishing, 2003).

———, *Posing Beauty: African-American Images 1980s to the Present* (New York: W.W. Norton & Company, 2009).

Womack, Ytasha L., *Post Black: How a New Generation is Redefining African American Identity* (Chicago: Chicago Review Press, 2010).

Youngman, Hennessey, 'ART THOUGHTZ: How to Be a Successful Black Artist', YouTube Video, 8:42, posted by Hennessey Youngman, 7 October 2010, https://www.youtube.com/watch?v=3L_NnX8oj-g.

Žižek, Slavoj, 'Tolerance as an Ideological Category', in *Critical Inquiry*, Vol. 34, No. 4 (Summer 2008), pp. 660–682.

———, *The Perverts Guide to Ideology*, Dir. Sophie Fiennes, Perf. Slavoj Žižek (Zeitgeist Films, 2012).

Index

The index is in word-by-word order, therefore 'black artists' comes before 'black arts'. Figures are represented by page number followed immediately by figure number, eg: *I Still Love You (You Still Love Me)* (2007) 131f29. Plates have not been indexed.